FOUR VIEWS ON THE BOOK OF
REVELATION

Books in the Counterpoints Series

Church Life

Exploring Theology

Stanley N. Gundry (S.T.D., Lutheran School of Theology at Chicago) is vice president and editor-in-chief of the Book Group at Zondervan. He graduated summa cum laude from both the Los Angeles Baptist College and Talbot Theological Seminary before receiving his Masters of Sacred Theology from Union College, University of British Columbia. With more than thirty-five years of teaching, pastoring, and publishing experience, he is the author or coauthor of numerous books and a contributor to numerous periodicals.

FOUR VIEWS ON THE BOOK OF
REVELATION

- Kenneth L. Gentry Jr.
- Sam Hamstra Jr.
- Robert L. Thomas
- C. Marvin Pate

- **Stanley N. Gundry** *series editor*
- **C. Marvin Pate** *general editor*

GRAND RAPIDS, MICHIGAN 49530 USA

ZONDERVAN™

Four Views on the Book of Revelation
Copyright © 1998 by C. Marvin Pate, Kenneth L. Gentry Jr., Sam Hamstra,
Robert L. Thomas

Requests for information should be addressed to:

Zondervan, *Grand Rapids, Michigan 49530*

Library of Congress Cataloging-in-Publication Data

Pate, C. Marvin
     Four views on the Book of Revelation / C. Mrvin Pate, general editor
        p. cm.
     Includes bibliographical references and index.
     ISBN: 0–310–21080-1 (softcover)
     1. Bible. N.T. Revelation—Criticism, interpretation, etc.. I. Pate, C. Marvin,
1952-. II. Series: Counterpoints (Grand Rapids, Mich.,).
     BS2825.2.F68 1998
     228'.07—dc21   97-33425
                                                   CIP

Printed in the United States of America

HB 05.09.2024

CONTENTS

PREFACE

One sage defined a classic as "a book everybody talks about, but which almost nobody reads." Unfortunately, that description could be applied to the last book of the Bible—Revelation. Who has not been captivated by the power of its drama and the poignancy of its message? And yet how many actually read the Apocalypse? Undoubtedly, there is a vast difference in the answers to those questions. The purpose of this volume is to help bridge the gap between the preceding responses; that is, to move people from being merely enamored with Revelation to engaging it through personal interaction. To this end, the present contributions offer four, we think, well-argued alternative viewpoints of the last book of the Bible.

All of the authors in this volume are evangelical scholars in theological studies. For each, the inspiration of the Scriptures is their framework for understanding the Apocalypse. Furthermore, while the contributors present their viewpoints with conviction, they do so in an irenic and Christian spirit. With that in mind, this book is dedicated to all those "who love his [Christ's] appearing," regardless of their eschatological persuasion.

I would like to acknowledge those who have assisted in this project. My sincere appreciation goes to the other participants—Ken Gentry, Sam Hamstra, and Robert Thomas—who have helped to transfer the vision for this work into reality. Personally this endeavor has afforded me the benefit of new friends and stimulating ideas. I hope my colleagues feel the same. I also wish to thank those of the Zondervan editorial staff who approved and guided the project to its completion—Ed van der Maas, Verlyn D. Verbrugge, and Stanley N. Gundry. Their input was enthusiastic and invaluable.

C. MARVIN PATE,
GENERAL EDITOR

ABBREVIATIONS

AB	Anchor Bible Commentary
BAR	*Biblical Archaeology Review*
BASOR	*Bulletin of the American Society for Oriental Research*
BSac	*Bibliotheca Sacra*
ICC	International Critical Commentary
JETS	*Journal for the Evangelical Theological Society*
JSNTSS	*Journal for the Study of the New Testament* Supplement Series
KJV	King James Version
LXX	Septuagint (Greek version of the Old Testament)
NASB	New American Standard Version
NICNT	New International Commentary on the New Testament
NIV	New International Version
NKJV	New King James Version
NovTSup	Supplements to *Novum Testamentum*
NRSV	New Revised Standard Version
NTS	*New Testament Studies*
RSV	Revised Standard Version
SNTSMS	Society of New Testament Studies Monograph Series
TNTC	Tyndale New Testament Commentaries
TrinJ	*Trinity Journal*

INTRODUCTION TO REVELATION

Of modern responses to the book of Revelation, three quickly come to mind. "Obsession" is the appropriate word to describe some eight million prophecy buffs today,[1] who pore over the prophecies of the Apocalypse in Nostradamus style, anachronistically correlating current events with its ancient cryptic warnings. Pursuing this angle, these interpreters equate Red China with the "kings from the East" (Rev. 16:12–16), the European Common Market with the "ten horns of the beast" (13:1–10), the mark of the beast (666) of Revelation 13 with everything from credit cards to the Internet, and the Antichrist with a parade of prominent people, including Adolf Hitler, Benito Mussolini, Henry Kissinger, and Mikhail Gorbachev. This intense fascination with Revelation by the doomsayers shows no sign of decreasing as the year 2000 approaches. Such a crystal ball reading of the last book in the Bible, however, has undoubtedly caused more harm than good and is best avoided by responsible hermeneuticians.[2]

A second modern response to Revelation can be expressed by the word "irrelevance." As the term indicates, too many consider the Apocalypse to be an antiquated anthology of bizarre images born out of paranoia and designed to moralize people by appealing to divine scare tactics. As a professor of religion once put it when speaking of apocalyptic literature, of which Revelation is a part, "It is foolishness!" One suspects that the first response of obsession might have contributed to the second response of irrelevance.

Many contemporary Christians, however, find themselves somewhere in between the two extremes, approaching Revelation with "dutiful, but hesitant" concern. On the one hand, they

---

[1]So, according to Paul Boyer, *When Time Shall Be No More: Prophecy Beliefs in Modern American Culture* (Cambridge, Mass.: Harvard Univ. Press, 1992), 2–3.

[2]For a critique of the doomsday mentality, see C. Marvin Pate and Calvin B. Haines Jr., *Doomsday Delusions: What's Wrong With Predictions About the End of the World* (Downers Grove, Ill.: InterVarsity, 1995).

revere the book as inspired of God and therefore pertinent to their lives; on the other hand, they find its meaning confusing and even potentially divisive. In large part, we hope that this work addresses these people—to bring clarity to a confusing but vital topic.

Yet we cannot gain perspicuity on any given subject simply by examining it from only one perspective. Such an approach runs the risk of being myopic and provincial. Rather, what is needed in examining Revelation is an interpretive reading of that book such that the sum total of the whole is greater than the individual parts. Not that an ancient text, biblical or otherwise, has more than one meaning, which is the claim of postmodernity. Instead, what is called for is the realization that we as humans, with finite understanding, need each other's insights, enlightened by the Holy Spirit, in order to grasp the intent of God's Word. Applying the analogy of the parts and the whole to Revelation permits one to state it this way: The four interpretations in this volume represent the interpretive parts while its readership, aided by the Spirit, forms the whole.

Before turning to the various perspectives offered in this book, however, we first need to survey introductory matters relative to the Apocalypse—namely, a general introduction, followed by a summary of the leading interpretations of the document. The bulk of this volume, then, will address the latter point, covering four current views: the preterist; the futurist, which can be delineated into classical dispensationalism and progressive dispensationalism; and the idealist. Hopefully, the sum total of the individual parts will extricate us from the hermeneutical criticism reflected in the famous quip by Mark Twain: "The researches of many commentators have already thrown much darkness on this subject, and it is probable that, if they continue, we shall soon know nothing at all about it!"

I. A GENERAL INTRODUCTION TO REVELATION

A. Genre

Before one can properly interpret any piece of literature, the Bible included, one must determine its genre or literary type.[3] This principle is acutely important for Revelation, and its neglect has resulted in a morass of conflicting viewpoints. The difficulty is heightened by the fact that Revelation consists of a mixture of three genres: apocalyptic, prophetic, and epistolary. Alan F. Johnson succinctly describes the first of these genres:

> Revelation is ... commonly viewed as belonging to the body of nonbiblical Jewish writings known as apocalyptic literature. The name for this type of literature (some nineteen books) is derived from the word "revelation" (*apocalypsis*) in Revelation 1:1. ... The extrabiblical apocalyptic books were written in the period from 200 B.C. to A.D. 200. Usually scholars stress the similarities of the Apocalypse of John to these noncanonical books—similarities such as the use of symbolism and vision, the mention of angelic mediators of the revelation, the bizarre images, the expectation of divine judgment, the emphasis on the kingdom of God, the new heavens and earth, and the dualism of this age and the age to come.[4]

While significant parallels do indeed exist between Revelation and early Jewish and Christian apocalyptic materials, there are critical differences between them as well, none the least of which is that Revelation is a prophetic book (1:3; 22:7, 10, 18–19), while the others make no such claim. As such Revelation is not pseudonymous (1:1; 22:8); neither is it pessimistic about God's intervention in history. Furthermore, while many apocalyptic writers recast past events as though they were futuristic prophecies (*vaticinia ex eventu*), thus lending credibility to their predictive prowess, John (the author of Revelation) does not follow this procedure. On the contrary, he places himself in the contemporary world of the first century A.D. and speaks of the coming eschatological consummation in the same manner as did the Old Testament prophets—a consummation that, for John, has already begun to break into history in the death and resurrection of Jesus Christ (1:4–8; 4–5).

---

[3]For an excellent "genre" approach to the Bible, see Gordon D. Fee and Douglas Stuart, *How to Read the Bible for All Its Worth: A Guide to Understanding the Bible*, 2d ed. (Grand Rapids: Zondervan, 1993).

[4]Alan F. Johnson, "Revelation," in *The Expositor's Bible Commentary*, ed. Frank E. Gabelein (Grand Rapids: Zondervan, 1981), 12:400. See also Johnson's helpful bibliography on the topic of apocalypticism, 400–401, n. 3.

In addition to being apocalyptic and prophetic in nature, Revelation is encased by an epistolary framework (1:4–8 and 22:10–21). This convention alone sets it apart from apocalyptic materials. The prescript (1:4–8) contains the typical epistolary components—sender, addressees, greetings, and the added feature of a doxology. The postscript (22:10–21), in good ancient letter form, summarizes the body of the writing, as well as legitimates John as its divinely inspired composer. The combined effect of the prescript and the postscript, not to mention the letters to the seven churches of the Roman province of Asia (chaps. 2–3), is to root Revelation in the real history of its day. How different from other ancient non-canonical apocalypses. Consider, for example, the opening statement in 1 Enoch, that what the author saw was "not for this generation but the distant one that is coming" (1 Enoch 1:2).

B. Authorship

In ascertaining the identity of the author of Revelation, two lines of evidence need to be assessed: external and internal.[5] The external evidence consists of the testimony of the church fathers, which is nearly unanimously in favor of the opinion that the apostle John was the author of the Apocalypse. These include Papias, Justin Martyr, the Muratorian Fragment, Irenaeus, Clement of Alexandria, Tertullian, Hippolytus, Origen, and Methodius. The notable exceptions to this testimony are Dionysius, bishop of Alexandria (247–264), and Eusebius, the church historian, who himself was persuaded by Dionysius' arguments against Johannine authorship of the book (though Eusebius expressed his doubts less vigorously than did Dionysius).

In turning to the internal evidence for determining the authorship of Revelation, Dionysius' four categories continue to convince many against Johannine authorship,[6] which we sum-

---

[5]The following discussion is indebted to Robert L. Thomas' work, *Revelation 1–7: An Exegetical Commentary*, ed. Kenneth Barker (Chicago: Moody, 1992), 2–19. The question of the authorship of Revelation is closely related to its canonicity, at least in terms of the discussion of the church fathers. Thus those who accepted the Johannine authorship of Revelation accepted its canonicity. Those, however, who questioned or even denied Johannine authorship, questioned or rejected its canonicity (notably Dionysius and, to a lesser degree, Eusebius).

[6]This influence can especially be seen in the monumental work by R. H. Charles, *The Revelation of St. John*, 2 vols. (ICC; Edinburgh: T. & T. Clark, 1920).

marize here: (1) the writer's self-identification; (2) the construction of Revelation as compared with the genuine writings of John the apostle; (3) the character of these writings; and (4) the writing style of these materials.

(1) The first internal argument offered by Dionysius is that whereas Revelation identifies its author as "John" (1:1, 4, 9; 22:8), neither the Gospel of John nor the letters of John do. The assumption here is that if the apostle John had written Revelation, he would not have felt any compulsion to identify himself as its author. This reasoning, however, is an argument from silence and therefore is not convincing. Moreover, the apocalyptic nature of the book may have necessitated the author identifying himself, even as other works fitting that genre do.

(2) With regard to the construction of Revelation and that of John's Gospel and letters, Dionysius argued that the former does not begin with the identification of Jesus as the "Word" nor with the author's eyewitness vantage point whereas the latter do (cf. John 1:1–18 with 1 John 1:1–4). But this observation overlooks Revelation 1:2 and its connection of the word of God with Christ. It also misses the significance attached to the concept of "witness" in Revelation and in the other Johannine literature (cf. Rev. 1:2; 22:16 with John 1:19ff.; 5:32; 8:18; 15:26; 1 John 1:1–4; 5:6–11).

(3) Dionysius also maintained that the vocabulary of Revelation differs significantly from the genuine Johannine writings. Yet Dionysius' assertion does not hold up under careful scrutiny. Twelve of the nineteen Johannine terms that are supposedly not found in Revelation do in fact occur (e.g., "life," "blood," "judgment," "devil"). Moreover, three of the terms not occurring in Revelation are also absent from the Gospel of John ("forgiveness," "Antichrist," "adoption"), and one of them ("conviction") is not present in 1 John. Furthermore, while "truth" is not in the Apocalypse, its synonym, "genuine," is. Also, while "joy" is absent in the Apocalypse, it only occurs once each in the three letters of John. We are left then with one term, "darkness," that occurs frequently in the other Johannine writings and not in Revelation—hardly enough evidence upon which to base a major distinction.

(4) Finally, Dionysius claimed that Revelation is written in poor Greek, in contrast to the good Greek style of the other Johannine materials. However, this overlooks two factors: (a) an

author's writing style is not always consistent; (b) John, like his contemporaries, may well have used an amanuensis (a professional secretary), through whom he composed his Gospel and the letters (cf. Rom. 16:22; 1 Peter 5:12). Exiled on the island of Patmos, however (cf. 1:9), he presumably did not have access to such an individual.

On balance, then, the external and internal evidence seems to point to the apostle John as the author of the Apocalypse or, at the very least, to a member of the Johannine School.[7]

C. Date

We will analyze the theories of the date of the Apocalypse later in this introduction with reference to the interpretive schemes of the book, but for the moment we note that two major periods qualify as candidates: emperor Nero's reign (A.D. 54–68) and Domitian's rule (A.D. 81–96). As will be developed later, the preterist school of interpretation argues for the former, while the futurist approach, especially classical dispensationalism, aligns itself with the latter. Progressive dispensationalism sees a combination of the two dates as operative in the book, while the idealist perspective is not bound by either time frame.

D. Unity

A generation or so ago some interpreters, enamored with source criticism, put forth the theory of multiple authorship for the Apocalypse, notably R. H. Charles and J. Massyngberde Ford.[8] Evidence that supposedly militates against single authorship falls into four categories: (1) the presence of doublets—the same scene or vision described twice; (2) sequence problems—persons or things introduced apparently for the first time when, in actuality, they had earlier been mentioned; (3) seemingly misplaced verses and larger sections; (4) distinc-

---

[7]The view that the Revelation and the Gospel of John were written by members of a Johannine school is argued by Elisabeth S. Fiorenza, "The Quest for the Johannine School: The Apocalypse and the Origin of Both Gospel and Revelation," *NTS* 23 (April 1977): 402–27.

[8]Charles, *The Revelation of St. John*; J. Massyngberde Ford, *Revelation* (AB; New York: Doubleday, 1975).

tive content within certain sections that does not fit the rest of the book.[9]

But, as Johnson observes, in each case there are satisfying alternative explanations. Moreover, there is an artificiality about assigning certain passages to an "interpolator" when they do not fit with the perceived unity of the book.[10] Even Charles, who applies a fragmentary approach to the document, admits to an overall unity of the work.[11] Likewise Ford who, although delineating three different authors for the Apocalypse, nevertheless ascribes the "final redaction" to a single editor.[12] In light of this, Johnson's conclusion about the unity of the Apocalypse seems justified:

> We may affirm that the book everywhere displays both the literary and conceptual unity to be expected from a single author. This does not eliminate certain difficult hermeneutical problems nor preclude the presence of omissions or interpolations encountered in the extant MSS of the book. Nor does the view of single authorship preclude that John in expressing in written form the revelation given to him by Christ used various sources, whether oral or written.... Yet, under the guidance of the Holy Spirit, who is of course the primary author, John has everywhere made these materials his own and involved them with a thoroughly Christian orientation and content.[13]

E. Structure

Like the question of the date of the Apocalypse, so too the issue of its structure is intimately related to one's interpretation of the book. Therefore, because we will cover the subject more extensively in the second part of this introduction, we only offer here the lowest common denominator among the various schools of thought, which consists of two structural elements.[14]

---

[9]See Johnson, "Revelation," 403.

[10]Ibid.

[11]Charles, *The Revelation of St. John*, 1:lxxxvii.

[12]Ford, *Revelation*, 46.

[13]Johnson, "Revelation," 403. G. Mussies' detailed analysis of the language of the Apocalypse has reaffirmed the unity of the book, *The Morphology of Koine Greek as Used in the Apocalypse of St. John* (Leiden: E. J. Brill, 1971), 351.

(1) In terms of content, after an introductory chapter, four series of sevens follow: seven letters (chaps. 2–3); seven seals (5:1–8:1); seven trumpets (8:2–11:19); and seven bowls (15:1–16:21). Interrupting these four series are several interludes (7:1–17; 10:1–11:13; 12:1–14:20). The book concludes with the judgment of "Babylon," worldwide apostasy, and the final triumph of God's kingdom (chaps. 17–21). (2) In terms of literary structure, Revelation consists of four visions, each of which involves John "seeing" the plan of God unveiled (1:19; 4:1; 17:1; 21:9). An epilogue concludes the book (22:6–21).

F. Traditional Materials in Revelation

While Revelation draws on various traditional materials (e.g., Greco-Roman court ceremonial, chaps. 4–5; Jewish apocalyptic, chaps. 4–5; the Olivet Discourse, chap. 6; the dragon drama, chap. 12; the Neronian story, chap. 13), by far the dominant source of its information is the Old Testament. While Revelation does not contain a single specific quotation of the Old Testament, nevertheless out of 404 verses in it, 278 contain allusions to the Old Testament. Johnson well summarizes the apostle John's usage of that material:

> The OT used by John is primarily Semitic rather than Greek, agreeing often with the Aramaic Targums and occasionally reflecting Midrashic background materials to the OT passages; and it can be shown that he used a text other than the Masoretic that has a close affinity with the Hebrew text of the Qumran MSS. From the Prophets, John refers quite frequently to Isaiah, Jeremiah, Ezekiel, and Daniel. John also refers repeatedly to the Psalms, Exodus, and Deuteronomy. Especially important are John's Christological reinterpretations of OT passages he alludes to. He does not simply use the OT in its pre-Christian sense but often recasts the images and visions of the OT. While there is an unmistakable continuity in Revelation with the older revelation, the new emerges from the old as a distinct entity.[15]

---

[14]See the summary by George Eldon Ladd, *A Commentary on the Revelation of John* (Grand Rapids: Eerdmans, 1972), 14.

[15]Johnson, "Revelation," 411. For further analysis of John's employment of the Old Testament in Revelation, see Austin Farrer, *A Rebirth of Images: The Making of St.*

G. The Text of Revelation

From a text-critical point of view, there are fewer extant Greek manuscripts for reconstructing the original reading of the Apocalypse than any other part of the New Testament. Nevertheless, there is a sufficient amount to accomplish the task with assurance (approximately 230 Greek manuscripts). The major witnesses to Revelation are: the uncials—Codex Sinaiticus (fourth century), Codex Alexandrinus (fifth century), Codex Ephraemic (fifth century); the papyri, the most important of which is p^{47} (third century); the minuscules (eighth to tenth centuries); the church father quotations (second to fifth centuries); and a Greek commentary on Revelation by Andreas (sixth century).[16]

II. A SURVEY OF LEADING INTERPRETATIONS OF REVELATION

Traditionally, four major interpretations have been put forth in attempting to unravel the mysteries of the Apocalypse: preterist, historicist, futurist, and idealist. The names encapsulate the essence of the respective approaches. The *preterist* (past) interpretation understands the events of Revelation in large part to have been fulfilled in the first centuries of the Christian era—either at the fall of Jerusalem in A.D. 70 or at both the falls of Jerusalem in the first century and of Rome in the fifth century. In effect the book was written to comfort Christians, who suffered persecution from both the imperial cult and Judaism.

The *historicist* school views the events of Revelation as unfolding in the course of history. This perspective was especially compatible with the thinking of the Protestant Reformers, who equated the papal system of their day with the Antichrist.

The *futurist* scheme argues that the events of Revelation are largely unfulfilled, holding that chapters 4–22 await the end times for their realization. If the preterist interpretation has dominated

---

John's Apocalypse (London: Darce, 1949). One of the most recent treatments of the subject is by Steve Moyise, *The Old Testament in the Book of Revelation* (JSNTSS 115; Sheffield: Academic Press, 1995).

[16]For further discussion of the manuscript evidence, consult Thomas, *Revelation 1–7*, 42–43.

among biblical scholars, then it may be said that the futurist reading is the preference of choice among the masses.

The *idealist* viewpoint, by way of contrast to the previous three theological constructs, is reticent to pinpoint the symbolism of Revelation historically. For this school of thought, Revelation sets forth timeless truths concerning the battle between good and evil that continues throughout the church age.

This volume incorporates the current, prevailing interpretations of Revelation. Thus, while the historicist approach once was widespread, today, for all practical purposes, it has passed from the scene. Its failed attempts to locate the fulfillment of Revelation in the course of the circumstances of history has doomed it to continual revision as time passed and, ultimately, to obscurity (a situation, one might add, if Jesus tarries, that contemporary doomsday prophets may eventually find themselves in!). Moreover, the lack of consensus among interpreters as to the identification of historical details that supposedly fulfill the prophecies of the Apocalypse contributed to the school's demise.

On the other hand, the other three interpretive approaches merit careful attention. The preterist view, always the favorite among scholars, has enjoyed a revival of interest at the popular level, thanks to the rise of Christian Reconstruction (more on this shortly). The futurist view, especially classical dispensationalism, will undoubtedly continue to hold the interest of many. Progressive dispensationalism, the "newest kid on the eschatological block," is beginning to capture the imagination of those who have grown weary over a sensationalist treatment of prophecy.[17] Finally, the idealist approach continues to hold considerable appeal because of the power of application to daily life that its system encourages. Those who are "burned out" by prophecy in general find in its schema a refreshing alternative for grasping the ever-present significance of Revelation.

We turn now to a survey of these four hermeneutical formats, covering the following points on each: its distinction; its origin; the time frame it presumes for the prophecies in Revelation; the structure that results for the book; and the philosophy of history operative in the approach. Handling these matters in

---

[17] That is not to say, however, that classical dispensationalism is to be equated with the doomsday mentality. Even though a good number of doomsayers come from this tradition, as we shall see, they need not be the same.

advance will better equip the reader to grasp the respective systems as a whole before analyzing the document in more detail. If the reader will permit us a little poetic license, we propose to treat these approaches according to the chronological order found in Revelation 1:19: "Write, therefore, what you have seen [preterist], what is now [idealist], and what will take place later [futurist]."

A. The Preterist Interpretation

The preterist viewpoint wants to take seriously the historical interpretation of Revelation by relating it to its original author and audience. That is, John addressed his book to real churches who faced dire problems in the first century A.D. Two quandaries in particular provided the impetus for the recording of the book. Kenneth L. Gentry Jr. writes of these:

> Revelation has two fundamental purposes relative to its original hearers. In the first place, it was designed to steel the first century Church against the gathering storm of persecution, which was reaching an unnerving crescendo of theretofore unknown proportions and intensity. A new and major feature of that persecution was the entrance of imperial Rome onto the scene. The first historical persecution of the Church by imperial Rome was by Nero Caesar from A.D. 64 to A.D. 68. In the second place, it was to brace the Church for a major and fundamental re-orientation in the course of redemptive history, a re-orientation necessitating the destruction of Jerusalem (the center not only of Old Covenant Israel, but of Apostolic Christianity [cp. Ac. 1:8; 2:1ff.; 15:2] and the Temple [cp. Mt. 24:1–34 with Rev. 11]).[18]

Thus, the sustained attempt to root the fulfillment of the divine prophecies of Revelation in the first century A.D. constitutes the preterist's distinctive approach.

---

[18]Ken Gentry Jr., *Before Jerusalem Fell: Dating the Book of Revelation* (Tyler, Tex.: Institute for Christian Economics, 1989), 15–16. It should be remembered, however, that preterism is comprised of two camps—one that locates the fulfillment of Revelation largely in the first century relative to the fall of Jerusalem, and another that sees the fulfillment of Revelation in *both* the first century (the fall of Jerusalem) and in the fifth century (the fall of Rome).

The origin of preterism can be traced to the theological system known as postmillennialism, which teaches that Christ will return after the Millennium, a period of bliss on earth brought about by the conversion of the nations because of the preaching of the gospel. The credit for formulating the postmillennial doctrine is usually given to Daniel Whitby (1638–1726), a Unitarian minister from England. Whitby's view of the Millennium was embraced by conservative and liberal theologians. John F. Walvoord observes:

> His views on the millennium would probably have never been perpetuated if they had not been so well keyed to the thinking of the times. The rising tide of intellectual freedom, science, and philosophy, coupled with humanism, had enlarged the concept of human progress and painted a bright picture of the future. Whitby's view of a coming golden age for the church was just what people wanted to hear. ... It is not strange that theologians scrambling for readjustments in a changing world should find in Whitby just the key they needed. It was attractive to all kinds of theology. It provided for the conservative a seemingly more workable principle of interpreting Scripture. After all, the prophets of the Old Testament knew what they were talking about when they predicted an age of peace and righteousness. Man's increasing knowledge of the world and scientific improvements which were coming could fit into this picture. On the other hand, the concept was pleasing to the liberal and skeptic. If they did not believe the prophets, at least they believed that man was now able to improve himself and his environment. They, too, believed a golden age was ahead.[19]

Such an acceptance on the part of many resulted in two types of postmillennialism, as Paul N. Benware notes: "liberal postmil-

---

[19]John F. Walvoord, *The Millennial Kingdom* (Findlay, Ohio: Dunham, 1963), 22–23. In a recent correspondence, Ken Gentry helpfully provides two clarifications of the presentation we have been providing here regarding the connection between preterism and postmillennialism. First, it is simplistic to restrict the preterist view to postmillennialism. Many amillennialists also align themselves with this interpretation (e.g., Jay Adams, Cornelis Vanderwaal). Second, although Whitby is credited as popularizing postmillennialism, actually it is Thomas Brightman (1562–1607) who deserves that credit. Moreover, there is a nascent postmillennialism/preterism in some of the church fathers (e.g., Origen, Eusebius, Athanasius, Augustine).

lennialism" and "biblical postmillennialism."[20] The former had its heyday in the nineteenth century in association with the "social gospel," whose mission was the liberation of humanity from societal evil (poverty, racism, disease, war, and injustice). The presupposition of this school of thought was that humanity was basically good and that ultimately society would get better and better, resulting in a golden age on earth. Laudable as this attempt was, however, the social gospel suffered from two flaws: It abandoned the preaching of the gospel, and it naively based its view of history on the evolutionary process. Time dealt a mortal blow to liberal postmillennialism—the catastrophic events of the twentieth century rendered it an untenable position (e.g., two world wars, the Great Depression, the threat of nuclear destruction).

Alongside liberal postmillennialism was its biblical counterpart. Those theologians of the eighteenth and nineteenth centuries following this approach maintained their commitment to the gospel and to its transforming power. Stanley J. Grenz writes of them:

> Their outlook differed fundamentally from both secular and liberal Christian utopianism. They were optimistic concerning the future to be sure. But their optimism was born out of a belief in the triumph of the gospel in the world and of the work of the Holy Spirit in bringing in the kingdom, not out of any misconception concerning the innate goodness of humankind or of the ability of the church to convert the world by its own power.[21]

Today, biblical postmillennialism has rebounded from the catastrophies of history and is currently experiencing a resurgence of influence, especially Christian Reconstructionism. Its conviction is admirable—as the church preaches the gospel and performs its role as the salt of the earth, the kingdom of God will advance until the whole world will one day gladly bow to the authority of Christ. The means for accomplishing this goal will be the law of God, which impacts the church and, in return, the world.[22]

---

[20]The following synopsis is taken from Paul N. Benware, *Understanding Endtimes Prophecy: A Comprehensive Approach* (Chicago: Moody, 1995), 120–22.

[21]*The Millennial Maze: Sorting Out Evangelical Options* (Downers Grove, Ill.: InterVarsity, 1992), 66.

[22]Authors who identify themselves with the preterist interpretation of Revelation include David Chilton, *The Days of Vengeance: An Exposition of the Book of Revelation*

Preterists locate the timing of the fulfillment of the prophecies of Revelation in the first century A.D., specifically just before the fall of Jerusalem in A.D. 70 (though some also see its fulfillment in both the falls of Jerusalem [first century] and Rome [fifth century]). Despite the opinion of many that Revelation was written in the 90s during the reign of Domitian (81–96), much of preterism holds the date of the book to be Neronian (54–68).

Three basic arguments are put forth to defend that period. (1) There are allusions throughout Revelation to Nero as the current emperor (e.g., 6:2; 13:1–18; 17:1–13).

(2) The condition of the churches in Asia Minor to which John writes his letters (chaps. 2–3) best correlates with pre-70 Jewish Christianity, a time that witnessed the rupture between Christianity and Judaism. In effect, Revelation attests to the twofold persecution of Jewish Christianity—by the Jews and by the Romans. The former persecuted Jewish believers because of their faith in Jesus as the Messiah, so that they were consequently expelled from the synagogues, thus exposing them to Caesar worship.[23] The latter, subsequently, tried to force Jewish Christians to revere Caesar. As judgment on the first-century Jews for persecuting Christians, John predicts that Christ will come in power to destroy Jerusalem, using the Roman empire to do so (e.g., 1:7–8; 22:20; chaps. 2–3; 11; 17–18)—a warning that came true with Jerusalem's fall in A.D. 70.

(3) According to Revelation 11, the temple seems still to be standing (that is, at the time of the writing of the book).

Based on the preceding arguments, we might outline Revelation as follows:

Chap. 1:   John's Vision of the Risen Jesus
Chaps. 2–3:   The Situation of Early Jewish Christianity
Chaps. 4–5:   The Heavenly Scene of Christ's Reign
Chaps. 6–18:   Parallel Judgments on Jerusalem
Chap. 19:   The Coming of Christ to Complete the Judgment of Jerusalem
Chaps. 20–22: Christ's Rule on Earth

(Fort Worth, Tex.: Dominion, 1987); Gary DeMar, *Last Days Madness: Obsession of the Modern Church* (Atlanta: American Vision, 1994).

[23] Judaism was permitted freedom of worship by Rome. To be separated from it was to lose that privileged status.

With regard to the philosophy of history presumed by most preterists, as noted before, it is a positive one (*contra* Jay Adams and Cornelis Vanderwaal). The world will get better and better because of the triumph of the gospel. In that sense, postmillennialism aligns itself more with the role of the Old Testament prophet, whose message proclaimed the intervention of God in history, than with the apocalypticist's doom and gloom forecasts of the future.

B. The Idealist Interpretation

The idealist approach to Revelation has sometimes been called the "spiritualist" view in that it interprets the book spiritually, or symbolically. Accordingly, Revelation is seen from this perspective as representing the ongoing conflict of good and evil, with no immediate historical connection to any social or political events. Raymond Calkins well describes this interpretation:

> If we understand the emergency which caused the book to be written, the interpretation of it for its time, for our time, and for all time, it becomes as clear as daylight. In the light of this explanation, how far from the truth becomes that use of it which finds the chief meaning of the book in the hints it gives us about the wind-up of creation, the end of the world, and the nature of the Last Judgment. ... To use Revelation in this way is to abuse it, for the book itself makes no claim to be a key to the future.[24]

Consequently, Calkins captures the chief message of Revelation in terms of five propositions:

1. It is an irresistible summons to heroic living.
2. It contains matchless appeals to endurance.
3. It tells us that evil is marked for overthrow *in the end.*
4. It gives us a new and wonderful picture of Christ.
5. It reveals to us the fact that history is in the mind of God and in the hand of Christ as the author and reviewer of the moral destinies of men.[25]

---

[24]Raymond Calkins, *The Social Message of Revelation* (New York: Woman's Press, 1920), 3.
[25]Ibid., 3–9.

While all four of the schools of interpretation surveyed here resonate with these affirmations, the idealist view distinguishes itself by refusing to assign the preceding statements to any historical correspondence and thereby denies that the prophecies in Revelation are predictive except in the most general sense of the promise of the ultimate triumph of good at the return of Christ.[26]

The origin of the idealist school of thought can be traced back to the allegorical or symbolic hermeneutic espoused by the Alexandrian church fathers, especially Clement and Origen. R. H. Charles writes of these Alexandrians that:

> under the influence of Hellenism and the traditional allegorical school of interpretation which came to a head in Philo, [they] rejected the literal sense of the Apocalypse, and attached to it a spiritual significance only. This theory dominates many schools of exegetes down to the present day. Thus Clement saw in the four and twenty elders a symbol of the equality of Jew and Gentile within the Church, and in the tails of the locusts the destructive influences of immoral teachers. Origen as well as his opponent Methodius rejects as Jewish the literal interpretation of chap. XX and in the hands of his followers the entire historical contents of the Apocalypse were lost sight of.[27]

Akin to the Alexandrian interpretation of Revelation was the amillennial view propounded by Dionysius, Augustine, and Jerome. Thus the Alexandrian school, armed with the amillennial method, became the dominant approach to Revelation until the Reformation.

As mentioned above, the idealist does not restrict the contents of Revelation to a particular historical period, but rather sees it as an apocalyptic dramatization of the continuous battle between God and evil. Because the symbols are multivalent in meaning and without specific historical referent, the application of the book's message is limitless. Each interpreter can therefore find significance for their respective situations.

---

[26]Merrill C. Tenney provides a helpful summary of the idealist interpretation of Revelation, as well as the other viewpoints, *Interpreting Revelation* (Grand Rapids: Eerdmans, 1957), 143–44.

[27]R. H. Charles, *Studies in the Apocalypse* (Edinburgh: T. & T. Clark, 1913), 11–12.

Two recent commentaries on Revelation nicely illustrate this method. The first is the work by Paul S. Minear,[28] whose interpretation of the symbols of Revelation is stimulating. For him the purpose of Revelation is to warn Christians of the enemy within—"the false Christian." The whole of the book is viewed from that perspective. The seven letters provide the context of the book—it is a divine challenge to the church to be faithful to Christ. The judgments thereafter are designed not to effect the ruination of those outside of Christendom, but of the unfaithful within it. But those who persevere in righteousness receive the promise of the new heaven and new earth. Read in this way, Revelation is to be taken not as an apocalyptic invective against the non-Christian but rather as a prophetic warning to the Christian.

A second work on Revelation illustrating the idealist interpretation is the challenging commentary by Elisabeth Schüssler Fiorenza, whose purpose in writing it is to "liberate the text from its historical captivity and rescue the message of Revelation for today."[29] In other words, the meaning of Revelation is not to be sought in the first century nor in the remote events of the end time, but rather in the ongoing struggle between those disadvantaged sociopolitically and their oppressors. Thus understood, Revelation is a powerful tool in the hands of liberation and feminist theologians for throwing off the yoke of capitalism and chauvinism, respectively.

The best way to appreciate Fiorenza's approach is to see her method at work. For example, she approvingly quotes from the poem, "Thanksgiving Day in the United States" by Julia Esquivel, which reworks Revelation 17–18 by applying it to her own third-world experience:

> In the third year of the massacres
> by Lucas and the other coyotes
> against the poor of Guatemala
> I was led by the Spirit into the desert
>
> And on the eve
> of Thanksgiving Day

---

[28]Paul S. Minear, *I Saw a New Earth: An Introduction to the Visions of the Apocalypse* (Cleveland: Corpus, 1968).

[29]Elisabeth Schüssler Fiorenza, *Revelation: Vision of a Just World* (Proclamation Commentaries; Minneapolis, Minn.: Fortress, 1991), 2.

I had a vision of Babylon:
The city sprang forth arrogantly
from an enormous platform
of dirty smoke produced
by motor vehicles, machinery
and contamination from smokestacks.

It was as if all the petroleum
from a violated earth
was being consumed
by the Lords of capital
and was slowly rising
obscuring the face
of the Sun of Justice
and the Ancient of Days. . . .

Each day false prophets
invited the inhabitants
of the Unchaste City
to kneel before the idols
of gluttony,
money,
and death:
Idolaters from all nations
were being converted to the American Way of Life. . . .

The Spirit told me
in the River of death
flows the blood of many peoples
sacrificed without mercy
and removed a thousand times from their lands,
the blood of Kekchis, of Panzos,
of blacks from Haiti, of Guaranis from Paraguay,
of the peoples sacrificed for "development"
in the Trans-Amazonic strip,
the blood of the Indians' ancestors
who lived on these lands, of those who
even now are kept hostage in the Great Mountain
and on the Black Hills of Dakota
by the guardians of the beast. . . .

My soul was tortured like this
for three and a half days

and a great weariness weighed upon my breast.
I felt the suffering of my people very deeply!
Then in tears, I prostrated myself
and cried out: "Lord, what can we do? . . .
Come to me, Lord, I wish to die among my people!"
Without strength, I waited for the answer.
After a long silence
and a heavy obscurity
The One who sits on the throne
to judge the nations
spoke in a soft whisper
in the secret recesses of my heart:

You have to denounce their idolatry
in good times and in bad.
Force them to hear the truth
for what is impossible to humans
is possible for God.[30]

Whether or not one agrees with the ideology informing this poem or, for that matter, with Fiorenza's radical feminist persuasion, the attempt here to capture and apply the symbolism of Revelation is engaging, if not arresting.

There does not seem to be a hard-and-fast rule for the idealist in delineating the structure of Revelation. For Minear, the key to outlining the book is to be aware that the running contrasts between the visions of heaven and earth are symbolic of the struggle within Christians between faithfulness to Christ (heaven) and unfaithfulness (earth). For Fiorenza, Revelation is chiastically structured such that the key to the book is to be found in 10:1–15:4, with its description of the struggle and liberation of the oppressed communities of the world.[31] The only notable structural feature in the idealist interpretative agenda is its disavowal of a literal and chronological reading of Revelation 20. Rather, in good amillennial fashion, that chapter is to be viewed as a symbolic description of the church's potential to reign with Christ in this age.

As to the worldview of the idealist school of thought, "realism" is its preferred perspective. Stanley Grenz encapsulates this mind-set of the idealist, amillennial position:

---

[30]Quoted in ibid., 27–28.
[31]Ibid., 35–36.

The result is a world view characterized by realism. Victory and defeat, success and failure, good and evil will coexist until the end, amillennialism asserts. The future is neither a heightened continuation of the present nor an abrupt contradiction to it. The kingdom of God does not come by human cooperation with the divine power currently at work in the world, but neither is it simply the divine gift for which we can only wait expectantly.[32]

Consequently, both unbridled optimism and despairing pessimism are inappropriate, amillennialism declares. Rather, the amillennialist worldview calls the church to "realistic activity" in the world. Under the guidance and empowerment of the Holy Spirit, the church will be successful in its mandate; yet ultimate success will come only through God's grace. The kingdom of God arrives as the divine action breaking into the world; yet human cooperation brings important, albeit penultimate, results. Therefore, God's people must expect great things in the present; but knowing that the kingdom will never arrive in its fullness in history, they must always remain realistic in their expectations.

C. Classical Dispensationalism

The most popular interpretation of Revelation among the masses during the twentieth century has been dispensationalism, one of the varieties of premillennialism. The name of the movement is derived from the biblical word "dispensation," a term referring to the administration of God's earthly household (KJV, 1 Cor. 9:17; Eph. 1:10; 3:2; Col. 1:25). Dispensationalists divide salvation history into historical eras or epochs in order to distinguish the different administrations of God's involvement in the world. C. I. Scofield, after whom the enormously popular *Scofield Bible* was named, defined a dispensation as "a period of time during which man is tested in respect of obedience to some specific revelation of the will of God."[33] During each dispensa-

---

[32]Grenz, *The Millennial Maze*, 187.

[33]*The Scofield Reference Bible* (New York: Oxford, 1909), note to Genesis 1:28, heading. For an updated definition that emphasizes faith as the means for receiving the revelations in the various dispensations, see Charles C. Ryrie, *Dispensationalism Today* (Chicago: Moody, 1965), 74.

tion, humankind fails to live in obedience to the divine test, consequently bringing that period under God's judgment and thus creating the need for a new dispensation. Read this way, the Bible can be divided into the following eight dispensations (though the number of names vary in this school of thought): innocence, conscience, civil government, promise, Mosaic law, church and age of grace, tribulation, millennium.[34]

The hallmark of dispensationalism has been its commitment to a literal interpretation of prophetic Scripture. This has resulted in three well-known tenets cherished by adherents of the movement. (1) A distinction between the prophecies made about Israel in the Old Testament and the church in the New Testament must be maintained. In other words, the church has not replaced Israel in the plan of God. The promises he made to the nation about its future restoration will occur. The church is, therefore, a parenthesis in the outworking of that plan. The dispensational distinction between Israel and the church was solidified in the minds of many as a result of two major events in this century: the holocaust (which has rightly elicited from many deep compassion for the Jewish people) and the rebirth of the State of Israel in 1948.

(2) Dispensationalists are premillennialists; that is, Christ will come again and establish a temporary, one-thousand-year reign on earth from Jerusalem.

(3) Dispensationalists believe in the pretribulation rapture; that is, Christ's return will occur in two stages: the first one for his church, which will be spared the Great Tribulation; the second one in power and glory to conquer his enemies.

Dispensationalism seems to have been first articulated by the Irish Anglican clergyman John Nelson Darby, an influential leader in the Plymouth Brethren movement in England during the nineteenth century. The movement was imported to the United States, receiving notoriety with the publication in 1909 of the *Scofield Reference Bible*. At least three developments have unfolded within the movement during this century. (1) The earliest stage was propounded by Darby and Scofield, a period that

---

[34]C. I. Scofield, *Rightly Dividing the Word of Truth* (New York: Loizeaux Brothers, 1896). Many modern dispensationalists, however, have grown uncomfortable with these periodizations, preferring rather to talk about the Bible in terms of its two divisions—the old and new covenants.

emphasized the dispensations themselves. (2) A second stage emerged in the 1960s, thanks to the work by Charles C. Ryrie, *Dispensationalism Today*. With this second development two noticeable changes transpired: (a) Faith was highlighted as the means of salvation in any of the dispensations *(contra* the old *Scofield Bible*'s statement about works being the means of salvation in the Old Testament; see the footnote on John 1:17). (b) The individual dispensations were no longer the focal point; rather, the emphasis now lay on the literal hermeneutic of dispensationalism. (3) In the 1980s a third development arose, commonly called progressive dispensationalism (more on this later). The middle stage, often labeled traditional dispensationalism, continues to find strong support today; it constitutes the fourth view offered in this volume on Revelation.

The classical dispensationalist's understanding of the time frame of Revelation and its structure go hand in hand. Because this school of thought interprets the prophecies of the book literally, their fulfillment, therefore, is perceived as still future (esp. chaps. 4–22). Moreover, the magnitude of the prophecies (e.g., one-third of the earth destroyed; the sun darkened) suggests that they have not yet occurred in history. The key verse in this discussion is 1:19, particularly its three tenses, which are thought to provide an outline for Revelation: "what you have seen" (the past, John's vision of Jesus in chap. 1); "what is now" (the present, the letters to the seven churches in chaps. 2–3); "what will take place later" (chaps. 4–22). In addition, the classical dispensationalist believes that the lack of mention of the church from chapter 4 on indicates that it has been raptured to heaven by Christ before the advent of the Great Tribulation (chaps. 6–18).

Intimately associated with premillennialism as dispensationalism is, one is not surprised that this perspective views the history of the world pessimistically. Grenz summarizes this interpretation:

> In contrast to the optimism of postmillennialism, premillennialism displays a basic pessimism concerning history and the role we play in its culmination. Despite all our attempts to convert or reform the world, prior to the end antichrist will emerge and gain control of human affairs, premillennialism reluctantly predicts. Only the catastrophic action of the returning Lord will bring about the

reign of God and the glorious age of blessedness and peace.

In keeping with this basic pessimism concerning world history, premillennial theologies emphasize the discontinuity, or even the contradiction between, the present order and the kingdom of God, and they elevate the divine future over the evil present. The kingdom is the radically new thing God will do. However it may be conceived, the "golden age"—the divine future—comes as God's gracious gift and solely through God's action.[35]

D. Progressive Dispensationalism

In discussing "progressive dispensationalism," the newest of the four interpretations surveyed here, we combine its origin and description. In the 1980s certain dispensational theologians launched a rethinking of the system and developed what has been called "progressive" or "modified" dispensationalism.[36] While it is too soon to call this approach a "school of thought," all the evidence indicates that this viewpoint will gain influence with time.

The umbrella concept informing this interpretation is its adherence to the "already/not yet" hermeneutic. First popularized by Oscar Cullmann, a Swiss theologian of a generation ago, this system views the first and second comings of Christ through the lens of eschatological tension. The former witnessed the inauguration of the kingdom of God, while the latter will result in its full realization. Until then, the Christian lives in the tension between the age to come (which dawned at the first coming of Christ) and this present evil age (which will only be transformed at the Parousia, or the second coming of Christ). Gordon D. Fee captures the essence of this approach:

> The absolutely essential framework of the self-understanding of primitive Christianity ... is an eschatological one. Christians had come to believe that, in the

---

[35]Grenz, *The Millennial Maze*, 185.

[36]Proponents of this approach include Craig Blaising and Darrell Bock, *Progressive Dispensationalism* (Wheaton: Victor, 1993); Robert L. Saucy, *The Case for Progressive Dispensationalism: The Interface Between Dispensational and Non-Dispensational Theology* (Grand Rapids: Zondervan, 1993).

event of Christ, the new (coming) age had dawned, and that, especially through Christ's death and resurrection and the subsequent gift of the Spirit, God had set the future in motion, to be consummated by yet another coming (*Parousia*) of Christ. Theirs was therefore an essentially eschatological existence. They lived "between the times" of the beginning and the consummation of the end. Already God had secured their ... salvation; already they were the people of the future, living the life of the future in the present age—and enjoying its benefits. But they still awaited the glorious consummation of this salvation. Thus they lived in an essential tension between the "already" and the "not-yet."[37]

As a result of interpreting the Bible in this manner, progressive dispensationalists part company with some of the points espoused by classical dispensationalism. (1) "Progressives" believe that Jesus began his heavenly, Davidic reign at the resurrection. Craig Blaising and Darrell Bock express this well:

Peter argues in Acts 2:22–36 that David predicted in Psalm 16 that this descendant would be raised up from the dead, incorruptible, and in this way He would be seated upon His throne (Ac. 2:30–31). He then argues that this enthronement has taken place upon the entrance of Jesus into heaven, in keeping with the language of Psalm 110:1 that describes the seating of David's son at God's right hand. Peter declares (Ac. 2:36) that Jesus has been made Lord over Israel (Ps. 110:1 uses the title Lord of the enthroned king) and Christ (the anointed king) by virtue of the fact that He has acted (or been allowed to act) from that heavenly position on behalf of His people to bless them with the gift of the Holy Spirit. ... Enthronement at the right hand of God, the position promised to the Davidic king in Psalm 110:1, is ascribed to Jesus in many New Testament texts. It is, of course, proclaimed in Acts 2:33–36.[38]

(2) The church is not a parenthesis in the plan of God; rather, like believing Jews in the Old Testament, it forms a part of the one

[37]Gordon D. Fee, *1 and 2 Timothy, Titus* (Peabody, Mass.: Hendrickson, 1988), 19.
[38]Blaising and Bock, *Progressive Dispensationalism*, 177–78.

people of God (e.g., Rom. 2:26–28; 11; Gal. 6:16; Eph. 2:11–22; 1 Peter 2:9–10).

(3) The new covenant is beginning to be fulfilled in the church (e.g., 2 Cor. 3:1–4:6; cf. also the book of Hebrews).

(4) Old Testament promises about the Gentiles' coming to worship the true God at the end of history is also experiencing partial realization in the church (e.g., Rom. 15:7–13).

With regard to the essentials of classical dispensationalism, however, progressives are in complete agreement, of which there are three: (1) Israel will be restored to God in the future (that is to say, there is a distinction, though not a dichotomy, between Israel and the church); (2) Christ will return to establish his millennial reign on earth (the premillennial view); (3) the church will not go through the Great Tribulation (the pretribulation interpretation).

Concerning Revelation in particular, progressives apply the already/not yet hermeneutic to its time frame as follows: The already aspect surfaces in the book in terms of historical fulfillment in the first century A.D. vis-à-vis Caesar worship and Jewish persecution of Christians (not unlike, though not to be equated with, the preterist approach). The not yet aspect of Revelation is to be found in those prophecies (the majority of the book) that await realization at the Parousia (the Great Tribulation, Antichrist, Parousia, Millennium).

Like classical dispensationalism, progressives also focus on Revelation 1:19 as the key to the book's structure, except, rather than view the verse as delineating three time frames (past, present, future), this viewpoint perceives only two periods at work. John is to write what he has seen (the visions of Revelation as a whole), which divide into two realities: the things that are—the present age; and the things that will be—the age to come. For John the church of his day lives in the present age (chaps. 1–3), but in heaven, by virtue of Jesus' death and resurrection, the age to come has already dawned (chaps. 4–5). In the future the age to come will descend to earth, effecting the defeat of the Antichrist (chaps. 6–19), the establishment of the temporary messianic kingdom on earth (chap. 20), and subsequently the eternal state (chaps. 21–22). Thus the overlapping of the two ages accounts for the continual shifting of scenes between earth (this age) and heaven (the age to come) in Revelation.

Because it is premillennial in perspective, progressive dispensationalism also views the unfolding of history pessimistically. However, the already/not yet hermeneutic tempers that pessimism with the optimistic belief that the kingdom of God has dawned spiritually, thereby giving great hope to the people of God. Progressive dispensationalists, therefore, are circumspect about not necessarily equating this current generation with the last one before Christ's return. It may be, or it may not be. Tony Campolo pinpoints the realism of the eschatological tension inherent in this mentality:

> Any theology that does not live with a sense of the immediate return of Christ is a theology that takes the edge off the urgency of faith. But any theology that does not cause us to live as though the world will be here for thousands of years is a theology that leads us into social irresponsibility.[39]

---

[39]"Interview: Tony Campolo," *The Door* (September/October 1993), 14.

Chapter One

A PRETERIST VIEW
OF REVELATION

Kenneth L. Gentry Jr.

A PRETERIST VIEW
OF REVELATION

Kenneth L. Gentry Jr.

INTRODUCTION

The closer we get to the year 2000, the farther we get from the events of Revelation. This claim, as remarkable as it may sound, summarizes the evangelical preterist view of Revelation.[1] "Preterism" holds that the bulk of John's prophecies occur in the *first century*, soon after his writing of them. Though the prophecies were in the future when John wrote and when his original audience read them, they are now in *our* past.

The format of the present book precludes a thorough analysis of Revelation and its intricate structure.[2] Yet I am firmly convinced that even an introductory survey of several key passages, figures, and events in John's majestic prophecy can demonstrate the plausibility of the preterist position. As to structure, suffice it to say that its movement suggests a spiraling forward of events, involving the recasting of earlier prophecies (e.g., notice the strong similarities between the seals and the trumpets, Rev. 6

---

[1]The word "preterist" is based on a Latin word "praeteritus," meaning "gone by," i.e., past.

[2]For more preterist detail on Revelation organized into an eschatological system, see my *He Shall Have Dominion*, 2d ed. (Tyler, Tex.: Institute for Christian Economics, 1996), esp. chaps. 8 and 14–17. See also David Chilton, *The Days of Vengeance: An Exposition of the Book of Revelation* (Fort Worth, Tex.: Dominion, 1987); Jay E. Adams, *The Time Is at Hand* (Phillipsburg, N.J.: Presbyterian and Reformed, 1966).

and 8). John's spiral structure allows occasional backward glances and a reconsidering of events from different angles, rather than a relentless chronological progression.

The reason for such a structure is interesting: Hermeneutics authority Milton S. Terry, a noted advocate of the grammatical-historical method of interpretation, a strong preterist, and a hermeneutics authority cited by Robert L. Thomas in his chapter (below), notes that "all such apocalyptic repetitions serve the twofold purpose of intensifying the divine revelation and showing 'that the thing is established by God and that he will shortly bring it to pass.'"[3] Of course, no interpreter takes the progress of Revelation as relentlessly forward working—even classic dispensationalist Robert Thomas allows some mingling of past and future, disjunctive intercalations, and so forth (e.g., in Rev. 11:15–19; 12:1ff.; 19:1–4, 7–9).[4]

Before beginning my survey, I must note what most Christians suspect and what virtually all evangelical scholars (excluding classic dispensationalists) recognize regarding the book: *Revelation is a highly figurative book that we cannot approach with a simple straightforward literalism.* That having been stated, however, the preterist view does understand Revelation's prophecies as strongly reflecting actual historical events in John's near future, though they are set in apocalyptic drama and clothed in poetic hyperbole. As even premillennialist commentator Robert Mounce notes: "That the language of prophecy is highly figurative has nothing to do with the reality of the events predicted. Symbolism is not a denial of historicity but a matter of literary

---

[3]Milton S. Terry, *Biblical Apocalyptics: A Study of the Most Notable Revelations of God and of Christ* (Grand Rapids: Baker, rep. 1988 [1898]), 22. See Genesis 41:25, 32.

[4]Robert L. Thomas, *Revelation 8–22: An Exegetical Commentary* (Chicago: Moody, 1995), 43, 103, 104, 106–7, 113, 355, 365–66. For example, "this passage is part of an intercalation which is not a part of Revelation's strict chronological sequence" (366). A remarkable peculiarity exists within classic dispensationalism's system of literalistic, chronological analysis of prophecy: Intercalations appear unexpectedly anywhere the system needs them. For example: (1) The unified image of Daniel 2 involves four successive world empires progressively developing one after the other, but with the fourth in two stages, including a "revived Roman empire" separated from its ancient Roman predecessor by 1500 years—so far (see ibid., 153). (2) The unified seventy weeks of Daniel, after developing progressively through the first sixty-nine weeks, suddenly stop in the first century, then picks up again at the Great Tribulation thousands of years later (see Thomas, *Revelation 1–7* [Chicago: Moody, 1992], 426).

genre."⁵ Note the following impediments to a preconceived literalism:

(1) *The statement as to content.* In his opening statement John informs us that his revelation has been given "to show" (Gk. *deixai*) the message being "signified [Gk. *esēmanen*] by His angel" (Rev. 1:1, NKJV). As Friedrich Düsterdieck notes: "The *deixai* occurs in the way peculiar to *semainein*, i.e., the indication of what is meant by significative figures."⁶ In fact, forty-one times John says he "sees" these prophecies (e.g., 1:12, 20; 5:6; 9:1; 20:1). Furthermore, some of the visions are obviously symbolic, such as the slain lamb (chaps. 4 and 14), the seven-headed beast (chaps. 13 and 17), and the Babylonian prostitute (chap. 17).

In his Gospel John shows the problem of literalism among Christ's early hearers: They misconstrue his teaching regarding the temple (John 2:19–22), being born again (3:3–10), drinking water (4:10–14), eating his flesh (6:51–56), being free (8:31–36), being blind (5:39–40), falling asleep (11:11–14), and Jesus' being king (18:33–37). Such an erroneous approach is magnified if used in John's Revelation. The visual nature of Revelation's content—not just the method of its reception—demands symbolic interpretation. That is, except for a very few instances (e.g., Rev. 1:20; 4:5; 5:6, 8; 7:13–14; 12:9; 17:7–10), the symbols are not interpreted for us. And in one of those instances where we do receive an angelic interpretation (17:9–12), the seven-headed beast is not literally a seven-headed beast at all.

(2) *The precedent of earlier prophets.* Old Testament prophets employ figurative language for one of two purposes: to majestically relate spiritual truths, or to dramatically symbolize historical events. For instance, God's riding on a cloud down into Egypt (Isa. 19:1, see below: "The Revelational Theme") and the decreation language (Rev. 13:10, see below: "The Sixth Seal") speak of the downfall of ancient cities. Terry offers many helpful insights in this regard,⁷ noting that "a rigid literal interpretation of apocalyptic language tends to confusion and endless

⁵Robert H. Mounce, *The Book of Revelation* (NICNT; Grand Rapids: Eerdmans, 1977), 218. For a helpful, succinct discussion of apocalyptic hermeneutics, see Vern S. Poythress, "Genre and Hermeneutics in Rev 20:1–6," *JETS* 36 (March 1993): 41–54.

⁶Friedrich Düsterdieck, *Critical and Exegetical Handbook to the Revelation of John*, 6th ed., trans. Henry Jacobs (Winona Lake, Ind.: Alpha, rep. 1980 [1884]), 96.

⁷Terry, *Biblical Apocalyptics*, chap. 19: "The Apocalypse of John"; see also Milton S. Terry, *Biblical Hermeneutics: A Treatise on the Interpretation of the Old and New*

misunderstandings."[8] Even literalist Robert Thomas admits "the fluidity of metaphorical language in Scripture is undeniable."[9]

(3) *The difficulty of consistent literalism.* Some instances of literalism seem to me strange, unreasonable, and unnecessary. For example, Robert Thomas holds that the eerie locusts of Revelation 9 and the strange frogs of Revelation 16 are demons who literally take on those peculiar physical forms, that the two prophets of Revelation 11 literally spew fire from their mouths, that every mountain in the world will be abolished during the seventh bowl judgments, that the fiery destruction of the literal city of Babylon will smolder for more than 1000 years, that Christ will return from heaven to earth on a literal horse, and that the new Jerusalem is literally a 1500-mile-high cube.[10]

THE TEMPORAL EXPECTATION (REV. 1:1–3)

I turn now to a survey of the book of Revelation. In his *Republic* Plato states an important maxim: "The beginning is the most important part of the work." This principle holds a special significance for the would-be interpreter of Revelation. Unfortunately, too many prophecy enthusiasts leap over the beginning of this book, never securing a proper footing for the treacherous path ahead. But stealing a line from Isaiah, the preterist asks: "Do you not know? Have you not heard? Has it not been told you from the beginning?" (Isa. 40:21). The preterist insists that the key to Revelation is found in its front door. Notice John's introduction:

> The revelation of Jesus Christ, which God gave him to show his servants what *must soon take place.* ... Blessed is the one who reads the words of this prophecy, and blessed are those who hear it and take to heart what is written in it, because *the time is near.* (Rev. 1:1a, 3, italics added)

Here—*before* the dramatic visions flash on the scene and the highly wrought imagery confound the reader—John provides an indispensable clue for interpreting his book: The events of

---

Testaments, 2d. ed. (Grand Rapids: Zondervan, rep. 1974 [n.d.]), chap. 26: "The Apocalypse of John."

[8]Terry, *Biblical Apocalyptics,* 228.

[9]Thomas, *Revelation 8–22,* 372.

[10]Thomas, *Revelation 1–7,* 455, and *Revelation 8–22,* 30, 46, 49, 90, 264, 360, 386, 467.

Revelation "must soon [Gk. *tachos*] take place" (v. 1) because "the time is near [Gk. *engys*]."[11]

Greek lexicons and modern translations agree that these terms indicate temporal proximity. Throughout the New Testament *tachos* means "quickly, at once, without delay, shortly."[12] The term *engys* ("near") also speaks of temporal nearness: of the future (Matt. 26:18), of summer (24:32), and of a festival (John 2:13). The inspired apostle John clearly informs his original audience nearly two thousand years ago that *they* should expect the prophecies to "take place" (Rev. 1:1) in *their* lifetime. As Milton Terry notes, the events of Revelation are "but a few years in the future when John wrote."[13]

The significance of these words lies not only in their introducing Revelation, but also in their concluding its drama. They bracket and, therefore, qualify the entire book. Notice how it ends:

> The angel said to me, "These words are trustworthy and true. The Lord, the God of the spirits of the prophets, sent his angel to show his servants the things that *must soon take place*". . . .
>
> Then he told me, "Do not seal up the words of the prophecy of this book, because *the time is near*." (Rev. 22:6, 10, italics added)

What is more, the terms appear frequently in Revelation, showing John's urgent emphasis on temporal expectancy. We find *tachos* ("soon") in 1:1; 2:16; 3:11; 22: 6, 7, 12, 20 and *engys* ("near") in 1:3; 3:10; 22:10.[14] Thus, as Robert Thomas, who opposes preterism, admits: "A major thrust of Revelation is its emphasis upon the shortness of time before the fulfillment."[15]

---

[11]Theologians note that references to "the time" often indicate a special "crisis time." The near crisis in Revelation, as I will show, is the "Day of the Lord" judgment on Israel in A.D. 67–70 (Acts 2:16–20; 1 Thess. 2:14–16).

[12]See Luke 18:8; Acts 12:7; 22:18; 25:4; 1 Tim. 3:14. Where *engys* is used in surprising contexts (Rom. 13:11; 16:20; Phil. 4:5), it opens the question of the meaning of the event expected, not of the temporal significance of *engys*.

[13]Terry, *Biblical Apocalyptics*, 277.

[14]Rev. 1:19 may also be helpful, though it is obscured in the NIV. It probably should be translated as in Marshall's *The Interlinear Greek-English New Testament*, 2d ed. (Grand Rapids: Zondervan, 1959), 959: "Write thou therefore the things which thou sawest and the things which are and the things which are *about to occur* after these things." See Kenneth L. Gentry Jr., *Before Jerusalem Fell: Dating the Book of Revelation* (Tyler, Tex.: Institute for Christian Economics, 1996), 141–42.

[15]Thomas, *Revelation 1–7*, 55.

John emphasizes these two clear terms with similar meanings, thereby preempting any confusion among his readers regarding *when* the prophecies will occur.

The preterist, then, argues that John himself positively asserts that the events are near in his day. Consequently, they must lie in *our* distant past. Preterism is exegetically based, being rooted in sound hermeneutical principle. But before moving on, I must briefly reckon with two common rejoinders to this analysis:

Objection 1: John is speaking of God's timing, not ours. Scripture informs us that a thousand years with the Lord is "as a day" (2 Peter 3:8).

This popular objection strains under the weight of the following evidence: (a) Revelation is personal-motivational. John is here writing to human beings, but not about God. Peter's statement in 2 Peter 3:8 is clearly a theological statement; Revelation 1:1, 3 are human directives, which are to be heard and acted upon. Peter is dealing with the opposite problem from John: He is explaining (on the basis of God's eternality) the *delay* of Christ's second advent (2 Peter 2:4), while John is warning (on the basis of human suffering) of the *nearness* of temporal judgment.

(b) Revelation is concrete-historical. John is writing to seven specific, historical churches (1:4, 11; 2:1–3:22) about *their* present dire circumstances (they are in "tribulation," 1:9; 2:9–10, 13), their need for patience (1:9; 2:2–3, 10, 13, 25; 3:10–11), and soon-coming judgments (2:5, 16, 25; 3:3, 11; 22:10, 18–19).

Robert Thomas, approvingly citing William Lee, notes concerning the letters to the seven churches in Revelation 2 and 3: "One cannot, however, overlook the historical character which is stamped on the Epistles throughout ... and which distinctly points to a state of things actually before St. John's mind as existing in the several churches."[16] That is, a number of the historical, geographical, and political allusions in the letters show that John does, in fact, have in view the specific churches he addresses. He would be taunting them mercilessly if he were discussing events two thousand or more years distant. God answers the anxious cry "How long?" by urging their patience

---

[16]Ibid., 515; cf. chaps. 3–9. See also William Ramsey, *The Letters to the Seven Churches* (Grand Rapids: Baker, 1963 [1904]); Robert H. Mounce, *The Book of Revelation*, chaps. 3 and 4; Steven Friesen, "Ephesus: Key to a Vision in Revelation," *BAR* 19:3 (May-June 1993): 24ff.

only a "little while longer" (6:10–11).[17] Revelation promises there will no longer be "delay" (10:6). The ad hoc nature of the book demands a preterist approach.[18]

(c) Revelation is emphatic-declarative. The expressions of imminence are didactic (nonsymbolic), frequent (in the introduction, conclusion, and elsewhere), and varied (see above discussions of *tachos* and *engys*). How else could John have expressed nearness in time if not by these terms? All English translations employ terms expressing temporal nearness.

(d) Revelation is parallel-harmonic. The temporal expectation in Revelation parallels New Testament teaching elsewhere. For instance, Robert Thomas parallels Revelation 6 with Matthew 24: "Jesus in His discourse was clearly anticipating what he was to show John in much greater detail." Pate concurs.[19] I agree. Interestingly, in Matthew 24:34 Jesus holds the same expectancy as John: "Assuredly, I say to you, *this generation* will by no means pass away till all these things take place" (NKJV, italics added; cf. 23:36). He urges his hearers, as John does his own, to expect these judgments in their own lifetimes.

In Mark 9:1 Jesus promises that some of his hearers will not "taste death" before witnessing "the kingdom of God come with power." This almost certainly refers to the destruction of the temple at the behest of Christ (rather than to his transfiguration, which is only six days away). Similar notes of the temporal proximity of divinely governed crises abound in the New Testament (see Matt. 26:64; Acts 2:16–20, 40; Rom. 13:11–12; 16:20; 1 Cor. 7:26, 29–31; Col. 3:6; 1 Thess. 2:16; Heb. 10:25, 37; James 5:8–9; 1 Peter 4:5, 7; 1 John 2:17–18). How else could the New Testament express nearness more clearly? As these verses so evidently

---

[17]Futurist Robert Thomas notes the potential "meaninglessness" of the prayers of these saints if their persecutors are not still alive when the prayer is uttered (Thomas, *Revelation 1–7*, 441). I would apply the same principle to the entire book of Revelation and place it in the first century.

[18]Of course, this does not preclude the contemporary relevance of Revelation today, in that it may still provide patterns illustrating certain divine principles for our instruction (e.g., Rom. 15:4; 1 Cor. 10:11; 2 Tim. 3:16–17) while maintaining its ad hoc character. See George W. Knight III, "The Scriptures Were Written for Our Instruction," in *JETS* 39 (March 1996): 3–14.

[19]Thomas, *Revelation 1–7*, 1:53–54. C. Marvin Pate and Calvin B. Haines Jr., *Doomsday Delusions: What's Wrong With Predictions About the End of the World* (Downers Grove, Ill.: InterVarsity, 1995), 44–45.

show, dramatic divine judgments are "soon," "near," "at hand," "at the door," "present"; "the hour has come"; "the time is short"; "the wrath of God is coming"; "the day is approaching" in "just a little while." These events are to occur in "this generation," before "some who are standing ... taste death."

Objection 2: These events do occur in the first century, but they occur again later in history, either through double fulfillment or through repeated recurrence until the end as the already/not yet nature of prophecy unfolds.

Three difficulties plague this type of response. (a) There is no exegetical warrant for it; the statement is pure theological assertion. What is more, this approach not only empties John's express declarations of meaning ("*these things* must shortly *come to pass*"), but it contravenes a specific angelic directive contrasting John's responsibility to Daniel's. An angel commanded Daniel to "seal up" his prophecy for later times (Dan. 12:4), but commands John (who lives in "the last hour," 1 John 2:18) to "*not* seal up the words of the prophecy of this book, *because the time is near*" (Rev. 22:10, italics added). Nevertheless, Marvin Pate holds that Revelation "does not imply that Nero filled the complete expectation of the coming antichrist, but, as a precursor to such, he is certainly a good starting place."[20] As I shall show, Nero does fulfill Revelation's prophecy. Why look for further fulfillment?

(b) It requires us to believe that the many specific events, things, and personages of Revelation will appear repeatedly on the scene of earth history. In the same order? In the same geographic regions? With continual groupings of 144,000 being sealed? With constant beasts designated by the same number 666? On and on I could go. For example, Pate suggests that "the signs of the times *began* with Jesus and his generation," and history witnesses "the coming intensification and culmination of those signs of the times," which began in the first century.[21] Such a position seems to stretch credulity to the breaking point.

The already/not yet theological principle, though valid and widely accepted by evangelicals, cannot govern whole, vast, complex works such as Revelation. The already/not yet principle applies to unitary, simple constructs: the kingdom, salvation,

---

[20]Pate and Haines, *Doomsday Delusions*, 43–44.
[21]Ibid., 36 (cf. 44, 57), 148–49. Italics added.

new creation, and so forth. The principle snaps apart when we stretch it over so massive a work as Revelation. Furthermore, how can this principle explain the simultaneous operation in one book of such allegedly global themes operating as judgment (Rev. 6–19) and blessing (Rev. 20–22)? Pate's use of this principle to explain Revelation seems more hopeful than helpful.[22]

(c) This approach not only denies what John expressly affirms, but confuses principial application with historic event. That is, even were the events of Revelation repeated, that would not diminish the fact of their direct first-century historical fulfillment—with all its pregnant meaning in that unique era that effects the closing of the sacrificial system, the setting aside of Israel, and the universalizing of the true faith. For instance, Exodus-like events occurring after the Mosaic Exodus do not remove the redemptive-historical significance of that original historical episode. Pate specifically notes that the mark of the beast "can be understood as pointing a guilty finger at those Jews in the first century."[23] Why, then, should we look for further fulfillments beyond this most relevant first-century one?

According to John, then, the prophetic events are "soon" (1:1) and "near" (1:3), so that his original audience must "hold fast" (2:25; 3:11, NKJV), waiting only "a little longer" (6:11). "I am coming soon. Hold on to what you have, so that no one will take your crown" (3:11). Modern students of prophecy must not let a presupposed theological scheme or predetermined interpretive methodology blunt these forceful assertions.

THE REVELATIONAL THEME (REV. 1:7)

What, then, does John expect in the near future of his original audience? How can any events in the first century meet up to the Revelational drama?[24]

---

[22]Ibid., 148–55.

[23]Ibid., 53.

[24]Due to space limitations I cannot here defend the pre-A.D. 70 date of Revelation's composition, which, though a minority viewpoint, claims many notable scholars. For detailed arguments see the published version of my doctoral dissertation on the subject: Gentry, *Before Jerusalem Fell*. Or see Terry, *Biblical Apocalyptics*, 237–42. The late-date view depends heavily on church tradition, a tradition deeply rooted in Irenaeus's famous statement found in his *Against Heresies* (5:30:5). But as Metzger notes: "Irenaeus's date is open to question" (Bruce M. Metzger, "Revelation, The

Revelation's main focus of attention (though not its only point) is this: God will soon judge the first-century Jews for rejecting and crucifying his Son, their Messiah. That is, the judgments of Revelation come especially against those who cried out: "Crucify him! . . . Let his blood be on us and on our children!" (Matt. 27:22, 25; cf. John 19:1–16). John states his theme in his introduction at Revelation 1:7, just after he declares the nearness of the events (1:1, 3), a theme that is directly relevant to the first-century circumstances. Note particularly the following literal translations:

> Lo, he doth come with the clouds, and see him shall every eye, even those who did pierce him, and wail because of him shall all the tribes of the land. Yes! Amen! (*Young's Literal Translation of the Holy Bible*)

> Behold he comes with the clouds, and will see him every eye and those who him pierced, and will wail over him all the tribes of the land. Yes, amen. (Alfred Marshall, *The Interlinear Greek-English New Testament*)

Many assume the Second Advent is in view here. And upon first reading such seems appropriate.[25] Nevertheless, in its contextual setting verse 7 points to the destruction of Jerusalem and her temple in A.D. 70, which produces several dramatic results: It brings God's wrath on the Jews for rejecting their Messiah (Matt. 21:33–44); it concludes the anticipatory old covenant era (John 4:20–23; Heb. 1:1; 12:18–29), which is becoming "obsolete" and "aging" and "will soon disappear" (Heb. 8:13); it finally and forever closes down the typological sacrificial system, reorienting the worship of God (Heb. 9–10); and it effectively universalizes the Christian faith by freeing it from all Jewish constraints (Matt.

Book of," in Bruce M. Metzger and Michael D. Coogan, eds., *The Oxford Companion to the Bible* [New York: Oxford Univ. Press, 1993], 653). Early date advocates include: Moses Stuart, B. F. Westcott, F. J. A. Hort, Joseph B. Lightfoot, F. W. Farrar, Alfred Edersheim, Philip Schaff, Milton Terry, F. F. Bruce, J. A. T. Robinson, J. A. Fitzmyer, J. M. Ford, C. F. D. Moule, Albert A. Bell, J. Christian Moberly, Cornelis Vanderwaal, and Christopher Rowland.

[25]I do believe Christ will come personally, visibly, and gloriously to end history with the resurrection of the dead and the great judgment of all humanity. See my *He Shall Have Dominion*, chap. 13. Thomas erroneously claims I do not see the Second Coming in the Olivet Discourse or Revelation; the Second Coming is found in Matt. 24:36–25:46 and Rev. 20:7-15.

28:18–20; Eph. 2:12–22) that tend to "pervert the gospel of Christ" (Gal. 1:7; cf. Acts 15:1; Gal. 4:10; Col. 2:16). Let me provide brief exegetical notations supporting this interpretation.

(1) The "coming with the clouds" language is common prophetic parlance for historical divine judgments on nations. Isaiah speaks of God's coming judgment against Egypt in similar terms: "An oracle concerning Egypt: See, the LORD rides on a swift cloud and is coming to Egypt. The idols of Egypt tremble before him, and the hearts of the Egyptians melt within them" (Isa. 19:1). Obviously, God does not literally and visibly ride down from heaven on a cloud against Egypt. But he does send a great judgment on the Egyptians—as by a terrible and destructive storm cloud. Other references confirm this type of statement, known as "apocalyptic metaphor" (see Ps. 18:7–15; 104:3; Isa. 13: 1, 9–13; Joel 2:1–2; Mic. 1:3–4).[26]

Interestingly, as Robert Thomas notes, John follows Jesus' merging of Zechariah 12:10 and Daniel 7:13.[27] Like John, Jesus mentions the "coming with [on] the clouds" (cf. Matt. 24:29–30) against Israel (23:36–24:2, 16), immediately before he says, "*This generation* will certainly not pass away until *all* these things have happened" (24:34, italics added). And just as Jesus says to the first-century high priest standing before him that he will "see" the Son of Man "coming on the clouds" (26:64), so here John tells his original audience, "Every eye will see him," that is, his judgment-coming will be a dramatic, public event, not done in a corner.[28]

(2) This coming will be especially directed against "those who pierced him," that is, the first-century Jews who demanded his crucifixion. Jesus' teaching lays the blame for the crucifixion primarily on the Jews (Matt. 20:18; 21:33–43; Luke 9:22), as does the apostle Peter's instruction: "Then know this, you and all the

---

[26] Even Dallas Theological Seminary's *Bible Knowledge Commentary: Old Testament*, ed. John F. Walvoord and Roy B. Zuck, (Wheaton, Ill.: Victor, 1985), recognizes this phenomenon in these Old Testament texts.

[27] Thomas, *Revelation 1–7*, 76.

[28] In various places in Revelation "seeing" does not demand a physical beholding, but sensing or realizing, just as we say, "I see," when a teacher shows us a math solution. Robert Thomas notes of John's own "beholding" in Rev. 4:1: "This action should not be equated with the physical eye. Rather, it is sight with the eye of ecstatic vision as throughout the Apocalypse" (Thomas, *Revelation*, 1:334). Yet this is a type of "seeing."

people of Israel: It is by the name of Jesus Christ of Nazareth, whom you crucified ..." (Acts 4:10; cf. John 19:5–15; Acts 2:22–23, 36; 3:14–15; 5:30; 10:39; 1 Thess. 2:14–16).[29]

Christ's judgment-coming will bring mourning on "all the tribes of the earth" (NIV). The literal translations cited above show John actually focuses on all the tribes of "the land" (Gk. *tēs gēs*), the well-known Promised Land in which the Jews lived. (We should probably translate the Greek word *hē gē* as "the land" rather than "the earth" in the great majority of the cases where this word occurs in Revelation.[30]) John's reference to Christ's piercing demands a first-century focus if the theme is to be relevant and true, for those who pierced him are now long since deceased. Note the important observation regarding Matthew 21:40 made by premillennialist scholar Henry Alford:

> We may observe that our Lord makes 'when the Lord cometh' *coincide with the destruction of Jerusalem*, which is incontestably the overthrow of the wicked husbandmen. This passage therefore forms an important key to our Lord's prophecies, and a decisive justification for those who like myself, firmly hold that *the coming of the Lord is*, in many places, to be identified, primarily, with that overthrow.[31]

(3) This interpretation fits perfectly with the Lord's Olivet Discourse, which begins with an inquiry regarding the destiny of the first-century temple in light of the Jewish rejection of Christ (cf. Matt. 23:34–24:2). The judgments focus particularly on the temple (24:2) in Judea (24:16) during that "generation" (24:34).[32]

---

[29]The Romans, in effect, were instruments of Jewish wrath against Christ. The Jews demanded that the Romans crucify him (Matt. 20:18–19; 27:11–25; Mark 10:33; 15:1; Luke 18:32; 23:1–2; John 18:28–31; 19:12, 15; Acts 3:13; 4:26–27; Rev. 17); Pilate sought to release him and lay the responsibility on the Jews (Matt. 27:24); Christ said that the Romans "do not know what they are doing" (Luke 23:34). For more information see Terry, *Biblical Apocalyptics*, 280–82.

[30]Alan James Beagley, *The "Sitz im Leben" of the Apocalypse With Particular Reference to the Role of the Church's Enemies* (New York: Walter de Gruyter, 1987). See also Gentry, *Before Jerusalem Fell*, chap. 8.

[31]Henry Alford, *The Greek New Testament*, 4 vols. (Chicago: Moody, 1958 [1849–1861]), 1:216 (emphasis his).

[32]See: Thomas D. Ice and Kenneth L. Gentry Jr., *The Great Tribulation: Past or Future?* (Grand Rapids: Kregel, 1997); Gary DeMar, *Last Days Madness: Obsession of*

As a result of the grave nature of God's judgment on Israel and its universal consequences, however, great disruptions will reverberate well beyond the narrow confines of Israel. The narrow focus is on Israel; the full scope encompasses the Roman empire. This is why John writes to the seven churches of Asia Minor. They not only must understand God's destruction of Jerusalem and the temple (a major event even for Christians[33]), but must brace themselves for the severe aftershocks associated with it. In fact, Christ urges the seven churches to repent, reform, and persevere (Rev. 2:5, 16, 21–22; 3:3, 19) because of impending judgments soon to erupt (2:5, 16; 3:11; 22:12, 20). In the case of the church in Philadelphia, for instance, Christ promises to shield them from that judgment: "Because you have kept the word of My perseverance, I also will keep you from the hour of testing, that *hour* which is *about to come* [italics added] upon the whole world, to test those who dwell upon the earth" (Rev. 3:10 NASB).

THE THRONE SCENE (REV. 4–5)

In 1:12–20 John's first vision shows Christ *in history* (spiritually) walking among the churches as their ever-present protector and head (cf. Matt. 18:20; 28:18, 20; Acts 18:9–10; Heb. 13:5). The focal judgments of Revelation do not begin until chapter 6. In chapters 4–5, however, God braces John for those coming fearsome judgment scenes by spiritually transporting him *above history* to God's throne room in heaven (Rev. 4:1–2).

In Revelation 4 John sees God sitting on his judicial throne and actively ruling over all creation (4:2–6, 11). The four "living creatures" closest to the throne seem to be angels of the highest order: They ever watch (being "covered with eyes," v. 6) over

---

the Modern Church (Atlanta: American Vision, 1994); David Chilton, *The Great Tribulation* (Fort Worth, Tex.: Dominion, 1987). Much helpful information is also found in Pate and Haines, *Doomsday Delusions*.

[33]Early believers continued to gravitate toward Israel: engaging in Jewish worship observances (Acts 2:1ff.; 24:11; 21:26), focusing on and radiating their ministry from Jerusalem (Acts 2–5) while frequenting the temple (Acts 2:46; 3:1ff.; 4:1; 5:21ff.; 21:26; 26:21), attending the synagogues (13:5, 14; 14:1; 15:21; 17:1ff.; 18:4, 7, 19, 26; 19:8; 22:19; 24:12; 26:11), designating themselves as the true heirs of Judaism (Gal. 3:27–29; 6:16; Phil. 3:3), and so forth.

creation (appearing as creatures and singing of creation, vv. 7, 11), ready to do God's holy bidding (having six wings to fly swiftly and singing of God's holiness, v. 8) in all of creation (their number represents the four points of the compass, v. 7; cf. 7:1; 21:13). Whatever John witnesses thereafter—however terrifying the judgments, however vicious the opposition—he may rest assured that not only does Christ concern himself with the affairs of his people in history (chap. 1), but God is actively controlling all things from above history (chap. 4; cf. Dan. 2:21; 4:35; Rom. 8:28; Eph. 1:11).

Interestingly, John mentions God's "throne" in eighteen of Revelation's twenty-two chapters. In fact, of the sixty-two appearances of the word "throne" in the New Testament, we find forty-seven of them in Revelation. Strong judicial tendencies characterize Revelation, not only because of this dramatic vision itself but because of all the judicial terminology therein (e.g., 6:10; 11:18; 15:3; 16:5-7; 18:8; 19:2, 11). The temporal judgment-coming of Christ, which dramatically concludes forever the Old Testament typological era (cf. 11:1-2, 19; 21:22), is directed from the throne of the universe.

In chapter 5 a remarkable claimant to the right to execute God's judgments appears before the throne: a slain but living Lamb. The strongly Judaic (and symbolic) description of Christ's appearance here underscores the thematic concern of Christ's coming in cloud-judgment against "those who pierced him," that is, the Jews (1:7). Thus he appears as a sacrificial lamb, "looking as if it had been slain" (5:6, 9, 12), who is "the Lion of the tribe of Judah, the Root of David" (5:5). The emphasis on his crucifixion (as in 1:7) is unmistakable ("lamb," "slain"). As Milton Terry observes, there is a certain irony in this imagery: "The great trouble with Judaism was that it looked for a mighty lion; and was scandalized to behold, instead, a little lamb" (cf. Luke 24:21, 25-27; John 6:15; 19:15).[34]

But what does the seven-sealed scroll represent? "Then I saw in the right hand of him who sat on the throne a scroll with writing on both sides and sealed with seven seals" (5:1). If we are to discern the proper meaning of this scroll, we must bear in mind four interpretive controls: (1) The scroll must apply to first-century events, for "the time is near" (1:3; 22:6, 10, 12; cf. 6:11). (2) The scroll

---

[34]Terry, *Biblical Apocalyptics*, 323.

must refer to Israel, for Revelation's theme refers to "those who pierced him" (1:7; 11:8). (3) The scroll should have Old Testament warrant, for, as Robert Thomas well notes: "The influence of the OT on Revelation is overwhelming."[35] (4) The scroll should be consistent with the flow of Revelation, for it is an intricately structured book with all of its numbered series and reappearing images.

In the Old Testament we find a scroll similarly described and in an analogous context. In Ezekiel 1 the prophet saw four living, winged creatures, much like those John sees (Ezek. 1:5–10; Rev. 4:6–8). Near Ezekiel's living creatures he saw a crystal-like expanse and a glorious throne overarched by a rainbow, much like that John sees (Ezek. 1:22–28; Rev. 4:2–6). In Ezekiel 2:9–10 we read: "Then I looked, and I saw a hand stretched out to me. In it was a scroll, which he unrolled before me. On both sides of it were written words of lament and mourning and woe." This reminds us of John's experience: "Then I saw in the right hand of him who sat on the throne a scroll with writing on both sides and sealed with seven seals" (Rev. 5:1). The strong similarities surely are not accidental; John seems to be intentionally following Ezekiel's pattern.

What, then, is the point of Ezekiel's vision? Judgment on Israel: "He said: 'Son of man, I am sending you to the Israelites, to a rebellious nation that has rebelled against me; they and their fathers have been in revolt against me to this very day'" (Ezek. 2:3). This supports our understanding of Revelation's main focus, especially when we consider how much greater is first-century Israel's sin in rejecting the Messiah himself (Matt. 21:33–45; 23:32–38; John 1:11; Acts 2:23, 36; cf. Matt. 13:17; 1 Peter 1:10–12). The sevenfold nature of the judgments on Israel (represented by the seven seals, trumpets, and bowls) reminds us of the covenantal curse God threatens on her in the Old Testament: "If after all this you will not listen to me, I will punish you for your sins seven times over" (Lev. 26:18; cf. vv. 24, 28).

When viewed against the backdrop of the theme of Jewish judgment, personages (a harlot and a bride), and the flow of Revelation (from the sealed scroll to capital punishment for "adultery" to a "marriage feast" to the taking of a new "bride" as the "new Jerusalem"), the covenantal nature of the transaction suggests that the seven-sealed scroll is God's divorce decree

---

[35]Thomas, *Revelation 1–7*, 41.

against his Old Testament wife for her spiritual adultery. In the Old Testament God "marries" Israel (see esp. Ezek. 16:8, 31–32),[36] and in several places he threatens her with a "bill of divorce" (Isa. 50:1; Jer. 3:8).

In the New Testament the final and conclusive destruction of the temple accomplishes this. In his divorce of Israel God disestablishes her: Redemptive history is no longer the story of a Jewish-focused, Israel-exalting, geopolitical work as in the Old Testament (Matt. 8:11; 21:43; cf. Ps. 147:19–20; Amos 3:2). God's work now reaches out to "all nations" (Matt. 28:19; Acts 1:8); Christ makes of two, one new man (Eph. 2:12–22), where there is no longer "Jew nor Greek" (Rom. 10:12; Gal. 3:28; Col. 3:11).

The "Lion of the tribe of Judah" reference (Rev. 5:5) harks back to Genesis 49. There we hear of the universalizing of God's work beyond the borders of Israel: Judah is "a lion's cub . . . the obedience of the nations is his" (Gen. 49:9–10). Furthermore, Christ's appearing before God's throne in heaven (Rev. 5:6) reminds us of Daniel's messianic vision: When the "son of man" appears before "the Ancient of Days," God grants him a kingdom so "that all peoples, nations and men of every language worshiped him" (Dan. 7:13–14; cf. Rev. 5:9; 7:9; 14:6).

Nevertheless, though God judges the first-century Jews and disestablishes Israel as the unique geopolitical focus of his kingdom, we know from other New Testament revelation that the Jews will also eventually return to the kingdom of God in full number, receiving the blessings of salvation (Rom. 11). But God will never exalt them above other blood-bought people (even the Old Testament anticipates such equality; see Isa. 19:23–25; Jer. 48:47; 49:6, 39; Zech. 9:7).[37] Jews and Gentiles merge into one body in Christ forever, forming one tree (Rom. 11:15, 25), one new man (Eph. 2:13–18), one new temple (2:19–22), and one new creation (Gal. 6:15).

THE SEVEN SEALS (REV. 6)

In Revelation 6 Christ begins opening the seals. As Robert Thomas, Marvin Pate, and other commentators note, there is a

---

[36]Isa. 54:5; 62:4; Jer. 3:14, 20; 31:32; Hos. 1:2; 2:2 ,7, 16; 5:4; 9:1, 10. She seeks marriage to foreign gods, Mal. 2:11.

[37]David E. Holwerda, *Jesus and Israel: One Covenant or Two?* (Grand Rapids: Eerdmans, 1995).

"close parallelism" between Jesus' Olivet Discourse and the seals of Revelation.[38] And as the preterist reminds them, the contexts of both of these prophecies relate to first-century events (cf. Rev. 1:1, 3 with Matt. 24:2–3, 34).[39] It is significant that church father Eusebius (A.D. 260–340) used Josephus's history of the Jewish War (A.D. 67–70) to illustrate the fulfilling of the Olivet prophecy (*Eccl. Hist.* 3:5–9).

The rider on the white horse "bent on conquest" (Rev. 6:2–3) represents the victorious Roman march toward Jerusalem to engage the Jewish war in the spring of A.D. 67.[40] The rider on the red horse (6:4), who takes the "peace from the earth" (6:4; cf. Matt. 24:6–7), speaks of the surprising disruption of the famous *pax Romana*, an enforced peace that prevailed throughout the Roman empire for many years. For example, Epictetus (A.D. 60–140) writes that "Caesar has obtained for us a profound peace. There are neither wars nor battles" (*Discourses* 3:13:9). The Jewish revolt against Rome temporarily interrupts this famous peace. The red horse especially highlights that civil war occurring in Jerusalem itself (where Jesus utters his prophecy, Matt. 24).

The riders on the black and pale horses represent famine and death issuing from the Jewish war. These tragic factors of this war are well-documented by Josephus (*Wars of the Jews* 4–7), the Jewish historian who participated in the war,[41] and by the Roman historians Tacitus (*Histories* 1) and Suetonius (*Vespasian*).

---

[38]Thomas, *Revelation 1–7*, 53; Pate and Haines, *Doomsday Delusions*, 37–44.

[39]For a detailed explanation of Matt. 24, see Ice and Gentry, *The Great Tribulation*.

[40]White here represents "victory," not purity: (1) It commonly does so in antiquity (Virgil, *Aeneid* 3:537; Plutarch, *Camillus* 7; Dio Cassius, *Roman History* 53:14). (2) The rider goes forth "bent on conquest" (6:2). (3) The bow is a symbol of victory (Zech. 9:13–14). (4) The color relates to its effect (conquering) like the other horses' colors (e.g., red=blood; black=famine; pale=death).

[41]Flavius Josephus is a non-Christian Jewish historian who lived from A.D. 37–101. He served as a general in the Jewish forces during the Jewish war against Rome in A.D. 67–70. During the war the Romans defeated him at Jotapata. Josephus surrendered to the Roman general Flavius Vespasian, whom he then befriended by interpreting a prophetic oracle to mean that Vespasian would one day be emperor of Rome. He then worked with Vespasian in attempting to persuade the Jews to surrender their hopeless cause. After the war Josephus moved to Rome and changed his name from the very Jewish Joseph Ben Matthias to a more Roman Flavius Josephus, taking on his benefactor's name. Vespasian became emperor of Rome in A.D. 69 and sponsored the writing of *The Wars of the Jews*, *The Antiquities of the Jews*, and

The fifth seal (6:9–11) gives a heavenward glance once again (cf. chap. 4), where we hear the martyrs crying for vengeance. God promises to vindicate them, but they must "wait a little longer" (v. 11; cf. Luke 18:6–8). Martyr vindication is crucial to understanding Israel's judgment (Matt. 23:34–24:2).

The decreation language in the sixth seal (Rev. 6:12–17) portrays Israel's world coming apart under the "wrath of the Lamb" on the "great day of wrath" (vv. 16–17).[42] Such language is common prophetic parlance regarding the collapse of God-cursed governments, such as Babylon (Isa. 13:1, 10, 19), Egypt (Ezek. 32:2, 7–8, 16, 18), Idumea (Isa. 34:3–5), and Judah (Jer. 4:14, 23–24).[43] Milton Terry writes of Revelation 6:

> The imagery and style of the Old Testament apocalyptists are most appropriately brought into use; sun, moon, and stars, and the heaven itself, are pictured as collapsing, and the crisis of the ages is signaled by voices and thunders and lightnings and earthquake. To insist on literal interpretation of such imagery is to bring prophecy into contempt and ridicule.[44]

The moving away of "every mountain" of the sixth seal (6:14) may allude to the Roman legions' construction crews removing mountainous impediments to the progress of the massive army, or else to their building banks to the tops of the protective walls surrounding Jewish cities. Josephus notes: "Accordingly [Vespasian] sent both footmen and horsemen to

---

other works by Josephus. Josephus completed *Wars* in A.D. 75, just five years after the fall of Jerusalem. In this work Josephus wrote as an eyewitness historian who happened to be in the action on both sides of the conflict. His work is extremely helpful for providing historical insights into the events of that war, so many of which are foretold in John's prophecy in Revelation.

[42]See the anticipation of this A.D. 70 judgment at the original A.D. 30 Pentecost (Acts 2:16–20). Tongues are a sign of judgment on the first-century Jews (1 Cor. 14:21–22; cf. Deut. 28:49; Isa. 28:11ff.; 33:19; Jer. 5:15; Ezek. 3:5). See Kenneth L. Gentry Jr., *The Charismatic Gift of Prophecy: A Reformed Response to Wayne Grudem* 2d ed. (Memphis, Tenn.: Footstool, 1989); O. Palmer Robertson, *The Final Word: A Biblical Response to the Case for Tongues and Prophecy Today* (Edinburgh: Banner of Truth, 1993).

[43]For expositions of Old Testament decreation imagery in preconsummational, historic Old Testament judgments, see Dallas Theological Seminary's commentary, *Bible Knowledge Commentary: Old Testament*, at Isa. 13:10; Jer. 4:23–28; Ezek. 32:11–16; Joel 2:10–11.

[44]Terry, *Biblical Apocalyptics*, 269.

level the road, which was mountainous and rocky, not without difficulty to be traveled over by footmen, but absolutely impracticable for horsemen. Now these workmen accomplished what they were about in four days" (*Wars* 3.7.3). After describing the mountainous setting of Jotapata and its natural impregnability (*Wars* 3.7.7), Josephus mentions Vespasian's decision to "raise a bank against that part of the wall which was practicable" (*Wars* 3.7.8).

In 6:15–16 many "hid in caves" and "called to the mountains and the rocks, 'Fall on us.'" Josephus frequently mentions that the Jews actually sought refuge underground during the A.D. 67–70 war: "And on this day the Romans slew all the multitude that appeared openly; but on the following days they searched the hiding places, and fell upon those that were underground, and in the caverns" (*Wars* 3.7.36; see also 3.2.3; 3.7.35; 5.3.1; 6.7.3; 6.9.4; 7.2.1).[45]

Jesus warns the women watching him carry his cross:

> For the time will come when you will say, "Blessed are the barren women, the wombs that never bore and the breasts that never nursed!" Then

> "they will say to the mountains, 'Fall on us!'
>   and to the hills, 'Cover us!'" (Luke 23:29–30; cf. Matt. 24:1–2, 19, 34)

The fate of the women and children in A.D. 70 was horrible:

> Then did the famine widen its progress, and devoured the people by whole houses and families; the upper rooms were full of women and children that were dying by famine; and the lanes of the city were full of the dead bodies of the aged; the children also and the young men wandered about the marketplaces like shadows, all swelled with the famine. (*Wars* 5.12.3)

The relevant fit of first-century events with the prophecy of Revelation 6 is so compelling that Marvin Pate admits their connection, even though he rejects the preterist conclusions.[46]

---

[45]An interesting archaeological study of the first-century caverns under Jerusalem appears in Leen Ritmeyer, "Locating the Original Temple Mount," *BAR* 18:2 (March-April 1992), 24–45.

[46]Pate and Haines, *Doomsday Delusions*, 44–55.

THE 144,000 SAINTS (REV. 7)

As the wrath of the Lamb against the Jews recorded in Revelation builds, we witness a surprising pause in the horrifying drama. Four angels hold back the wind from "the land," that is, from Israel (7:1–3). This act is symbolic imagery, relating what Robert Thomas calls (at another place) "picturesque apocalyptic."[47] The angels are not holding back literal winds, but the winds of destruction (cf. Jer. 49:36–37; 51:1–2). The first six seals represent the early stage of the Jewish war, wherein Vespasian fought his way through Galilee toward Jerusalem. But before he has an opportunity to besiege Jerusalem, the action pauses as these angels seal the 144,000 from the twelve tribes of Israel (Rev. 7:3).

The number 144,000, as most commentators agree, is surely symbolic. In fact, in Revelation perfectly rounded thousands all appear to be symbolic. Ten is the number of quantitative perfection, and one thousand is the cube of ten. Frequently Scripture uses the number 1,000 as a symbolic value, not expressing a literal enumeration (e.g., Ex. 20:6; Deut. 1:11; 7:9; 32:30; Josh. 23:10; Job 9:3; Ps. 50:10; 84:10; 90:4; 105:8; Eccl. 7:28; Isa. 7:23; 30:17; 60:22; 2 Peter 3:8). Furthermore, in this highly symbolic book we should note that exactly 12,000 people come from each one of the twelve tribes. But what does the number symbolize? And who are these people? What is the significance of this episode?

To properly assess these questions, we must keep in mind the following facts: (1) The events are occurring in the first century, as John so clearly demands (1:1, 3; 22:6, 10). (2) The judgments are falling on Israel and moving toward Jerusalem (see discussion above on 1:7 and chaps. 5–6). (3) Apostolic Christianity tended to focus on Jerusalem (cf. Acts 1:4, 8; 18:21; 20:16; 24:11[48]). (4) John considers non-Christian Jews as only "so-called Jews" and members of the "synagogue of Satan" (Rev. 2:9; 3:9; cf. John 8:31–47).

Therefore, these "servants of God" from the "twelve tribes of Israel" (7:4–8) are racial Jews who accept the Lamb of God for salvation (they later appear with him on Mount

---

[47]Thomas, *Revelation 1–7*, 465.
[48]See note 33 above.

Zion, 14:1–5).[49] When we compare their specifically defined number (144,000) to the "great multitude that no one could count" (7:9), it is relatively small. But they are a perfect number, especially loved by God and belonging to him (they are true Jews, the remnant; see Rom. 2:28–29; 9:6, 27; 11:5). Thus, the Lord places his (spiritual) seal on them (Rev. 7:3; cf. 2 Cor. 1:22; Eph. 1:13; 4:30; 2 Tim. 2:19). In a sense, their sealing is the answer to the question: "Who can stand?" (Rev. 6:17). The answer: Only those whom God protects—precisely as per the Old Testament backdrop (Ezek. 9:4–9).

In other words, before the Jewish war reaches and overwhelms Jerusalem, God providentially causes a brief cessation of hostilities, allowing the Jewish Christians in Judea to escape (as Jesus urges in Matt. 24:16–22). This happened when the emperor Nero committed suicide (A.D. 68), causing the Roman generals Vespasian and Titus to cease operations and withdraw for a year because of the turmoil in Rome.[50] We know from the church fathers Eusebius and Epiphanius that Christians fled to Pella before the war overwhelmed Jerusalem (Eusebius, *Eccl. Hist.* 3.5.3; Epiphanius, *Heresies* 29.7).

THE SEVEN TRUMPETS (REV. 8–9)

After a dramatic pause in the action for literary effect (8:1), the seventh seal initiates a new series of judgments under the imagery of seven trumpets (chaps. 8–9). These judgments spiral forward, rehearsing from different angles the preceding judgments

[49]Thomas has misunderstood the presentation in my book *Before Jerusalem Fell*, erroneously charging me with contradiction regarding the identity of the 144,000. He says I state in one place that they represent the entire church and in another place only the Jewish converts from Israel. In my view, the 144,000 represent the firstfruits of the gospel from Jewish converts in Israel. Of course, as such they are the beginning of the new covenant phase of the church, but they do not symbolize the church.

[50]Luke translates the Hebraic terminology of Matthew 24:15 so that we understand it occurs when "you see Jerusalem being surrounded by armies, you will know that its desolation is near" (Luke 21:20), and at that time his followers are to flee (Luke 21:21; cf. Matt. 24:16). In A.D. 68 generals Vespasian and Titus "had fortified all the places round about Jerusalem ... encompassing the city round about on all sides" (Josephus, *Wars* 4.9.1). But when Vespasian and Titus are "informed that Nero was dead" (4.9.2), they "did not go on with their expedition against the Jews" (4.9.2; cf. 4.10.2) until after Vespasian became emperor in 69. Then "Vespasian turned his thoughts to what remained unsubdued in Judea" (4.10.5).

but intensifying the crises. For example, the devastation grows from one-fourth in 6:8 to one-third in 8:7–12; this is in response to the continuing imprecatory prayers of the saints (cf. 8:3–4 with 6:9–11). Here Israel's judgments begin to reflect the Egyptian plagues (cf. Rev. 8 with Ex. 9–10; see also Rev. 8:10–11 with Ex. 15:23–25). This marvelously drawn scene shows a reversal of Israel's Exodus experience, in that now she herself suffers through exodus-like judgments. Later in Revelation John specifically calls Jerusalem "Egypt" (Rev. 11:8), showing her acting like Egypt, the enemy of God.[51]

The First Four Trumpets

If we consult Josephus's eyewitness account of the Jewish war, we discover remarkable correspondences with Revelation's imagery. Let me cite a few illustrations. (1) In 8:5 we read of "peals of thunder, rumblings, flashes of lightning and an earthquake." Josephus informs us of a

> prodigious storm in the night, with the utmost violence, and very strong winds, with the largest showers of rain, and continual lightnings, terrible thunderings, and amazing concussions and bellowings of the earth, that was in an earthquake. These things were a manifest indication that some destruction was coming upon men, when the system of the world was put into this disorder; and any one would guess that these wonders foreshewed some grand calamities that were coming. (*Wars* 4.4.5)

(2) The burning up of one-third of the trees of "the land" (Gk. *hē gē*; 8:7) reminds us of the Romans' setting villages on fire in conjunction with their denuding the land of its trees.

- Note what Josephus writes about the policy of the Romans: "He also at the same time gave his soldiers leave to set the suburbs on fire, and ordered that they should bring timber together, and raise banks against the city" (*Wars* 5.6.2).
- The Romans destroyed the trees in Israel for fuel and for building their weapons: "All the trees that were about the city had been already cut down for the mak-

---

[51]Interestingly, in one of Josephus's speeches to Israel seeking her continued existence through surrender, he alludes to the Egyptian plagues (*Wars* 5.9.4).

ing of the former banks" (*Wars* 5.12.4). "They cut down all the trees that were in the country that adjoined to the city, and that for ninety furlongs round about" (*Wars* 6.1.1; cf. 3.7.8; 5.6.2).

- Of Vespasian's march on Gadara, Josephus writes: "He also set fire, not only to the city itself, but to all the villas and small cities that were round about it" (*Wars* 3.7.1; cf. 4.9.1). "Galilee was all over filled with fire and blood" (*Wars* 3.4.1). Vespasian "went and burnt Galilee and the neighboring parts" (*Wars* 6.6.2).
- When the temple finally burns, Josephus moans: "One would have thought that the hill itself, on which the temple stood, was seething hot, as full of fire on every part of it" (*Wars* 6.5.1).
- And, of course, ultimately the whole city of Jerusalem goes up in flames so that as the Romans take the Jews captive to Rome, they relate that they are from "a land still on fire upon every side" (*Wars* 7.5.5).

(3) The destroying of ships and the turning of the seas and waters into blood (8:8–9) remind us of fights at the various bodies of water in and around Israel. Josephus records one scene in which the Jews "built themselves a great many piratical ships, and turned pirates upon the seas near to Syria, and Phoenicia, and Egypt, and made those seas unnavigable to all men" (*Wars* 3.9.2). Unfortunately, for these men "a violent wind [blew] upon them; it is called by those that sail there 'the black north wind,' and there dashed their ships one against another" with such great destruction that "although the greatest part of them were carried by the waves, and dashed to pieces against the abrupt parts of the rocks, insomuch that the sea was bloody a long way, and the maritime parts were full of dead bodies" (*Wars* 3.9.3).

The same happens at the Sea of Galilee: "One might then see the lake all bloody, and full of dead bodies" (*Wars* 3.10.9). Elsewhere we read: "Not only the whole of the country through which they had fled was filled with slaughter, and Jordan could not be passed over, by reason of the dead bodies that were in it, but because the lake Asphaltitis [Dead Sea] was also full of dead bodies, that were carried down into it by the river" (*Wars* 4.7.6).

(4) Regarding the waters turning bitter and poisonous (8:10–11), we might think of such scenes as those associated with the sea battles mentioned above:

One might then see the lake all bloody, and full of dead bodies, for not one of them escaped. And a terrible stink, and a very sad sight there was on the following days over that country; for as for the shores, they were full of shipwrecks, and of dead bodies all swelled; and as the dead bodies were inflamed by the sun, and putrefied, they corrupted the air. (*Wars* 3.10.9)

The Fifth Trumpet

When the fifth trumpet sounds, the Abyss ("bottomless pit," KJV) opens, belching forth smoke like "the smoke of a great furnace" (9:2, KJV). Out of this smoke swarm terrifying locusts armed with the sting of scorpions; they torment people for five months (9:3–6). As Robert Thomas notes, these must be demons—though I do not agree with his notion that they literally take on the grotesque shape of these images.[52] I would use Thomas's term employed elsewhere: "picturesque apocalyptic."[53]

We have sufficient warrant from the words of our Savior to see this prophecy applying to the Jewish war era. Jesus comes to Israel preaching the nearness of "the kingdom of heaven" (Matt. 4:17). This, of course, represents a threat to Satan's kingdom, thereby sparking a strong demonic response. Satan even tempts Jesus to acknowledge Satan's rule (4:8–10). An important aspect of Jesus' ministry, then, is to confront Satan and to exorcize demons in response to Satan's arraying his forces against him (e.g., 4:24; 8:16; 10:8; 12:27).

Jesus warns Israel that his exorcism ministry will have only a temporary effect if the people do not repent. In fact, he warns them by parable that their own generation will experience a renewed outburst of demonic affliction:

When an evil spirit comes out of a man, it goes through arid places seeking rest and does not find it. Then it says, "I will return to the house I left." When it arrives, it finds the house unoccupied, swept clean and put in order. Then it goes and takes with it seven other spirits more wicked than itself, and they go in and live there. And the final condition of that man is worse than

---

[52]Thomas, *Revelation 8–22*, 30, 46, 49.
[53]Thomas, *Revelation 1–7*, 465.

the first. *That is how it will be with this wicked generation.* (Matt. 12:43–45, italics added)

Within forty years of Jesus' warning, the Jewish war erupted. During the particularly grueling final siege of Jerusalem, an evil gloom settled over the city. F. F. Bruce comments: "Titus began the siege of Jerusalem in April, 70. The defenders held out desperately for five months, but by the end of August the temple area was occupied and the holy house burned down" (cf. *Wars* 5).[54] This five months of the Jewish war happens to be its most gruesome and evil period (*Wars* 5.1.1, 4–5; 10.5; 12.4; 13.6), fitting well the imagery of Revelation 9:5: "They were not given power to kill them, but only to torture [Gk. *basanizō*] them for five months. And the agony they suffered was like that of the sting of a scorpion when it strikes a man" (cf. v. 10).

Although Josephus does not mention demonic involvement, the cruel barbarity of the Jews' internal strife seems to reflect such. He writes: "For the present sedition, one should not be mistaken if he called it a sedition begotten by another sedition, and to be like a wild beast grown mad, which for want of food from abroad, fell now upon eating its own flesh" (*Wars* 5.1.1).

> And now, as the city was engaged in a war on all sides, from these treacherous crowds of *wicked men*, the people of the city, between them, were like a great body torn in pieces. The aged men and the women were *in such distress by their internal calamities*, that they wished for the Romans, and earnestly hoped for an external war, in order to deliver them from their *domestic miseries*. The citizens themselves were under a *terrible consternation and fear. . . .* The noise also of those that were fighting was incessant, both by day and by night; *but the lamentation of those that mourned exceeded the other*; nor was there ever any occasion for them to leave off their lamentations, because *their calamities came perpetually one upon another*, although *the deep consternation they were in prevented their outward wailing*; but, being constrained by their fear to conceal their inward passions, they were *inwardly tormented* [Gk. *ebasanizonto*, as in Rev. 9:5], without daring to open their lips in groans. . . . *Everyone despaired of himself*; for those that were not among the seditious had no great

[54] F. F. Bruce, *New Testament History* (Garden City, N.Y.: Anchor, 1969), 382.

desires of anything, as expecting for certain that they should very soon be destroyed; but, for the seditious themselves, they fought against each other, while they trod upon the dead bodies as they lay heaped one upon another, and taking up a mad rage from those dead bodies that were under their feet, became the fiercer thereupon. They, moreover, were still inventing somewhat or other that was pernicious against themselves; and when they had resolved upon anything, they executed it without mercy, and *omitted no method of torment or of barbarity.* (*Wars* 5.1.5, italics added)

John of Giscala "filled his entire country with ten thousand instances of wickedness, such as a man who was already hardened sufficiently in his impiety towards God would naturally do" (*Wars* 5.6.2).

But these men, and these only, were incapable of repenting of the wickedness [cf. Rev. 16:9, 11] they had been guilty of; and separating their souls from their bodies, they used them both as if they belonged to other folks and not to themselves. For no gentle affection could touch their souls, nor could any pain affect their bodies, since they could still tear the dead bodies of the people as dogs do, and fill the prisons with those that were sick. (*Wars* 5.12.4)

Neither did any other city ever suffer such miseries, nor did any age ever breed a generation more fruitful in wickedness than this was, from the beginning of the world. (*Wars* 5.10.5)

Josephus continues:

The madness of the seditious did also increase together with their famine, and both those miseries were every day inflamed more and more; for there was no corn which anywhere appeared publicly, but the robbers came running into, and searched men's private houses; and then, if they found any, they tormented them, because they had denied they had any; and if they found none, they tormented [Gk. *basanizō*, as in Rev. 9:5] them worse, because they supposed they had more carefully concealed it. (*Wars* 5.10.2)

They also invented terrible methods of torment [Gk. *basanismos*, noun form of *basanizō*] to discover where any food was ... and this was done when these tormentors were not themselves hungry; for the thing had been less barbarous had necessity forced them to it; but this was done to keep their madness in exercise. (*Wars* 5.10.3)

This seems strongly indicative of a wicked demonic undercurrent. It surely fulfills Christ's parable-prophecy on that first-century "generation" that denied him (Matt. 12:44). Many of the Jews desired to die but suffered long (Rev. 9:6): "Those that were thus distressed by the famine were very desirous to die; and those already dead were esteemed happy, because they had not lived long enough either to hear or to see such miseries" (*Wars* 6.3.4).

The Sixth Trumpet

Revelation 9:14–16 introduces the sixth trumpet:

[The angel] said to the sixth angel who had the trumpet, "Release the four angels who are bound at the great river Euphrates." And the four angels who had been kept ready for this very hour and day and month and year were released to kill a third of mankind. The number of the mounted troops was two hundred million. I heard their number.

Because of mounting space pressures I can only offer a brief insight into this passage. Josephus reports a phenomenon that may indicate the angelic forces behind this earthly judgment in A.D. 70:

A certain prodigious and incredible phenomenon appeared; I suppose the account of it would seem to be a fable, were it not related by those that saw it, and were not the events that followed it of so considerable a nature as to deserve such signals; for, before sun setting, chariots and troops of soldiers in their armor were seen running about among the clouds, and surrounding of cities. (*Wars* 6.5.3)

And the Roman historian Tacitus writes: "In the sky appeared a vision of armies in conflict, of glittering armour" (*Histories* 5.13).

In Revelation 9 the "four angels" (v. 15) immediately become "mounted troops" of an incalculable number (v. 16).

Besides the supernatural backdrop involving four angels, this imagery portrays in the most terrifying form the overwhelming forces arrayed against Israel during the Jewish war. Nero sent Vespasian "to take upon him the command of the armies that were in Syria," where he "gathered together the Roman forces" (*Wars* 3.1.3). Interestingly, the Euphrates River (Rev. 9:14) touches Syria, where the Romans normally keep four legions (Tacitus, *Annals* 4.5). Josephus notes that four legions assaulted Jerusalem: "The works that belonged to the four legions were erected on the west side of the city" (*Wars* 6.8.1; cf. Tacitus, *Histories* 5.1).

Josephus mentions these well-organized legions intentionally employed psychological warfare by displaying their military order, weaponry, and horses before the walls of Jerusalem in order to terrify the Jews:

> So the soldiers, according to custom, opened the cases wherein their arms before lay covered, and marched with their breastplates on; as did the horsemen lead their horses in their fine trappings. Then did the places that were before the city shine very splendidly for a great way; nor was there anything so grateful to Titus's own men, or so terrible to the enemy as that sight; for the whole old wall and the north side of the temple were full of spectators, and one might see the houses full of such as looked at them; nor was there any part of the city which was not covered over with their multitudes; nay, a very great consternation seized upon the hardiest of the Jews themselves, when they saw all the army in the same place, together with the fineness of their arms, and the good order of their men. (*Wars* 5.9.1; cf. 3.7.4)

Revelation 9:17 presents an apocalyptically enhanced description of these tormentors: "The horses and riders I saw in my vision looked like this: Their breastplates were fiery red, dark blue, and yellow as sulfur. The heads of the horses resembled the heads of lions, and out of their mouths came fire, smoke and sulfur." Here we discover the implements of the fiery destruction that Jerusalem will undergo from the Roman's armored horsemen, iron-plated towers, battering rams, and catapults, producing their fire and smoke (a description of the Roman armament appears in *Wars* 3.5.2, 5–6; 6.2). For instance:

> At the same time such catapults as were intended for that purpose, threw at once lances upon them with great

noise, and stones of the weight of a talent were thrown by the engines that were prepared for that purpose, together with fire, and a vast multitude of arrows, which made the wall so dangerous that the Jews durst not to come upon it. (*Wars* 3.7.9, cf. 3.7.10)

THE MEASURING OF THE TEMPLE (REV. 11:1–2)

Jumping ahead in Revelation, we come to John's visionary command to measure the temple and its worshipers (Rev. 11:1–2). Again we clearly see Revelation's focus on Israel: This "holy city" with a "temple" must be Jerusalem (Neh. 11:1; Isa. 48:2; 52:1; 64:10; Matt. 4:5; 27:53).[55] In verse 8 John unmasks this "holy city" for what she becomes: an Egypt, a Sodom, the slayer of Christ: "Their bodies will lie in the street of the great city, which is figuratively called Sodom and Egypt, where also their Lord was crucified." Indeed, second-century Christians called Jews "Christ-killers" and "murderers of the Lord."[56]

Significantly this passage strongly reflects Jesus' prophecy in the Olivet Discourse (compare the italicized words):

- Luke 21:24: "*Jerusalem* will be *trampled* on by the *Gentiles* until the *times* of the Gentiles are fulfilled" (italics added).
- Revelation 11:2: "But exclude the outer court; do not measure it, because it has been given to the *Gentiles*. They will *trample* on the *holy city* for 42 *months*" (italics added).

These twin passages inform us that the "holy city/Jerusalem" will be "trampled" by the "Gentiles" until the "times of the Gentiles are fulfilled," that is, after "42 months."

Evidently Revelation 11:1–2 prophesies the impending destruction of the temple in A.D. 70, for its source in Luke 21:24

---

[55] Here we have one clear line of evidence that John writes Revelation while the temple is still standing. Otherwise, he would surely mention its destruction, as do Christian writers shortly afterward (e.g., *Barnabas* 16:1ff.; Ignatius, *Magnesians* 10; Justin Martyr, *First Apology* 32). To assume this is a "rebuilt temple" is just that, an assumption—and an assumption that goes contrary to the conclusion of the sacrificial system (Heb. 9–12).

[56] E.g., Ignatius, *Magnesians* 11; Justin Martyr, *First Apology* 35; Irenaeus, *Against Heresies* 3.12.2.

(cf. parallels in Matt. 24 and Mark 13) prophesies that very event. Note the context: (1) Jesus particularly speaks of the first-century temple (Luke 21:5–7; cf. Matt. 23:38–24:3; Mark 13:1–4), and (2) he ties his prophecy to his own generation (Luke 21:32; cf. Matt. 24:34; Mark 13:30). And again, the events of Revelation are "soon" (Rev. 1:1) and "near" (1:3).

What of "the times of the Gentiles"? Daniel 2 prophesies that four successive Gentile empires (Babylon, Medo-Persia, Greece, Rome) will dominate God's people; they are able to do so because they can strike at the material temple in the specifically defined land. But after one final period of rage, the Gentiles will no longer be able to trample God's kingdom, for it will become universal and disassociated from a central temple (Eph. 2:19–21), a localized city (Gal. 4:25–26), a circumscribed land (Matt. 28:19; Acts 1:8), and a distinguishable race (Gal. 3:9, 29). As Jesus puts it: "A time is coming when you will worship the Father neither on this mountain nor in Jerusalem," but everywhere (John 4:21).

In other words, the trampling of the temple in A.D. 70 (Dan. 9:26–27)[57] after its "abomination" (9:27; cf. Matt. 24:15–16; Luke 21:20–21) ends the Gentiles' ability to stamp out the worship of God. In Daniel 9:24–27, Matthew 23:38–24:2, and Revelation 11:1–2, the "holy city" and its temple end in destruction.

But how do the "times of the Gentiles" relate to the forty-two months (Rev. 11:2)? In late A.D. 66 Israel revolted against her oppressive Roman procurator Gessius Florus. By November the Roman governor of the province of Syria, Cestius Gallus, attempted to put down the uprising, but withdrew prematurely for reasons that are unclear (Josephus, *Wars* 2.17–22; Tacitus, *Histories* 5.10). A few months later Vespasian was "sent to Judea by Nero early in 67 to put down the revolt."[58] By August of 70 the Romans breached the inner wall of Jerusalem, transforming the temple and city into a raging inferno. From spring of 67 to August of 70, the time of formal imperial engagement against Jerusalem, is a period of forty-two months.

---

[57]Daniel 9:26–27 must refer to A.D. 70, for the temple rebuilt in the first sixty-nine weeks is destroyed in 70. To assume some other temple following that one defies the logic of the text.

[58]Bruce, *New Testament History*, 380, cf. 381. Tacitus, *The Histories*, trans. Kenneth Wellesley (New York: Penguin, 1986), 277, n. 4.

John "measures" for protection (Ezek. 22:26; Zech. 2:1–5) the inner temple (Gk. *naos*), altar, and worshipers (Rev. 11:1); the "outer court" is excluded for destruction (11:2). The imagery here involves the protecting of the *essence* of the temple, its heart (appearing as the worshiping of God by his faithful people), while the externalities of the temple (the husk, the actual material property itself) perish.[59] This mix of physical and spiritual is rooted in the very idea of the temple. For instance, Hebrews 8:5 mentions an earthly "sanctuary that is a copy and shadow of what is in heaven." The earthly or external temple is a copy or shadow of the heavenly and spiritual reality. The "man-made sanctuary" is a "copy of the true one" (9:24). In Revelation 11 God removes the shadow or copy so that the essential remains, which John here portrays as the worshipers in the heart of the temple.

This is much like Paul's imagery in Galatians 4:22–26, where he contrasts "Jerusalem below" (literal, historical Jerusalem) with the "Jerusalem above" (the heavenly city of God). Or it is like the writer of Hebrews comparing historical Mount Sinai, which can be touched (Heb. 12:18–21), with spiritual Mount Zion, the home of "the spirits of men" that "cannot be shaken" (12:22–27). This mixture of literal and figurative should not alarm us, for all interpreters find such necessary from time to time. Even literalist Robert Thomas, for instance, while insisting that Revelation 19 teaches the return of Christ on a literal horse, urges that his sword and the rod are figurative.[60] And everyone sees a mixing of physical eating and spiritual eating in John 6:49–50 and physical resurrection and spiritual resurrection in 5:25–29.

THE BEAST (REV. 13)

Skipping ahead once again, we notice a new player enter the scene of Revelation: "And the dragon stood on the shore of the sea. And I saw a beast coming out of the sea. He had ten horns and seven heads, with ten crowns on his horns, and on

---

[59]This protecting of the inner temple and giving of the outer temple to destruction is akin in purpose to the sealing/protecting of the Jewish Christians in Rev. 7 in preparing for the destroying of the non-Christian Jews. God is making a separation.

[60]Thomas, *Revelation 8–22*, 387–89.

each head a blasphemous name" (Rev. 13:1). As with the rest of the temporally confined prophecies, this evil character must have a direct relevance to the first-century Christians. Previously John focused on Israel; now he turns to see—Rome.[61]

The Identity of the Beast

Most commentators agree with Robert Thomas that this beast imagery "allows the interchangeability of the head with the whole beast—i.e., the king with his kingdom—as vv. 12, 14 require." I understand the beast to portray the Roman empire (kingdom) generally and Emperor Nero Caesar (king) specifically. I do so for several reasons. (1) The events and characters of Revelation are in the time of John's original audience (1:1, 3; 22:6, 10, 12). Interestingly, the beast arises from the sea (13:1), which reflects the geographical perspective of Rome when considered either from Patmos (from where John writes) or Israel (of which John writes).

(2) The beast possesses great "authority" (13:2) and power (13:4). Rome was the largest and mightiest of the empires of the ancient world and the one currently in power as John wrote. Josephus calls the Romans "the lords of the habitable earth" (*Wars* 4:3:10) and Rome "the greatest of all cities" (*Wars* 4.11.5).

(3) The beast has a blasphemous character (13:5–6) and demands worship (13:8). The Romans considered many of their emperors as gods (cf. Matt. 22:21). Nero thought of himself as the god Apollo; for instance, an inscription from Athens speaks of him as "All powerful Nero Caesar Sebastos, a new Apollo."[62]

(4) According to 13:18 the number of the beast's name equals six hundred and sixty and six (*not* a series of three individual sixes). In the ancient world prior to the invention of Arabic numerals, alphabets serve as numbering systems. As scholars note, a first-century spelling of Nero Caesar's name (*NRWN QSR*), written in Hebrew characters, adds up to that exact value.[63]

---

[61]For detailed information on the material in this section, see Kenneth L. Gentry Jr., *The Beast of Revelation* (Tyler, Tex.: Institute for Christian Economics, 1989), chap. 6.

[62]Mary E. Smallwood, *Documents Illustrating the Principates Gaius Claudius and Nero* (Cambridge: Cambridge Univ. Press, 1967), 52 (entry #145).

[63]D. R. Hillers, "Revelation 13:18 and a Scroll from Murabba'at," *BASOR* 170 (April 1963): 65. The evidence may be seen by consulting the French work edited by

(5) The seven heads of the beast represent both "seven mountains" and "seven kings" (17:9–10). Despite Robert Thomas's surprising denial of the literalness of this reference,[64] the interpreting angel clearly informs John that the seven heads represent seven mountains.[65] The seven mountains obviously refer to the famous seven hills of Rome, well-known to Revelation's original recipients as the seat of imperial rule. Oddly, Thomas drops his literalism at this point: He says the seven mountains represent kingdoms, not mountains. If that is so, the interpretation requires a figure of a figure. That is, the heads represent mountains and the mountains represent kingdoms.

According to the angel who interprets the vision for John (17:7), the heads "are also seven kings. Five have fallen, one is, the other has not yet come; but when he does come, he must remain for a little while" (17:10). The first seven Caesars of Rome are Julius, Augustus, Tiberius, Gaius, Claudius, Nero, and Galba, according to ancient historians Suetonius (*Lives of the Twelve Caesars*), Dio Cassius (*Roman History* 5), and Josephus (*Antiquities* 19.1.11; cf. 18.2.2; 18.6.10).[66] The first five of these "have fallen" (they are dead); the sixth one "is" (Nero is alive). The seventh will come and "remain a little while": The emperor following Nero's thirteen-year rule was Galba, who reigned only seven months (June, A.D. 68–January, A.D. 69).

The Persecution by the Beast

The beast's "war" with the saints for "forty-two months" (13:5–7) refers to the Neronian persecution. Roman historian Tacitus provides a gruesome account of Nero's persecution in Rome, noting that he "inflicted unheard-of punishments on those who, detested for their abominable crimes, were vulgarly called Christians" (*Annals* 15.44). The persecution broke out in

---

P. Benoit, J. T. Milik, and R. DeVaux, *Discoveries in the Judean Desert of Jordan* II (Oxford: Oxford Univ. Press, 1961), 18, plate 29; Bruce M. Metzger, *A Textual Commentary on the Greek New Testament* (London: United Bible Societies, 1971), 751–52.

[64]Thomas, *Revelation 8–22*, 296.

[65]The perplexing nature of the vision in Revelation 17 is due to the surprising twofold referent: The seven heads represent *both* seven mountains *and* seven kings. Revelation 17:9–10 is a part of the angel's explication of the vision, not further visual material causing difficulty.

[66]This is another evidence for a pre-A.D. 70 date of composition.

November, A.D. 64, claiming the lives of "an immense number" (Tacitus), "a vast multitude of the elect" (1 Clement 6). This first ever Roman assault on Christianity claimed the apostles Peter and Paul, who died in A.D. 66 or 67.

Noted church historian L. von Mosheim writes of Nero's persecution:

> The dreadful persecution which took place by order of this tyrant, commenced at Rome about the middle of November, in the year of our Lord 64. . . . This dreadful persecution ceased but with the death of Nero. The empire, it is well known, was not delivered from the tyranny of this monster until the year 68, when he put an end to his own life.[67]

Remarkably the persecution ceased after forty-two months (but for a few days; i.e., November, A.D. 64–June, A.D. 68). John wrote while banished to Patmos under Nero's persecution (1:9); he informs his readers that the persecution will last only forty-two months. C. Marvin Pate admits the relevant fit, though he rejects the preterist implications of the fit.[68]

The Death and Revival of the Beast

But now what of the death and revival of the beast? "One of the heads of the beast seemed to have had a fatal wound, but the fatal wound had been healed. The whole world was astonished and followed the beast" (13:3). The significance of this prophecy is rooted in first-century political events.

Nero committed suicide on June 8, A.D. 68, early in the Roman civil wars that were erupting against him. The peril Rome faced and the upheaval spreading like a fault line throughout the empire were well-known in that era, as Josephus notes: "I have omitted to give an exact account of them, because they are well known by all, and they are described by a great number of Greek and Roman authors" (Wars 4.9.2).

Introducing the months following Nero's death, Tacitus writes: "The history on which I am entering is that of a period rich in disasters, terrible with battles, torn by civil struggles, hor-

---

[67]L. von Mosheim, *Historical Commentaries*, vol. 1, trans. Robert S. Vidal (New York: Converse, 1854), 138–39.

[68]Pate and Haines, *Doomsday Delusions*, 42–44.

rible even in peace. Four emperors were felled by the sword; there were three civil wars, more foreign wars and often both at the same time" (*Histories* 1.2). These upheavals struck both the subjects and the enemies of the vast empire as being the very death throes of Rome (the beast generically considered). Indeed, in Tacitus's estimation, it very nearly was so: "This was the condition of the Roman state when Serius Galba, chosen consul for the second time, and his colleague Titus Vinius entered upon the year that was to be for Galba his last and *for the state almost the end*" (*Histories* 1.11, italics added).

Before the world's startled eyes, the seven-headed beast (Rome) was toppling to its death as its sixth head (Nero) received his mortal wound. These events impacted not only John's Christian audience in Asia Minor but the Jewish war, for as Josephus notes:

> [Vespasian and Titus] were both in suspense about the public affairs, the Roman empire being then in a fluctuating condition, and did not go on with their expedition against the Jews, but thought that to make any attack upon foreigners was now unseasonable, on account of the solicitude they were in for their own country. (*Wars* 4.9.2)

The reports of the destruction and rapine were so horrible that Vespasian's "sorrow [was so] violent, he was not able to support the torments he was under, nor to apply himself further in other wars when his native country was laid waste" (*Wars* 4.10.2). Josephus agrees that Rome was near "ruin" (*Wars* 4.11.5): "The state of the Romans was so ill" (*Wars* 7.4.2); "every part of the habitable earth under them was in an unsettled and tottering condition" (*Wars* 7.4.2).

But what eventually happened? Roman historian Suetonius writes: "The empire, which for a long time had been unsettled and, as it were, drifting through the usurpation and violent death of three emperors, was at last taken in hand and given stability by the Flavian family" (*Vespasian* 1). Josephus concurs: "So upon this confirmation of Vespasian's entire government, which was now settled, and upon the unexpected deliverance of the public affairs of the Romans from ruin, Vespasian turned his thoughts to what remained unsubdued in Judea" (*Wars* 4.11.5). In other words, after a time of grievous civil war, the empire revived. The pseudo-prophecy of 4 Ezra 12:16–19 (A.D. 100) reflects the amazement of the ancient world: "In the midst of the time of that kingdom great struggles shall arise, and it shall be in danger of falling; nevertheless it shall not fall then, but shall regain its former power."

In light of John's original audience (1:4, 11), his call for their careful consideration (1:3; 13:9), and his contemporary expectation (1:1, 3), these verses must apply to the earthshaking historical events of the late A.D. 60s. Rome died, as it were, then returned again to life.

ISRAEL'S JUDGMENT RESUMES (REV. 14–16)

After mentioning the redeemed/sealed of Israel in 14:1–5, John turns his attention to further judgments on the land by means of the three woes (14:6–21) and the seven bowls (chaps. 15–16). Though the prophecies are crafted in dramatic hyperbole, they refer to historical events. For instance, consider the reaping of the grapes of wrath: "They were trampled in the winepress outside the city, and blood flowed out of the press, rising as high as the horses' bridles for a distance of 1,600 stadia" (14:20).

For compelling reasons "the city" here appears to be Jerusalem: (1) John defines "the city" earlier as Jerusalem (11:8); (2) the "harvest" is in "the earth/land" (Gk. hē gē; 14:15–19); (3) this judgment falls on the place where Jesus was crucified: "outside the city" (John 19:20; cf. Heb. 13:11–13); and (4) the Son of Man "on the cloud" (Rev. 14:14–15) rehearses Revelation's theme regarding Israel (1:7). The distance of the blood flow is 1600 stadia, which is roughly the length of the land as a Roman province: The *Itenerarum* of Antonius of Piacenza records Palestine's length as 1664 stadia. This prophecy refers to the enormous blood flow in Israel during the Jewish war. Allow me to document this.

In his *Wars* Josephus writes: "the sea was bloody a long way" (3.9.3); "one might then see the lake all bloody, and full of dead bodies" (3.10.9); "the whole of the country through which they had fled was filled with slaughter, and Jordan could not be passed over, by reason of the dead bodies that were in it" (4.7.6); "blood ran down over all the lower parts of the city, from the upper city" (4.1.10); "the outer temple was all of it overflowed with blood" (4.5.1); "the blood of all sorts of dead carcasses stood in lakes in the holy courts" (5.1.3); and "the whole city ran down with blood, to such a degree indeed that the fire of many of the houses was quenched with these men's blood" (6.8.5).

The dividing of "the great city" into three parts (16:19; cf. 11:8) seems to refer to the internal strife in Jerusalem. As they fought against the Romans, the Jews fragmented into three warring camps:

> And now there were three treacherous factions in the city, the one parted from the other. Eleazar and his party, that kept the sacred firstfruits, came against John in their cups. Those that were with John plundered the populace, and went out with zeal against Simon. This Simon had his supply of provisions from the city, in oppositions to the seditious. (*Wars* 5.1.4; cf. 5.1.1)

This situation caused serious problems for the defense of the city, even resulting in their destroying their own food supplies (*Wars* 4:1:4).

John is presenting the dramatic covenant lawsuit against Israel for her adultery. The punishment in God's law for adultery is death (Lev. 20:10), which in biblical law is by stoning. Thus, we witness enormous hailstones raining down on Jerusalem in Revelation 16:21: "From the sky huge hailstones of about a hundred pounds [Gk. *talantiaia*, talent, KJV] each fell upon men. And they cursed God on account of the plague of hail, because the plague was so terrible." Josephus records its historical fulfillment in the Roman catapulting of Jerusalem:

> The stones that were cast, were of the weight of a talent [Gk. *talantiaia*], and were carried two furlongs and further. The blow they gave was no way to be sustained, not only by those that stood first in the way, but by those that were beyond them for a great space. As for the Jews, they at first watched the coming of the stone, for it was a white colour. (*Wars* 5.6.3)

But I must move on.

THE PROSTITUTE AND THE BEAST (REV. 17–18)

In this grand vision John sees a richly adorned prostitute sitting on the scarlet beast (17:1–5). She is drunk "with the blood of the saints, the blood of those who bore testimony to Jesus" (v. 6). At first John is perplexed, but then the interpreting angel explains the vision (vv. 7–18; cf. Dan. 9:20–23). It brings together two leading historical characters, showing their ironic connection: the Roman empire (the beast) and Jerusalem (the "prostitute," called "Babylon the great," Rev. 17:5).

Many suppose the Babylonian prostitute represents the city of Rome because she sits on seven hills. The evidence, however, suggests otherwise. As Professor Iain Provon of the University of Edinburgh observes: "The case of Babylon as Jerusalem, then, is in my view a compelling one."[69] (1) Revelation designates the prostitute as "Babylon the great" (17:5), that is, "the great city" (17:18; cf. 14:8; 16:19; 18:10, 16, 21). The first mention of "the great city" is 11:8, which indisputably points to Jerusalem, "where also their Lord was crucified" (cf. Luke 18:31). A cruel irony arises in this reverse imagery: In the Old Testament historical Babylon burns down the temple (2 Chron. 36:18–20); now Israel herself becomes a "Babylon," causing the destruction of her own temple. Josephus records the tragic reality of A.D. 70: The Jews "had begun with their own hands to burn down that temple" (*Wars* 6.3.5).

Jerusalem was a "great city" because of her covenantal status (Ps. 48:1–2; 87:3; Matt. 5:35). Referring to her coming destruction by Old Testament Babylon, Jeremiah twice calls her the "great" city: "How deserted lies the city, once so full of people! How like a widow is she, who once was *great among the nations*! She who was queen among the provinces has now become a slave" (Lam. 1:1, italics added; cf. Jer. 22:8). John's description is similar: "Give her as much torture and grief as the glory and luxury she gave herself. In her heart she boasts, 'I sit as queen; I am not a widow, and I will never mourn'" (Rev. 18:7).

(2) John's apparent backdrop for this prostitute (17:1–6; 19:1–2) is an Old Testament text also dealing with Israel—Jeremiah 3. Not only are there remarkable correspondences of words and images but of themes as well. The theme of Jeremiah 3 is God's divorce of the northern kingdom, Israel, and his threat

---

[69]Iain Provon, "Foul Spirts, Fornication and Finance: Revelation 18 From an Old Testament Perspective," *JSNT* 64 (December 1996): 96. His whole discussion of Revelation is extremely helpful. See also Cornelis Vanderwaal, *Search the Scriptures: Hebrews–Revelation* (St. Catherines, Ont.: Paideia, 1979), 10:79–111. Terry, *Biblical Apocalyptics*, 426–39. J. Massyngberde Ford, *Revelation* (AB; Garden City, N.Y.: Doubleday, 1975), 54–55, 93, 259–307 .

of divorce to the southern kingdom, Judah. Revelation's theme is God's divorce of New Testament Jerusalem/Israel (Rev. 5). Space forbids an in-depth treatment of these remarkable correspondences, but let me quickly summarize the parallels (LXX is the abbreviation for the Greek translation of the Old Testament).

In Jeremiah 3:1–2 God charges Judah with acting as a prostitute (LXX: *porneuō*), as does John in Revelation 17:1–2 (Gk. *porneuō*). Her wickedness "defiled the land" (Jer. 3:1–2, 9): "the land" (LXX, *hē gē*, 3:2) "defiled" in Jeremiah becomes the "the land" (Gk. *hē gē*) "corrupted" in Revelation (Rev. 19:2). God warns Old Testament Judah on the basis of Israel's experience: He "gave faithless Israel her certificate of divorce and sent her away because of all her adulteries" (Jer. 3:8)—that is, when he allowed the Assyrians to destroy her (Jer. 50:17). The fate of Revelation's harlotrous Jerusalem/Israel will be the same (Rev. 17:16; 19:2). When justifying Old Testament Judah's overthrow by Babylon, Jeremiah says: "You had a harlot's forehead" (Jer. 3:3, NASB; cf. KJV, NRSV); when declaring New Testament Jerusalem's rebellious character, John notes her forehead that marks her as "BABYLON THE GREAT, THE MOTHER OF PROSTITUTES" (Rev. 17:5). Surely John is dealing with the same people.

(3) The Babylonian prostitute fills herself with the blood of the saints (Rev. 16:6; 17:6; 18:21, 24): "In her was found the blood of prophets and of the saints, and of all who have been killed on the earth [land]" (18:24). Of course, with the Neronian persecution currently under way (1:9; 13:5–7), Rome was stained with the blood of the saints. Yet Rome had only recently entered the persecuting ranks of God's enemies; throughout Acts Jerusalem and the Jews were the main persecutor.[70] Furthermore, Rome was not guilty of killing any of "the prophets" of the Old Testament, as was Jerusalem.[71] Of Jerusalem's authorities Stephen asks: "Was there ever a prophet your fathers did not persecute? They even killed those who predicted the coming of the Righteous One. And now you have betrayed and murdered him" (Acts 7:52).

---

[70]See, for example: Acts 4:3; 5:18–33; 6:12; 7:54–60; 8:1ff.; 9:1–4, 13, 23; 11:19; 12:1–3; 13:45–50; 14:2–5, 19; 16:23; 17:5–13; 18:12; 20:3, 19; 21:11, 27; 22:30; 23:12, 20, 27, 30; 24:5–9; 25:2–15, 24; 26:21. See also 2 Cor. 11:24; 1 Thess. 2:14–15; Heb. 10:32–34; Rev. 2:9; 3:9; etc.

[71]Jer. 2:30; Matt. 5:12; 23:29–31, 34–35, 37; Luke 6:23, 26; 11:47–50; 13:34; Rom. 11:3; 1 Thess. 2:15; Heb. 11:32–38.

In the context of the Olivet Discourse Jesus specifically reproached Jerusalem in words remarkably like those of Revelation:

> Therefore I am sending you prophets and wise men and teachers. Some of them you will kill and crucify; others you will flog in your synagogues and pursue from town to town. And so upon you will come *all the righteous blood that has been shed on earth*, from the blood of righteous Abel to the blood of Zechariah son of Berekiah, whom you murdered between the temple and the altar. (Matt. 23:34–35, italics added)

Or as Luke records it:

> Therefore *this generation* will be held responsible for the blood of *all the prophets* that has been shed *since the beginning of the world*, from the blood of Abel to the blood of Zechariah, who was killed between the altar and the sanctuary. Yes, I tell you, *this generation will be held responsible* for it all. (Luke 11:50–51, italics added)

Jesus mentions both Israel's New Testament and Old Testament era persecutions of the saints.

Remember that throughout Revelation the slain Lamb acts in judgment on his slayers, the Jews (5:6; cf. 5:12; 13:8; this Lamb appears twenty-seven times in Revelation[72]). Why should this surprise us? Jerusalem literally calls down judgment on herself for slaying the Lamb of God: "All the people answered, 'Let his blood be on us and on our children!'" (Matt. 27:25).

(4) The prostitute's array reflects the Jewish priestly colors of scarlet, purple, and gold (Ex. 28),[73] indicating her priestly status with the temple in her midst: "The woman was dressed in purple and scarlet, and was glittering with gold, precious stones and pearls. She held a golden cup in her hand" (Rev. 17:4). Josephus carefully describes the temple's tapestry as "Babylonian tapestry in which blue, purple, scarlet and linen were mingled" (*Wars* 5.5.4).

The prostitute's gold cup reminds us of the temple's implements: "The greatest part of the vessels that were put in them was

---

[72]See Rev. 5:6, 8, 12–13; 6:1, 16; 7:9–10, 14, 17; 12:11; 13:8; 14:1, 4, 10; 15:3; 17:14; 19:7, 9; 21:14, 22–23; 22:1, 3.

[73]Cf. Rev. 17:4–5 with Ex. 25:2, 4; 26:1, 31, 36; 27:16; 28:1–2, 5–12, 15, 17–23, 33.

of silver and gold" (*Wars* 5.4.4). Even the temple itself was "dressed" with gold plates and white stone reminiscent of the prostitute "glittering with gold, precious stones and pearls" (17:4):

> Now the outward face of the temple in its front ... was covered all over with plates of gold of great weight, and, at the first rising of the sun, reflected back a very fiery splendor, and made those who forced themselves to look upon it to turn their eyes away, just as they would have done at the sun's own rays. But this temple appeared to strangers, when they were at a distance, like a mountain covered with snow; for, as to those parts of it that were not gilt, they were exceeding white. (*Wars* 5.5.6)

The prostitute's blasphemous inscription on her forehead gives a reverse image of the holy inscription on the Jewish high priest. On the high priest's forehead we read: "HOLY TO THE LORD" (Ex. 28:36–38); on the prostitute's forehead we read: "MYSTERY, BABYLON THE GREAT, THE MOTHER OF PROSTITUTES AND OF THE ABOMINATIONS OF THE EARTH" (Rev. 17:5).

(5) An obvious literary contrast exists between the drunken prostitute and the coming chaste bride. This juxtaposition suggests an intentional contrast between the Jerusalem below (11:8) and the Jerusalem above (21:2) and should be familiar to New Testament students (cf. Gal. 4:24–31; Heb. 12:18–24). Revelation 17 and 21 provide remarkable negative and positive images. Remember that John specifically calls the bride the "new Jerusalem" from heaven (21:1–2), suggesting her contrast to the old Jerusalem (cf. new order/old order contrasts elsewhere, Matt. 9:16–17; 13:52; 2 Cor. 3:7–14; Heb. 1:1–2; 3:1–6; 8:1–13). As Robert Thomas notes of the correspondences between the prostitute and the bride: "The resemblances are too close and too many to be accidental."[74] Consider just three samples of the many available (see top of p. 78).

(6) Revelation elsewhere ascribes the pagan names "Sodom and Egypt" to Jerusalem, names quite compatible with "Babylon" (11:8; cf. Isa. 1:9–10). In other words, rather than conducting herself as the wife of God, Jerusalem has become one of his enemies—like Sodom, Egypt, and Babylon. The new Jerusalem obviously replaced the old Jerusalem.

---

[74]For more information, see Thomas, *Revelation 8–22*, 569–74.

An angel intro-duces John to the prostitute and to the bride in the same way:	17:1: "One of the seven angels who had the seven bowls came and said to me, 'Come, I will show you the punishment of the great prostitute, who sits on many waters.'"	21:9: "One of the seven angels who had the seven bowls full of the seven last plagues came and said to me, 'Come, I will show you the bride, the wife of the Lamb.'"
The two women have contrasting character:	17:1b: "Come, I will show you the pun-ishment of the great prostitute, who sits on many waters."	21:9b: "Come, I will show you the bride, the wife of the Lamb."
The two women appear in contrast-ing environments:	17:3: "Then the angel carried me away in the Spirit into a desert. There I saw a woman sit-ting on a scarlet beast."	21:10: "And he car-ried me away in the Spirit to a mountain great and high, and showed me the Holy City, Jerusalem, coming down out of heaven from God."

The prostitute's sitting on the beast (17:3) is ironic: It indicates not identity with Rome, but dependence on Rome. The image reminds us of Israel's past dependence on Rome so that she could attack Christ and his followers. Josephus writes: "It seems to me to be necessary here to give an account of *all the honors that the Romans and their emperors paid to our nation*, and of *the leagues of mutual assistance* they have made with it" (*Antiquities* 14.10.1–2, italics added). Using this leverage ("we have no king but Caesar," John 19:15), the Jews demanded Christ's crucifixion (Matt. 23:37–39; John 19:12–16) and constantly agitated against the Christians so as to involve the Romans in their per-secution (Acts 4:27; 16:20; 17:7; 18:12; 21:11; 24:1–9; 25:1–2). "And they began to accuse him, saying, 'We have found this man sub-verting our nation. He opposes payment of taxes to Caesar and claims to be Christ, a king'" (Luke 23:2). But now Jerusalem's former ally against Christ turns and destroys her (Rev. 18:16).

THE MARRIAGE SUPPER AND THE BRIDEGROOM (REV. 19)

In Revelation 19 John draws together four important factors necessary for developing his glorious, hope-filled conclusion, toward which he now takes great strides.

(1) Whereas the preceding chapter was virtually a mournful dirge for Jerusalem by the merchants of the earth,[75] John now hears the heavenly interpretation of her fall (19:1–5):

> Hallelujah!
> Salvation and glory and power belong to our God,
>   for true and just are his judgments.
> He has condemned the great prostitute
>   who corrupted the earth by her adulteries.
> He has avenged on her the blood of his servants. (19:1–2)

Jerusalem, the unfaithful wife of God, suffers capital punishment as a spiritual adulteress for denying her Messiah (notice her harlotrous immorality, v. 2). Her destruction avenges "the blood of his servants" (19:1–2; cf. 6:10–11; also Matt. 23:34–36; 1 Thess. 2:14–16), causing the saints to rejoice in witnessing the conquering of the first great enemy of Christ and his people.

(2) Following the judgment of prostitute-Jerusalem as an unfaithful wife, heaven announces the marriage supper of the Lamb (19:6–10). The merging of a king's victory celebration with a joyous nuptial feast reminds us of the royal wedding song in Psalm 45, which probably serves as the backdrop to Revelation 19. The punishment of God's unfaithful wife (19:1–5) publicly and securely establishes Christ's kingdom (19:6), leading to the announcement of the festal presentation of the Lord's new bride (19:7–8; cf. chap. 21).

Jesus teaches the significance of Jerusalem's judgment for establishing his kingdom: "I tell you the truth, some who are

---

[75]Josephus mentions Jerusalem's "vast riches" (*Wars* 6.10.1) and the temple's "immense quantity of money" (*Wars* 6.5.2). See also Tacitus, *Histories* 5:5. Jeremias notes that "foreign trade had considerable importance for the Holy City" (Joachim Jeremias, *Jerusalem in the Times of Jesus: An Investigation into Economic and Social Conditions During the New Testament Period* [Philadelphia: Fortress, 1969], 38).

standing here will not taste death before they see the kingdom of God come with power" (Mark 9:1). Though from A.D. 30 to 70 two redemptive eras overlap, Christ's judgment of the first-century Jews and the destruction of the temple system dramatically secured the kingdom (Rev. 19:6) and vindicated the universal church's message (19:9–10) in festal celebration: "I say to you that many will come from the east and the west, and will take their places at the feast with Abraham, Isaac and Jacob in the kingdom of heaven. But the subjects of the kingdom will be thrown outside, into the darkness, where there will be weeping and gnashing of teeth" (Matt. 8:11–12).

The events of A.D. 70 vindicated Christianity against Judaism—as many early church fathers proclaimed.[76] Pointing to A.D. 70 the Lord warned the Sanhedrin about to judge him: "I say to all of you: In the future you will see the Son of Man sitting at the right hand of the Mighty One and coming on the clouds of heaven" (Matt. 26:64).

The New Testament records the gradual establishment of the kingdom (cf. Matt. 13:31–33; Mark 4:26–29): from its ministerial announcement (Matt. 12:28; Mark 1:15) to its legal securing at the cross (Matt. 28:18; Rom. 1:3–4; Phil. 2:1–11; Col. 1:13; 2:14–15) to its public vindication in Israel's overthrow (Matt. 23:32–24:21; Gal. 4:21–31; 1 Thess. 2:16; Rev. 6–19). God's removal of the temple system—physically breaking down the "dividing wall of hostility" legally broken in Christ (Eph. 2:14)—conclusively ended the early Zionistic tendencies of many first-century Christians (e.g., Acts 11:1–3; 15:1; Rom. 14:1–8; Gal. 1–5; Col. 2:16; Tit. 3:9) and established Christianity as a separate religion in its own right (this is why Jesus likens the great tribulation to "birth pains," Matt. 24:8).

(3) In conjunction with the marriage feast preparations, the bridegroom appears. In fact, his divorce and the capital punishment of his adulterous wife-prostitute provide the very justification for this celebration and new marriage (19:11–18). The lesson of Revelation now becomes clear: Christ gloriously

---

[76]See Melito of Sardis; Tertullian's *Apology* 21 and 26; *On Idolatry* 7; *An Answer to the Jews* 9 and 13; *Against Marcion* 3.6, 23; 5.15; Hippolytus's *Treatise on Christ and Antichrist* 30 and 57; *Expository Treatise Against the Jews* 1, 2 and 7; and *Against Noetus* 18; Cyprian's *Treatises* 9.7; 10.5; 12.2.14; 12.2.20; Lactantius's *Divine Institutes* 4.18; *Epitome of the Divine Institutes* 46; *On the Manner in Which the Persecutors Died* 2.

appears as a warrior-bridegroom, punishing faithless Jerusalem and taking a new bride.

Christ is Israel's ultimate judge (Matt. 24:29–30; 26:64); he is the one who makes war against her (Rev. 19:11; cf. Matt. 21:40–45; 22:1–7). He so severely judges her that her citizens receive no proper burial, being consumed by birds (Rev. 19:17–18). Robert Thomas well remarks: "The worst indignity perpetrated on a person in that culture was to be left unburied after death (cf. Ps. 79:2–3)."[77] Josephus notes that the bodies of the dead in Jerusalem were "cast down from the walls into the valleys beneath" (*Wars* 5.12.3). Indeed, "those valleys [were] full of dead bodies, and the thick putrefaction running about them" (*Wars* 5.12.4).

The vision of Christ's "many crowns" (Rev. 19:12) is the apocalyptic way of affirming that he has "all authority in heaven and on earth" (Matt. 28:18), that he is "far above all rule and authority, power and dominion" (Eph. 1:21), that has "the name that is above every name" (Phil. 2:9), and that "angels, authorities and powers [are] in submission to him" (1 Peter 3:22). In short, as John forthrightly declares at the beginning of Revelation, already in the first century Christ is "the ruler of the kings of the earth" (Rev. 1:5).

Though the imagery of this passage suggests to many the Second Advent (and there certainly are many correspondences), it more likely refers to A.D. 70, which is a distant adumbration of the Second Advent. Actually Revelation 19 more fully explicates the theme John announces in 1:7, which itself originates in Christ's teaching in Matthew 24:29–30. And remember: This judgment-coming of Christ, mentioned in both Revelation and Matthew 24, are near in time to the original audiences (Matt. 24:34; Rev. 1:1, 3; 22:6, 10).

(4) Because of Revelation's primary interest in the judgment of Israel, John mentions almost in passing the destruction of the beast who warred against God (Rev. 19:19–21). Nero (the personification of the beast) died in A.D. 68, which was during God's three and one-half year judgment on Israel (A.D. 67–70). In fact, he died in the devastating Roman civil wars (A.D. 68–69), which almost brought down mighty Rome herself. After Nero and the three short reigning emperors during the Roman civil wars, the next two emperors (Vespasian and Titus) left the Christians unmolested.

---

[77] Thomas, *Revelation 8–22*, 93.

THE MILLENNIUM (REV. 20)

The closer John approaches his conclusion, the more glorious the outcome appears. In Revelation 20 he glances into the distant future (the Millennium begins in the first century, but its length necessarily requires its extension beyond the near/soon time frame of the book). In fact, it provides the long-lasting consequence of Israel's destruction and the securing of the kingdom of Christ. Once again, space forbids a thorough analysis of this interesting text, so I will only highlight some of the more important features for the preterist viewpoint, which are subject to debate: the "thousand years," the binding of Satan, the rule of Christ, and the resurrections.[78]

The Thousand Years

Only one place in all of Scripture limits Christ's rule to a thousand years: Revelation 20:1–10, a half chapter in the most highly figurative book in the Bible. As I pointed out above in my treatment of the 144,000, the number 1000 is surely a symbolic sum representing quantitative perfection. Scripture frequently employs this number in a nonliteral fashion: Does God, for example, own the cattle on only one thousands hills (Ps. 50:10)? The length of the Millennium could actually be thousands of years, as hermeneutics authority Milton Terry ably argues.[79]

The Binding of Satan

John here picks up and reverses an earlier theme. In 9:1 Satan *has fallen* from heaven (Gk. *ouranos*) and *is given the key* to the *Abyss*. In 20:1 Christ *descends* from heaven (Gk. *ouranos*), *having possession of the key* in order to bind Satan and throw him into the *Abyss*.

Scripture explicitly informs us that Christ bound Satan during his first-century ministry. In response to charges he was exorcizing demons by the power of Satan, the Lord responded: "But if I cast out demons by the Spirit of God, then the kingdom

---

[78]For more information see my chapter, "Postmillennialism," in Darrell L. Bock, ed., *Three Views of the Millennium and Beyond* (Grand Rapids: Zondervan, forthcoming).

[79]Terry, *Biblical Apocalyptics*, 451.

of God has come upon you. Or how can anyone enter the strong man's house and carry off his property, unless he first binds the strong man? And then he will plunder his house" (Matt. 12:28–29, NASB). Christ's promotion of the kingdom of God involved his exercising power over Satan's kingdom (cf. v. 26): He snatched men and women from Satan's control. In that we are still in the Millennium, Christ continues his plundering of Satan's house today by the preaching of the gospel, which rescues people from darkness and brings them into his kingdom (Col. 1:13; cf. Acts 26:17–18).

Christ bound Satan for a well-defined purpose: "to keep him from *deceiving the nations* anymore" (Rev. 20:3, italics added). In Old Testament times only Israel knew the true God (Ps. 147:19–20; Amos 3:2; Luke 4:6; Acts 14:16; 17:30). But Christ's incarnation changed this as the gospel began flowing to all nations (e.g., Isa. 2:2–3; 11:10; Matt. 28:19; Luke 2:32; 24:47; Acts 1:8; 13:47). In fact, Christ judged the Jews and opened his kingdom to the Gentiles (Matt. 8:11–12; 21:43; 23:36–38). (Note, however, that the New Testament elsewhere promises the eventual reentry of the Jews into God's kingdom, thereby encouraging our evangelizing them; see Acts 1:6–7; Rom. 11:11–25; 15:12.)

Thus, Christ bound Satan with the result that his deceptive power over the nations is fading as the gospel advances into all the world. In fact, the Great Commission necessitates this new state of affairs. Despite Satan's "authority" before Christ's coming (Luke 4:6; John 12:31; 14:30; 16:11; Eph. 2:1–2), Christ now claims: "All authority in heaven and on earth has been given to me. Therefore go and make disciples of all nations" (Matt. 28:18–19). Christ commissioned Paul for this very task: "I will rescue you from your own people and from the Gentiles. I am sending you to them to open their eyes and turn them from darkness to light, and from the power of Satan to God" (Acts 26:17–18).

Consequently, the New Testament speaks frequently and forcefully of Satan's demise in this regard (see Matt. 12:28–29; Luke 10:18; John 12:31; 16:11; 17:15; Acts 26:18; Rom. 16:20; Col. 2:15; Heb. 2:14; 1 John 3:8; 4:3–4; 5:18). Jesus' own words harmonize well with Revelation 20: "Now is the time for judgment on this world; now the prince of this world will be driven out [Gk. *ekballō*]" (John 12:31). Revelation 20:3 says that Christ "threw" [Gk. *ballō*] Satan into the Abyss. Other New Testament writers agree. Paul wrote: "Having disarmed the powers and authorities, he made a public spectacle of them, triumphing over them by the cross" (Col. 2:15). The author of Hebrews noted: "Since the children have flesh and blood, he too shared in their humanity so that by his death he might destroy him who holds the power of death—that is, the devil" (Heb. 2:14). And John expressed it this way: "The reason the Son of God appeared was to destroy the devil's work" (1 John 3:8).

The binding of Satan, then, began in the first century. Christ initiated it during his ministry (Matt. 12:24–29), secured it in legal fact at his death and resurrection (Luke 10:17; John 12:31–32; Col. 2:15; Heb. 2:14–15), and dramatically "proved" it in the collapse of Christianity's first foe, Judaism (Matt. 23:36–24:3; 1 Thess. 2:14–16; Rev. 3:9). Jerusalem's demise is significant in that the satanic resistance to Christ's kingdom first comes from the Jewish persecution of Christ and Christianity.

The Rule of Christ

The preceding comments have already suggested the preterist understanding of Christ's rule. Revelation's "ruling and reigning" with Christ demand two important, present spiritual realities. (1) Christ established his kingdom in the first century.[80] Matthew 12:28–29 clearly parallels the thought of Revelation 20:1–6, for in both places we see the relationship of Christ's kingdom and the binding of Satan (see above). Indeed, the kingdom came near in the early ministry of Christ because "the time [had] come" (Mark 1:14–15). Christ's power over demons shows the kingdom's presence during his earthly ministry (Matt. 12:28; cf. 8:29; Mark 1:24; 5:10; Luke 8:31); his kingdom does not await some future, visible coming (Luke 17:20–21; Col. 1:13).

Consequently, Christ claimed to be king while on earth (John 12:12–15; 18:36–37), and God enthroned him as king following his resurrection and ascension (Acts 2:30–36). Since his resurrection Christ has "all authority in heaven and on earth" (Matt. 28:18), for he is at the right hand of God, ruling over his kingdom.[81] As a result, first-century Christians proclaimed him king (Matt. 2:2; Acts 17:7; Rev. 1:5), and new converts entered his kingdom (John 3:3; Col. 1:12–13; 1 Thess. 2:12).

---

[80]See my essay "Postmillennialism" in *Three Views of the End of History.*

[81]Mark 16:19; Luke 22:69; Acts 2:33; 5:31; 7:55–56; Rom. 8:34; 14:11; Eph. 1:20–23; Col. 1:18; 3:1; Heb. 1:3, 13; 8:1; 10:12; 12:2; 1 Peter 3:22; Rev. 17:14; 19:16.

(2) The other reality involves our present rule with him in his kingdom. John tells the seven churches of the first century that Christ "has made us to be a kingdom and priests to serve his God and Father" (Rev. 1:6). This present priestly kingship is exactly what Revelation 20 relates of the millennial kingdom: "They will be priests of God and of Christ and will reign with him for a thousand years" (20:6).

Paul mentions our present rule as well: "And God raised us up with Christ and seated us with him in the heavenly realms in Christ Jesus" (Eph. 2:6; cf. 1:3; Col. 3:1–4). Whatever surprised responses might arise against this viewpoint, the fact remains: The Bible teaches we are presently "seated with him."

The Resurrections

Revelation 20 associates two resurrections with the millennial kingdom of Christ. One resurrection is spiritual and present; the other is physical and future.

Revelation 20:4–6 mentions two groups who rule with Christ and who are "blessed" by means of "the first resurrection" (v. 6).[82] John first sees "the souls of those who had been beheaded because of the testimony of Jesus and because of the word of God." These "souls" are deceased saints who have died in the service of Christ. He then also sees "those who had not worshiped the beast or his image, and had not received the mark upon their forehead and upon their hand." These are living saints who presently live for Christ on the earth.

This first resurrection is—salvation. Note how John, the author of Revelation, earlier recorded Christ's instruction in which he parallels spiritual resurrection unto present salvation and physical resurrection unto eternal destiny:

> I tell you the truth, whoever hears my word and believes him who sent me has eternal life and will not be condemned; *he has crossed over from death to life.* I tell you the truth, *a time is coming and has now come when the dead will hear the voice of the Son of God and those who hear will live.* . . .
>
> Do not be amazed at this, for *a time is coming when all who are in their graves will hear his voice and come out—* those who have done good will rise to live, and those

---

[82]On this point I will use the NASB translation, which is more precise.

who have done evil will rise to be condemned. (John 5:24–29, italics added)

In fact, because of Christ's physical resurrection, we are spiritually resurrected (Rom. 6:4–14; Eph. 2:5–6; Col. 3:1).

John does not expressly mention the second resurrection in Revelation 20. We imply that from three factors in the text: (1) reference to "the first resurrection" (which language requires a "second" resurrection); (2) the "rest of the dead [not coming] to life" until after the thousand years; and (3) the judgment scene in verses 12–13. The second resurrection happens to be the second one mentioned in John 5:28–29: It is the physical resurrection from "the grave" (cf. Job 19:25–27; John 6:38–50, 54; 11:24–25; Acts 24:15; Rom. 8:11; 1 Thess. 4:14–17). In Revelation 20:7–15 we witness the Second Coming and final judgment. But since this is so distant from John's day, he only quickly mentions them.

John's mixing of spiritual and literal realities here in comparing the spiritual resurrection and the physical resurrection is not unprecedented. For instance, as I noted above, John records Christ's words regarding eating bread (John 6:49–50), where he parallels the *spiritual* eating of Christ's body with the *literal* eating of the manna in the desert—which in turn parallels spiritual death and physical death: "Your forefathers ate the manna in the desert, yet they died. But here is the bread that comes down from heaven, which a man may eat and not die." The same words "eat" and "die" occur in both statements, but they carry different connotations. The same is true of "come to life" in Revelation 20:4–5.

THE BRIDE FROM HEAVEN (REV. 21–22)

John now comes to his conclusion—and a glorious conclusion it is! As the reader may expect by now, the preterist understands this passage quite differently from the futurist and is at this point more like the idealist. In chapter 21 John witnesses Christ's bride in glorious array descending out of heaven into a new creation: "Then I saw a new heaven and a new earth, for the first heaven and the first earth had passed away, and there was no longer any sea. I saw the Holy City, the new Jerusalem, coming down out of heaven from God, prepared as a bride beautifully dressed for her husband" (21:1–2).

The Bride Identified

To understand this passage requires analyzing the new creation/new Jerusalem imagery in light of prior Scriptures. Once we do so, we will see that the new creation begins in the first century.

(1) John's time frame demands a first-century context. The description of the new creation and new Jerusalem bride-city extends from Revelation 21:1 to 22:5. Following immediately upon that, we read: "The angel said to me, 'These words are trustworthy and true. The Lord, the God of the spirits of the prophets, sent his angel to show his servants the things that *must soon take place'*" (22:6, italics added). And for good measure, four verses later John adds: "Then he told me, 'Do not seal up the words of the prophecy of this book, because *the time is near'*" (22:10, italics added). A delay of several thousand years would override sound exegesis of these clear temporal statements.

(2) Revelation's flow expects a first-century setting. As Robert Thomas notes, there is a "major antithesis between the two women in the closing chapters of the Apocalypse."[83] My understanding of this antithesis is that the new Jerusalem is replacing the old Jerusalem. The coming of the new Jerusalem down from heaven (chaps. 21–22) logically should follow soon upon the destruction of the old Jerusalem on the earth (Rev. 6–11, 14–19), rather than waiting thousands of years.

Remember, Revelation's judgment scenes focus primarily on Israel, God's Old Testament wife. God is judging her for rejecting her Messiah (Rev. 1:7; 5:1ff.; 11:8; cf. Matt. 23:37–24:2; John 19:12–16; Gal. 4:25–31) and for persecuting his followers (Rev. 6:10–12; 16:6; 17:6; 18:24; cf. Matt. 23:34–36; 1 Thess. 2:14–16). That is, she is being punished for committing spiritual adultery. The angel tells John that she intoxicates the inhabitants of the land "with the wine of her adulteries" (Rev. 17:2), which includes being "drunk with the blood of the saints" (17:6). After God issues his divorce decree (chap. 5), he puts the harlotrous Jerusalem away by capital punishment (chaps. 6–11; 14–18) and hosts the royal wedding feast (19:7–20); thereupon the new Jerusalem appears "as a bride beautifully dressed for her husband" (21:2).

---

[83]Thomas, *Revelation 8–22*, 569.

(3) The new creation language suggests a first-century setting. The new creation begins flowing into history before the final consummation (which will establish a wholly new physical order, 2 Peter 3:10–13). The paradigmatic new creation passage that serves as John's backdrop is Isaiah 65:17, 20:

> Behold, I will create
>> new heavens and a new earth.
> The former things will not be remembered,
>> nor will they come to mind. . . .
> Never again will there be in it
>> an infant who lives but a few days,
>> or an old man who does not live out his years;
> he who dies at a hundred
>> will be thought a mere youth;
> he who fails to reach a hundred
>> will be considered accursed.

Here Isaiah clearly writes that this new creation still experiences sin, aging, and death. Thus, it cannot refer either to heaven or the consummate, eternal new creation. Paul uses similar language to John's (Rev. 21:1) when he describes the Christian's new condition in Christ: "Therefore, if anyone is in Christ, he is a new creation; the old has gone, the new has come!" (2 Cor. 5:17; cf. Eph. 2:10; 4:24; Gal. 6:15).

(4) New Testament theology supports a first-century setting. In the New Testament the church appears as the bride of Christ (Eph. 5:25–28; 2 Cor. 11:2; cf. John 3:29). This new bride (the international church) must replace the old wife (the racially based church, Israel). This change is dramatically finalized in A.D. 70, when God removed the physical temple from the earth. John even portrays the finality of Israel's judgment as a marriage feast (Rev. 19).

The New Testament anticipates this imminent change of the old typological temple era into the new final era of spiritual worship:

> Jesus declared, "Believe me, woman, a time is coming when you will worship the Father neither on this mountain nor in Jerusalem. . . . A time is coming and has now come when the true worshipers will worship the Father in spirit and truth, for they are the kind of worshipers the Father seeks." (John 4:21, 23)

The Pentecost experience in Acts 2 itself anticipates the fast approaching day of the Lord against Jerusalem for crucifying Christ (Acts 2:16–23, 36–40).[84] See the expectancy in Matthew 23:36–24:3, 34; 26:64; Mark 9:1; John 4:20–24; Romans 13:11–12; 16:20; 1 Corinthians 7:26, 29–31; Colossians 3:6; 1 Thessalonians 2:16; Hebrews 2:5; 10:25, 37; 12:18–29; James 5:8–9; 1 Peter 4:5, 7; and 1 John 2:17–18.

The Bride Described

But what of all the majestic expressions in Revelation 21–22? The preterist believes that John is expressing, by means of elevated poetic imagery, the glory of salvation. In this we differ from interpreters who strive for literalism. Robert Thomas, for example, writes of the 1,500-mile cube city (21:16): "Though staggering to the human mind ... a city fifteen hundred miles high and fifteen hundred miles on each side is no more unimaginable than a pearl large enough to serve as a city-gate or gold that is as transparent as glass."[85] (We should note that on the literalist exegesis, this city reaches 1,200 miles higher than the space shuttle orbits!) Again, page constraints allow only a quick survey of the material.

The absence of the sea (21:1) speaks of harmony and peace within. In Scripture the sea often symbolizes discord and sin (13:1–2; cf. Isa. 8:7–8; 23:10; 57:20; Jer. 6:23; 46:7; Ezek. 9:10). Christianity offers the opposite: peace with God and among humankind (Luke 2:14; Rom. 5:1; Eph. 2:12–18; Phil. 4:7, 9).

The bride-church is the tabernacle-temple of God (Rev. 21:3) because God dwells within her; no literal temple is needed (21:22; cf. Eph. 2:19–22; 1 Cor. 3:16; 6:19; 2 Cor. 6:16; 1 Peter 2:5, 9). The old Jerusalem with its tabernacle/temple "made with hands" is passing away as the new Jerusalem temple supplants it (Heb. 8:13; 9:11, 24; 12:18–28). This was finalized in A.D. 70.

Hebrews 12 is an important passage for showing the change of eras (which is the message of the whole letter). The author is writing to Jewish Christians who were in danger of

---

[84]The presence of foreign tongues in Israel is evidence of God's judgment (Deut. 28:49; Isa. 28:11; Jer. 5:15; 1 Cor. 14:21–22). Thus, the New Testament tongues experience serves as a sign of God's wrath on her.

[85]Thomas, *Revelation 8–22*, 467.

apostatizing away from Christ back into Judaism. As he draws near his conclusion, he compares the two worlds of Judaism (12:18–20) and Christianity (12:22–28). His description of Christianity has points of contact with John in Revelation:

> But you have come to Mount Zion, to the heavenly Jerusalem, the city of the living God. You have come to thousands upon thousands of angels in joyful assembly, to the church of the firstborn, whose names are written in heaven. You have come to God, the judge of all men, to the spirits of righteous men made perfect, to Jesus the mediator of a new covenant, and to the sprinkled blood that speaks a better word than the blood of Abel. . . .
> Therefore, since we are receiving a kingdom that cannot be shaken, let us be thankful, and so worship God acceptably with reverence and awe. (Heb. 12:22–24, 28)

Revelation 21:1–8 informs us that this new creation salvation removes grief (v. 4; cf. 1 Cor. 15:55–58; 1 Thess. 4:13; James 1:2–4), introduces one into the family of God (Rev. 21:7; cf. John 1:12–13; 1 John 3:1–3), and brings eternal life (Rev. 21:6).

Revelation 21:9–22:5 speaks of the majesty of the bride-church. She shines brilliantly like light (21:10–11; cf. Matt. 5:14–16; Acts 13:47; Rom. 13:12; 2 Cor. 6:14; Eph 5:8–14). She is precious to God as costly gold and jewels (Rev. 21:11, 18–21; cf. 1 Cor. 3:12; 1 Peter 1:7; 2:4–7). She has a sure foundation and impregnable walls (Rev. 21:12–21; cf. Isa. 26:1; 60:18; Matt. 16:18; Acts 4:11; 1 Cor. 3:10–15; Eph. 2:19–20). Thus, she is destined to have a massive influence in the world (Rev. 21:16; cf. Isa. 2:2–5; Ezek. 17:22–24; 47:1–11; Dan. 2:31–35; Mic. 4:1; Matt. 13:31–32; 28:18–20; John 3:17; 1 Cor. 15:20–28; 2 Cor. 5:19). She is cared for by God's provision with the water of life (Rev. 21:22; 22:1–5; cf. John 4:14; 7:37–38; 6:32–35). Thus, she brings healing to the nations by her presence (Rev. 22:2–3; cf. Isa. 53:5; Ezek. 47:1–12; Matt. 13:33; Luke 4:18; John 4:14; Gal. 3:10–13; Heb. 5:12–14; 1 Peter 2:2, 24).

CONCLUSION

Despite centuries of discussion, debate, and confusion regarding Revelation, the book is still one of the sixty-six books of God's canon. It deserves our attention, even if sometimes in bewilderment. This is the only book in the New Testament that has a blessing attached to its reading (Rev. 1:3). We need to read carefully and study this wonderful work of art. In the process we need to be wary of the incautious extravagance of many modern populists.

The preterist understanding of Revelation is rooted in sound hermeneutical and theological principles—and receives surprising historical verification. It takes seriously the temporal remarks of Revelation (1:1, 3; 22:6, 10, 12), observes carefully Revelation's historical setting (chaps. 2-3), and listens intently to the prophets' Old Testament apocalyptic (Isa. 13; 34; Ezek. 32). It explains the enormous redemptive-historical change from the old covenant economy to the new covenant. In the process preterism also provides encouragement to believers today, showing the great judgments of Revelation are already fulfilled, allowing our hope-filled anticipation of the future as the church's glory unfolds in history.

The idealist position of Sam Hamstra, also called the "time-less symbolic" or "poetic-symbolic," denies Revelation is painting an objective, historical portrait at all. Rather, John intends to provide a nonhistorical, allegorical summation of various significant redemptive truths or historical principles. Revelation, then, attempts to provide the scene behind the scene. That is, it offers a look at the philosophical/spiritual issues involved in history rather than at historical events themselves.

Of course, in a certain, limited sense this view could be true at the same time as any of the other views, for history is in fact the outworking of divinely established principles. It cannot, however, serve as an appropriate interpretation while standing alone. Revelation appears to be so concerned with concrete history that to wholly overlook historical events seems to defy the facts. Revelation is so long and complex that it would seem that such a view as idealism, if that were John's intent, could have been presented in a shorter space and without giving such an appearance of historical reality. Furthermore, it downplays the time-frame indicators of the book.

The futurist view of dispensationalist Robert Thomas approaches Revelation as a series of prophecies (beginning at Rev. 4:1) dealing with the remote future from John's time. This view understands Revelation as concerned with the ultimate historical issues that the world and/or the church will face just prior to Christ's return.

The weaknesses of futurism include the following: It almost totally removes the relevance of Revelation from John's original audience, especially at a time of their great suffering. It has to reinterpret phenomena in John's day to make them fit modern times. It overlooks the claims of the nearness of the events in Revelation. It is not subject to historical verification presently and thus is incapable of falsification; in this way it fails the philosophical verification principle, which according to some philosophers renders it philosophically meaningless.

The now/not yet view of progressive dispensationalist C. Marvin Pate attempts to adapt elements of each of the views into one system. As I indicated early in my presentation, however, the now/not yet principle cannot be sustained over so vast a work as Revelation. Furthermore, Revelation specifically claims to relate events "shortly to come to pass," in that "the time is at hand." Why not accept John's statements at face value—especially since he presents them in his didactic sections, which both introduce and conclude his work?

Preterism seems to me to provide the most coherent, relevant, and exegetically sound approach to this most difficult book of the Bible. The preterist principle can be abused, of course—some liberals adopt it (devoid of its supernaturalism, of course). But so can the futurist principle—some millennialist cults adopt it (e.g., Mormonism, Jehovah's Witnesses). The same can be said about the idealist and progressivist principles. The task of the serious Christian is to carefully weigh the issues in the balance of the whole of Scripture.

Chapter Two

AN IDEALIST VIEW
OF REVELATION

Sam Hamstra Jr.

AN IDEALIST VIEW
OF REVELATION[1]

Sam Hamstra Jr.

APOCALYPSE NOW[2]

In times like these you need assurance. At this moment in
your struggle, you need hope, for all is not as it is supposed to
be; your life is afflicted in every way.[3] Personally, your wife is
dying of cancer, your son has rejected the faith you would die
for, your daughter is being abused by a husband who holds
office in the church, and your middle management position has
been eliminated by a force called downsizing. Added to those
calamities, lust, greed, and pride are entrenched in the deep

---

[1]This chapter is a summary of the work of several outstanding scholars in the
idealist tradition. For additional study I recommend Raymond Calkins, *The Social
Message of the Book of Revelation* (New York: The Womans Press, 1920); William Hendriksen, *More Than Conquerors: An Interpretation of the Book of Revelation* (Grand
Rapids: Baker, 1944), and *Three Lectures on the Book of Revelation* (Grand Rapids: Zondervan, 1949); William Milligan, *The Revelation of St. John* (London: MacMillan, 1886),
Lectures on the Apocalypse (London: MacMillan, 1892), and *Discussions on the Apocalypse* (London: MacMillan, 1893); and Arne Unjhem, *The Book of Revelation* (Philadelphia: Lutheran Church Press, 1967).
[2]The title of the 1979 motion picture written by John Milius and Francis Cop-
pola serves as a good title for this section, though any similarities between the two
is coincidental.
[3]Cornelius Plantinga Jr., *Not the Way It's Supposed to Be: A Breviary of Sin* (Grand
Rapids: Eerdmans, 1995).

recesses of your being and affect your every thought and action. Your hope for Christlikeness is fading.

Politically, it is clear you live in a post-Christian society. Your public schools have no place for God. Your legal courts wrestle with the right to choose and the right to die. Special interest groups lobby for same-sex marriage. The Judeo-Christian heritage of your country is a memory. Globally, famine, hunger, and disease indiscriminately take the lives of children and adults, believers and unbelievers. Basic human rights are violated as the rich oppress the poor, the powerful the powerless. The major industry on the planet is war, robbing the world of a new generation of gifted leaders as young men and women lie dead, not on open fields of battle as in centuries past, but on city streets flanked by innocent bystanders.

Finally, the church of Jesus Christ, your love and your life, has compromised its convictions, lost its saltiness, and diminished its influence to the point where the word of a pope goes unattended while the word of a missionary results in his death. Each generation of believers is further removed from the passion and conviction of those who preceded them. Your local body of believers isn't any better, having suffered its second split—the first because the pastor was caught in bed with the church organist, the second because some prefer heaven for everyone over hell for some. Neighboring congregations offer little hope. They suffer from lukewarmness, a condition worse than open opposition to the faith.

You live on an island called Patmos. With David you cry, "My God, why have you forsaken me?" With Job you wonder why the heathen prosper and evil flourishes. With saints throughout the ages, you question the sovereignty of a God who has promised abundant life through Jesus Christ. You need a word from the Lord.

The God of grace, who has established a covenant with his children, hears your cry and responds with a series of visions collected in a book called The Apocalypse of John. The message carried by these visions is simple: While at this moment the children of God suffer in a world where evil appears to have the upper hand, God is sovereign and Jesus Christ has won the victory. Yes, you suffer as a resident of this world that bears the imprint of Adam's sin. Yes, you experience persecution as a light-bearer of the gospel, but God the Father will preserve and protect you as well as each one of his children so not one will be lost.[4] In addition, Christ will achieve ultimate victory over Satan and his hosts when he judges and punishes the wicked. So, hold on. Don't give up. Remain faithful to your calling as a child of God. Live by faith, not by sight, for your sovereign Lord has defeated Satan. You will reign with Christ, for the kingdom of this world has become the kingdom of our Lord and of his Christ.

This word from the Lord comes like no other. It does not come in the form of a letter like that from the apostle Paul, with assuring words of hope, such as "nothing . . .will be able to separate us from the love of God that is in Christ Jesus" (Rom. 8:39), and "in all things God works for the good of those who love him, who have been called according to his purpose" (8:28). You do not receive a simple statement of truth like that found in Ephesians 6:12: "Our struggle is not against flesh and blood, but against the rulers, against the authorities, against the powers of this dark world and against the spiritual forces of evil in the heavenly realm." Nor do you receive a comforting word of victory from the historical accounts of the life of Christ, who proclaimed victory over the world (John 16:33). Rather, by the inspiration of the Holy Spirit, you receive God's message through a series of visions that roll before your eyes like an animated motion picture, impressing you with graphic designs and colorful symbols.

Scholars describe this pictorial presentation of truth as apocalyptic, a style of communication and writing characterized by bold colors, vivid images, unique symbols, a simple story line, a hero, and a happy ending. Thus, in Revelation you meet angels, animals, and numbers. You see lightning and hear thunder. You witness earthquakes and battles. You see the sparkle of jewels and a woman clothed with the sun facing a terrifying dragon. You see a rider on a white horse and hear the lyrics of the Hallelujah Chorus.

You approach apocalyptic literature differently than you would a letter or one of the Gospels. In Revelation words take the place of pigments and brushes to create a portrait designed to visualize great principles, not particular incidents. Resisting

---

[4]The Heidelberg Catechism Question and Answer 54.

the temptation to dissect the portrait described in each vision, you let the vision as a whole impress you. And impress you it will. The Apocalypse of John, as part of the biblical canon, the inspired Word of God to his children, will illuminate in a fresh way relevant teachings found throughout Scripture.

In times like these, you need a word from the Lord. You don't need a history lesson of the militant church of either the first or last century. You don't need a prophetic vision of a day you will never experience in this life. At this moment in your struggle with sin and evil, you need a hope-filled word from the Lord. You need the Apocalypse of John now.

Some approach Revelation differently. Perhaps, naively secure in their luxurious homes, they turn their eyes from the evil and sin that ravages their brothers and sisters in Christ throughout the world. They think they are at peace, having learned the habit of a positive mental attitude. They don't need a word of comfort and hope. So, they approach Revelation like a history lesson, memorizing trumpets and bowls like presidents and wars. Or they approach the Apocalypse like a puzzle with a thousand small pieces. At their leisure, they try to piece together the seals, the beasts, the prostitute, and the plagues. They are not blessed by the colorful visions, for they are never impressed by the vision as a whole. They are only confused because they cannot fit the pieces together.

Let the troubles come, however, and Revelation becomes as precious as it was to John on the island of Patmos. The book of Revelation is for believers like you and the apostle John, who find that following the Lord is a way of contradiction that pierces your inmost thoughts, even as it heals them with peace.[5] It is for believers like those in the first century, whose only conquest was their steadfast endurance with no tangible evidence of victory. It is for the believer who doubts the sovereignty of God, questions the influence of the church, and fears the power of evil. To these readers Revelation offers a message of assurance, hope, and victory.

---

[5]Wilfrid J. Harrington, *Understanding the Apocalypse* (Washington, D.C.: Corpus Books, 1969), 56–58.

REVIEW OF REVELATION[6]

Introduction (Rev. 1:1–20)

The opening chapter of the Apocalypse introduces the reader to the entire book and holds the key to its interpretation. It may be divided into three parts: the preface, the salutation, and the initial vision of the risen Jesus.

The *preface* (vv. 1–3) conveys five important concepts. (1) It informs us that the book did not originate with any human being. It is a revelation of God the Father and God the Son, sent to one called John through the supernatural agency of an angel. This fact will prove helpful to the reader when tempted to dismiss key elements of the Apocalypse, such as the total destruction of the wicked, that seem inconsistent with our limited understanding of the Deity.

(2) The recorder or author of Revelation is John. While the book contains little biographical information about the author, nearly every scholar throughout the centuries has concluded that John is the beloved apostle of Jesus, the author of the fourth Gospel and three letters. The internal evidence of the book seems consistent with such a conclusion.

(3) The preface informs us that Revelation contains a mixture of literary styles. It is predominantly apocalyptic (v. 1), but also prophetic (v. 3) and epistolary, as evidenced by the traditional bookends of salutation and benediction. As an apocalyptic book the symbols employed in the various visions are tools for the communication of precepts. They may have no historic connection with any particular event. Yet, a symbol may find fulfillment in an historical event or person without exhausting its meaning.

(4) The book is designed to bless the reader. For many, including myself, Revelation has been a source of frustration. Christians have spent hours wrestling with the identity of the Antichrist, the time of the Tribulation, and the nature of the Millennium. In the end, the reading of the text seldom ushered

---

[6]Since there is no consensus regarding the outline of the book, I utilize, for the most part, the outline provided in the study notes for the book of Revelation in *NIV Study Bible* (Grand Rapids: Zondervan, 1985).

blessing, only confusion. John assures us that his visions are recorded to bless us. In so doing, he illustrates his literary propensity for triads: blessed are those who read, hear, and take to heart what is written.

(5) The preface relates urgency. The Apocalypse reveals "what must soon take place" (1:1; 22:6), for the "the time is near" (1:3). These words confirm several approaches to Revelation, including that of the idealist, who is convinced that Revelation describes the entire era from Christ's first to second appearing.[7]

The *salutation* (vv. 4–8), following typical epistolary style, introduces the recipients of the letter. John selects seven congregations for reasons known only to him. He may have visited each of them during his years in Ephesus, for all seven are located in the district of Asia Minor of which Ephesus was the capital.

John intentionally addressed the letter to seven congregations rather than five, nine, or eleven. The number seven appears frequently throughout the book. Its use is not accidental. In much of the ancient world certain numbers, especially among the first ten, were universally associated with certain ideas. As we progress we will find this true of the numbers three, four, seven, ten, and twelve. The number seven, however, surpasses all others both in the frequency in which it occurs and in the importance of the objects with which it is associated. The number seven represents totality, fullness, and completeness. In the salutation, then, the seven congregations represent the church of Jesus Christ in every country of the world to the end of time.

The salutation also includes a beautiful blessing, in which John prays that the readers receive the grace of peace, that deep assurance in the depth of one's being that remains undisturbed by outward trouble. This is the peace of Christ imparted by the Holy Spirit, the seven spirits, as it operates in the church.

---

[7]Observe the inconsistency of the other viewpoints outlined in this book with respect to Rev. 1:1, 3. Ironically, Thomas proposes a literal interpretation of Revelation but then offers a symbolic understanding of "what must soon take place." Gentry proposes a symbolic approach to Revelation but offers a literal interpretation of 1:3. For Thomas, then, "what must soon take place" has not yet taken place, while for Gentry it already has. Pate's already/not yet approach allows him to say yes to both Gentry and Thomas, but his interpretation does not allow for any fulfillment of Revelation between the first and second coming of Christ. The idealist approach affirms that Gentry is right: Soon means soon! The idealist also affirms Pate: The period of fulfillment should not be limited to the writer's day.

Finally, the salutation is noteworthy for its comforting snap-shot of a sovereign God, the Alpha and the Omega, who reigns with Jesus Christ, the ruler of the kings of the earth. The theme of a sovereign God is central to the book and will reappear in a variety of forms. Here John combines the first and last letter of the Greek alphabet as a symbolic expression that affirms the Lord as the first and the last, the beginning and the end and any-thing in between. This affirmation confronts the harsh reality that may cause even the most devoted believer to question whether this is our Father's world. Furthermore, God the Son, the victorious head of the church, is also reigning supreme. Now, in the midst of our suffering, he is hidden from view, but, as we will see, he will appear in glory.

The *initial vision of the exalted Christ* (vv. 9–20) is the focal point or center of the first vision. Our imagination is taxed beyond capacity as we try to imagine the Christ described by John, whose frequent use of the word "like" warns us that we should not take him literally. He is using earthly language to describe what is beyond description. The end result is a brilliant picture of the exalted Christ that knocks John to the ground. One truth is clear: The Christ in this vision is not the Jesus of John's Gospel, that is, Jesus in a state of humiliation. Here, Jesus is the Son of Man clothed with majesty and armed with a two-edged sword, the Word, for battle against those who refuse to repent (2:16).

There are several additional key elements to John's first vision. (1) John connects with his readers by assuring them that he shares the triad of suffering, the kingdom, and patient endurance (1:9). Together, as disciples of Jesus, they bear the bur-dens foretold by their Master (John 15:20; 16:2).

(2) John is commissioned as a New Testament prophet in the honored tradition of the Old Testament. Like Ezekiel, God commissioned John through a vision and called him to bring a prophetic word to the people. The voice instructed John to write what he saw—that is, the vision of the Son of Man, the condi-tion of the seven congregations, and what is to come.

(3) John is commanded to record his vision on one scroll for believers in seven named communities. The fact that there is only one scroll, instead of seven, confirms that the book is for the entire Christian church. The upcoming seven messages, then, should be read together, not in isolation.

(4) The exalted Christ walks among the seven golden lamp-stands (v. 12), which represent the seven congregations in Asia Minor. Furthermore, he holds seven stars in his right hand, perhaps a reference to the pastoral leadership of those Christian communities. The lesson is clear: The true church is ever the light-bearer, causing the light of Christ's glorious gospel to be poured out in a dark world.[8]

The Letters to the Churches (Rev. 2:1–3:22)

Since the exalted Christ has a two-edged sword coming from his mouth, we expect a word from the Son of Man. The first message is to the seven congregations of Asia Minor (1:11). These congregations may have been selected for a practical reason.[9] If we draw a line on the map through the seven cities in the order in which they are named, we find that we have followed a roughly circular route through what were doubtless the most important parts of the province of Asia. If John's book was sent along this route, it would reach the greatest number of people in the shortest period of time, and this fact may have played a part in the selection and naming of the churches. Yet, the fact that seven were named, rather than eight or nine, suggests that another idea is at work here.[10] As previously noted, the symbolic meaning of seven as completeness suggests the author is speaking of the church at all times and in all places.

The description of the seven churches, then, is a candid picture of what can happen in congregational life at all times and in all places. The letters provide a closer look at the bride of Christ, which helps the reader understand her divine origin and human frailty. Through the letters, we witness her grace and defects, her zeal and lukewarmness, her joys and sorrows, her guardianship by Christ and final victory after many struggles.[11] Of course, the seven vignettes of congregational problems do not equal a complete catalog of the possibilities of failure. The dangers for the churches of Asia were related to conditions in

---

[8]Hendriksen, *Three Lectures on the Book of Revelation*, 15.

[9]Unjhem, *Book of Revelation*, 66.

[10]Edwin A. Schick, *Revelation: The Last Book of the Bible* (Philadelphia: Fortress, 1977), 27.

[11]William Milligan, *The Book of Revelation* (New York: A. C. Armstrong, 1893), 838.

that part of the world at that time. The dangers for the churches in North America are related to conditions of life as they exist here and now. But the meaning of these dangers is always the same: Something else (and it does not matter what) diverts attention from Christ, who is the true life and meaning of the church, wherever it is.[12]

Christ is the appropriate messenger, for he is the Lord of the church (1:12–13), who knows (2:2) the character and life of each congregation, as well as the position and problems of each individual member. He is aware of the frailty of life and sympathetic to those who struggle, but he does not tolerate any form of counterfeit Christianity. As a result, the church must subject itself to critical scrutiny at all times. Self-examination, confession, repentance, and renewal characterize its life. This sacred ritual is made possible by a compassionate Savior, who meets every repentant backslider while steadfastly condemning the unrepentant.

The Throne, Scroll, and Lamb (Rev. 4:1–5:14)

As we move to the third section of the book, John provides a vision that affirms the sovereignty of God, who holds the affairs of this world in his hands. This vision serves as a postscript to the previous vision and a prelude to all that follows. The church that brings the light of Christ's gospel to the world, as prescribed in the previous vision, will experience tribulation (cf. the vision of the seals). Yet, no matter what the church endures on earth, it should never forget that God is sovereign. In the midst of trial, the church should gaze on the One who is King of Kings and Lord of Lords.

This vision provides several additional lessons. (1) With chapter 4 we enter the main body of the book. Immediately, we recognize a change in literary style. We are now reading apocalyptic literature. Our first indication is John's reference to his vision. Another is the manner in which the picture takes the place of words. As apocalyptic literature we seek to understand the impressions that the vision makes rather than analyzing every detail. We look for the main point so as not to be confused

---

[12]Abraham Kuyper, *The Revelation of St. John* (Grand Rapids: Eerdmans, 1964), 27–31.

by the particulars. In addition, we will not establish unique doctrinal teachings on symbols that are difficult for a twentieth-century Christian to understand. Following good hermeneutical guidelines, we recognize that doctrine must be established by the clear teaching of Scripture. Revelation, then, will support doctrines found outside itself rather than create new ones.

(2) These chapters serve an important function as an introduction to chapters 6–20. The vision contained within them establishes the perspective that must govern the remainder of the visions. They provide an ever-present vision of hope and victory with God on the throne, which should hold the reader from discouragement or despair as he or she continues through the remainder of the book.

(3) The word "throne" dominates this vision. The term occurs forty-six times in the book, nineteen times in this vision, and seventeen times with reference to the throne of God in heaven. Notice that the throne in heaven is positioned in the center, not of heaven, but of the universe. "Every creature in heaven and on earth and under the earth and on the sea, and all that is in them" worships the Lamb (5:13). The universe is theocentric.

(4) God the Father sits on the throne, but John cannot describe him. Thus, he describes his radiant appearance as jasper and carnelian (4:3). The flash of jewelry portrays God's majesty.

(5) Worship dominates the vision. A large and diverse congregation joins in worship. The group includes four living creatures, who represent all living creatures. It also includes the entire community of the redeemed, represented by twenty-four elders wearing garments of holiness and crowns of victory: the twelve patriarchs of the Old Testament era and the twelve apostles of the New Testament period (21:12, 14).

(6) Jesus Christ is the triumphant redeemer who governs the entire universe from the throne (Eph. 1:22–23). The seven horns and seven eyes symbolize his complete authority, omnipotence, and omnipresence in the world. He holds the future, the scroll, in his hands. Now the Lamb moves into action and breaks the seals one by one.

The Seven Seals (Rev. 6:1–8:1)

The vision of the seals takes us from the glorious perspective of the universe centered around the throne of God to a world teeming with trouble. This earthly travail is as expected. Whenever the church is faithful to its calling as light in the world, tribulation follows. Aside from this, the church is in the world and suffers along with it the difficulties of war, disease, and famine.[13] The church suffers both direct attack from the world and the common woes of a world infected by sin.

The seals do not follow in chronological succession. Each does not belong to a particular time. Remember, for John the time between the first and second coming is short, and whatever happens must shortly come to pass. So the vision deals with the whole history of the church and of the world throughout the Christian age.[14] The vision provides no details of particular wars, diseases, slaughters, or difficulties. Everything has been described in general terms. The symbols represent forces that have been with us all the time. We all know them, and all generations before us knew them too. They may have ridden silently across the stage and off into the darkness, but we will not forget them.

The vision of the seals illustrates the calamities that fall upon the children of God even while the provident God sits on his throne. The calamities require illustration. Statistics on moral and natural disasters can be shrugged off. John shocks us with symbols beginning with four horsemen borrowed from the prophet Zechariah (Zech. 6:1–8). The opening of the first seal introduces the first of four wondrous riders who come across the stage without a word or action. The first rider bears a crown and holds a bow while he travels ready for conquest on a white horse. There are several options concerning his identity but the most compelling is Jesus Christ.[15] This assertion is founded on the portrayal of Christ as conqueror in 5:5 and on the color of the horse. White is a color normally associated with that which is holy and heavenly, such as garments, clouds, and a throne. In addition, this option fits with the Christus Victor theme that runs like a thread throughout the book.[16]

The opening of the next three seals introduces three additional riders on different colored horses. There is consensus

[13]Hendriksen, *More Than Conquerors*, 99.
[14]Milligan, *The Book of Revelation*, 860.
[15]Hendriksen, *More Than Conquerors*, 114.
[16]See Rev. 1:13ff.; 2:26–27; 3:21; 5:5; 6:16; 7:9–10; 11:15; 12:11; 14:1ff., 14ff.; 17:14; 19:11; 20:4; 22:16.

among idealist interpreters of Revelation concerning their identities. The three riders illustrate the disintegration of both human civilization and creation as a result of the rejection of the Lamb of God. The red horse represents slaughter or war; the black horse represents economic hardship and poverty, perhaps because of injustice; the pale horse represents death, famine, and disease. Together these riders highlight the woes that afflict sinful human beings, who live in a world filled with evil. The riders are instruments of God's moral government.[17] While the problems come because of the unrighteous rejection of the Lamb, they are free to afflict the righteous even while God sits on his throne.

The fifth seal illustrates the persecution of the faithful. The souls may be those persecuted by the slaughter and hardship represented in the previous seals. The faithful, wearing white robes that symbolize righteousness and holiness, must endure until the time of judgment. That day will not come until every elect person has been brought into the fold and the number of martyrs is full.

The sixth seal, accordingly, introduces the Day of Judgment. It describes one great catastrophe at the end of this age. The terror of this day is pictured through the twofold symbol of a crashing universe and a frightened human race. Here we learn that the Lamb of God is victorious, that God will judge each adversary who persecutes the church, and that the wrath of God is so terrible that each opponent of the Lord seeks refuge beneath falling rocks.

Now we expect the seventh seal to be opened, but John's style is such that before any critical manifestation of God's wrath, he provides a vision of comfort and hope.[18] John follows the pattern of Ezekiel, who, just before the destruction of Jerusalem, described the preservation of the faithful in the midst of the judgment of the wicked. The message of this vision is simple: The universal church—that is, the sealed 144,000—are safe in the midst of the judgment of the wicked brought about by the four winds.

The identity of the sealed as the universal church needs substantiation.[19] (1) Revelation does not distinguish between

---

[17]Albertus Pieters, *Studies on Revelation* (Grand Rapids: Eerdmans, 1950), 117.
[18]Milligan, *The Book of Revelation*, 861.
[19]Ibid.

Jewish and Gentile Christians. John does not exhibit a particularistic tendency at variance with the universalism of the gospel. For John, the church is one. (2) John tends to spiritualize Jewish names and images, as in 21:12, where the twelve tribes clearly include all believers. (3) The number of the redeemed, a multiple of one thousand, is symbolic of a large number of individuals who, in spite of the world's rejection, have accepted the Lamb and have the seal of God upon their foreheads.[20] The number, a multiple of twelve, is also symbolic of completeness, indicating that not one member of the church will be lost.[21]

While a host of individuals reject the Lamb and discover that their way of life has been a colossal mistake, there are those who accept the Lamb, who have the seal of God on their foreheads and the inheritance of the future. This perspective gives meaning and purpose to the followers of the Lamb on earth. As in the first six seals, this vision does not point to any particular period in history, nor does it describe any particular set of events in the near or distant future. Rather, it speaks of the situation in all historical periods. The description of natural disasters is not a preview of the end of the world, but a vivid way of saying that even nature itself will not sustain those who reject God's redemption in Christ.[22]

The Seven Trumpets (Rev. 8:2–11:19)

Now that the two visions of comfort and hope are complete, John returns to the seventh seal, whose opening introduces the next vision, that of the seven trumpets. This vision portrays the punishment awaiting the wicked persecutors of the church.[23] It begins with silence in heaven, which focuses attention on what is about to be revealed (8:1). The presence of trumpets lends additional emphasis to the importance of what is to happen, for in the Old Testament the sound of the trumpet often symbolized God's intervention in the world (Isa. 27:12–13). The prayers of all the saints (Rev. 8:3–5) reflect that the fate of the chosen people is a major concern in all that is about to happen.[24] They also draw

---

[20]Unjhem, Book of Revelation, 103.

[21]Milligan, The Book of Revelation, 863.

[22]Unjhem, Book of Revelation, 103–5.

[23]Hendriksen, Three Lectures on the Book of Revelation, 17.

[24]Unjhem, Book the Revelation, 105.

a connection to the vision of the seals: God has heard the prayers of the persecuted saints and responded with the punishment of the wicked.

We must resist the temptation to link each trumpet with a particular date or person in history.[25] The trumpets indicate a series of happenings or calamities that will occur again and again throughout the earthly existence of the church. For example, the hail and fire mingled with blood that destroy one-third of the earth is a symbol of all those land disasters that are used by God to warn the wicked to refrain from their wickedness (9:21). Similarly, the great mountain ablaze symbolizes all sea disasters by means of which God threatens to destroy the unrepentant. The Lord uses the land, sea, rivers, sun, moon, stars, the pit of the abyss, the field of battle, and the threat of coming judgment to warn the enemies of his beloved ones. He afflicts them with warning judgments in seven departments of the universe, each one pictured by a trumpet. So, the trumpets do not symbolize single and separate events but trials that may be found at any time and at any place.

Several important observations should be made about the trumpets. (1) The judgment of the trumpet is not final and complete. Notice the pervasive use of the fraction "one-third," which occurs sixteen times in Revelation, fifteen times in this scene. The punishment of each trumpet, while incomplete, is a sufficient notice to the wicked.

(2) The trumpets of judgment affect every part of the universe. Nowhere is there safety for the wicked.[26]

(3) The judgments are expressed in language similar to the ten plagues in Egypt, yet the description in Revelation is more terrible. The hail and fire, for example, are mingled with blood; the locusts inflict, not the grass of the earth, but the wicked themselves. One similarity between the plagues and the trumpets is that neither set of plagues harms believers.[27]

The first four trumpet blasts (8:7–12) call forth various kinds of physical disasters. The entire universe is used by the Lord to warn those who reject the Lamb of God and persecute God's children. One need not explain these phenomena as nat-

[25]Hendriksen, *Three Lectures on the Book of Revelation*, 18.
[26]Hendriksen, *More Than Conquerors*, 141.
[27]Ibid.

ural events that someday take place. For one, the common view at that time was that the earth is flat, the sky is above, and the world is like an inverted bowl, whose perimeter contains all the heavenly bodies. The physical disasters point beyond themselves to divine justice. As in the Old Testament stories of the Flood or the ten plagues, natural calamities are the consequence of disobedience and rebellion. God has good reason to employ nature as an instrument of warning and punishment. After all, those who rebel against God often turn to the world for meaning and purpose. Used in such a way, nature is a foundation for rebellion against God. God, however, reminds the unrepentant that nature does not offer humanity security and hope.[28]

There is a brief intermission after the fourth trumpet. John sees and hears an eagle, whose loud and clear voice tells the world that the next three judgments will be worse than the first four. The fifth and sixth trumpets add demonic terrors as John describes the brutal despair and horror of human existence apart from God (9:1–21). The fifth trumpet offers a vision of terror and destruction as it reveals God's permissive decree that allows the prince of darkness to fill the world with the influence and activity of demons, symbolized by the destructive power of the locusts who harm the unsealed. The hearts of men and woman are so filled with hopelessness that they seek death but cannot find it (9:6–10). The sixth trumpet describes war, which serves as a punishment and warning for unbelievers. God permits four evil angels to plunge humanity into war (9:20). A tremendous host of warriors, horsemen on horses, bring destruction on every side, killing one-third of humanity.

The general meaning of the first six trumpets is clear. The Lord will punish the persecutors of the church by inflicting on them disasters in every sphere of life, physical and spiritual. The blood of the martyrs is precious in the Lord's sight. The prayers of the saints are heard. God sees their tears and suffering. Yet, in spite of the warnings, humankind in general does not repent (9:21). The disintegration of life away from God does not automatically lead to the experience of redemption. Encouraged by the dragon and his allies, the persecuting world is impenitent. That disposition brings the outpouring of the bowls.[29]

[28]Unjhem, *Book of Revelation*, 105–6.
[29]Hendriksen, *More Than Conquerors*, 148.

Now, as two visions preceded the seventh seal, so two visions precede the seventh trumpet. The first vision (10:1–11), reminiscent of the Old Testament apocalyptic imagery of Ezekiel (9:4), describes a giant angel descending from heaven with a little scroll in his hand. The symbolism associates but does not identify the angel with Christ (1:7; 4:3; 1:17; 1:15). The angel stands on both sea and land with a message for the entire universe: "There will be no more delay." The time for judgment has come. The mystery of God's permissive will shall be revealed. The wicked will be punished and God's children will receive their final inheritance as promised by the prophets.[30]

The angel holds a scroll or a little book. Perhaps it is a reminder for the church.[31] If it experiences bitter trials, that is not because God has forgotten to be gracious or has shut up his mercies. Rather, it is because the church has sinned and must be taught to live in direct dependence upon the voice of the Lord. More likely, the scroll symbolizes the good news of salvation.[32] The gospel is glorious and sweet, but its proclamation brings bitter persecution. The prophet must eat the scroll; that is, the apostle must experience both the sweetness and suffering of the gospel. His suffering for Christ's sake will enable believers to persevere in their proclamation of the Word. Hence, the prophet is encouraged to prophesy again and again.

The next vision, then, describes the bitter experiences attending the gospel. It depicts the effect on the church of the faithful proclamation of the sweet gospel of Christ. The apostle measures the sanctuary of God, the altar, and those who worship in it (11:1–14). The sanctuary symbolizes the true church, that is, all those in whose hearts Christ dwells in the Spirit (1 Cor. 3:16–17). The task of measuring implies that all true children of God who worship him in spirit and truth are measured or protected from all harm,[33] especially that which will come during a special time, the three and a half years of pressure and hardship.[34]

Now the seventh angel sounds the trumpet. The new vision provides an open view of heaven; nothing is hidden or veiled.

---

[30]Milligan, *The Book of Revelation*, 881.

[31]Ibid., 873.

[32]Hendriksen, *More Than Conquerors*, 151.

[33]Ibid., 154.

[34]Schick, *Revelation: The Last Book of the Bible*, 47.

The ark is safe and secure in the heavenly temple. The entire redeemed community, represented by the twenty-four elders, join with the angels in worship of the sovereign God. While at times it appears as though this is Satan's world, God is sovereign, and he will reveal his supremacy at the Day of Judgment when all opposition is abolished.

Various Personages and Events (Rev. 12:1–14:20)

This section is the most difficult of the entire book. Three introductory comments are helpful.[35] (1) This section, like those preceding, covers the entire course of time from the first to second coming of Christ. In unmistakable symbolism the prophet carries us back to the birth and ascension of Christ (12:1–5) and concludes the vision with Christ prepared to judge with a golden crown and a sickle in his hand (14:14).

(2) This section inaugurates the second major division of the book, which continues through chapter 22. This major portion of the Apocalypse, describing the conflict between the church and Satan, may be called "The Drama of the Woman and the Dragon."[36] It introduces the reader to the main characters who oppose Christ and his church: the dragon (chap. 12), the beast out of the sea (13:2), the beast out of the earth (13:11), Babylon (14:8), and those who have the mark of the beast (14:9). The introduction is followed by visions that illustrate the doom awaiting each of those anti-Christian forces: those who have the mark of the beast (chaps. 15–16), the harlot Babylon and the two beasts (chaps. 17–19), and the dragon (chaps. 20–22).

(3) The predominant theme of the second half of the book (chaps. 14–22) is similar to that of the first half (chaps. 1–13): Christ is victorious over Satan and his hosts. The difference between the two segments is that the first pictures the outward struggle between the church and the world, while the second reveals the deeper reality of a war between Christ and Satan. After witnessing the four visions of this section, the believer will know that the outward struggle between good and evil in this world, in which we suffer as Christians, is part of a larger conflict in the spiritual realm. The unseen conflict is the fundamental

---

[35]Hendriksen, *More Than Conquerors*, 162–63.
[36]Pieters, *Studies on Revelation*, 151.

battle where the enemy has already been defeated by the victorious Christ through his atoning work on the cross. Now, for a short time, Satan and his forces will muster up their final attacks on the church, but their end is sure.

The first vision of this section (12:1–14:20) introduces the main characters in the struggle between Christ and Satan (12:1–13:1). The first character is the woman, who symbolizes the seemingly insignificant people of God or the church (Eph. 5:32; cf. Isa. 50:1; Hos. 2:1). From heaven's perspective, they are radiant and glorious. This church brings forth the child, the seed of the woman, the Christ. The final character is the dragon, symbolizing Satan (20:2), who has dominion over the world (seven crowns) and who has tremendous destructive power (ten horns). The action of this vision involves the attempt of the huge red dragon to devour the seed of the radiant woman just as she gives birth, and the protection and preservation of both the woman and her child by Almighty God. This apocalyptic rendering of Genesis 3:15 summarizes as one story the entire history of God's people through the life of Christ: the original and ultimate struggle between good and evil, between the seed of the woman and the dragon, with Christ crushing the head of Satan.[37]

In 12:7–12, we witness the effect of Christ's birth, atonement, and ascension to the throne in heaven. There is a battle in heaven, with two opposing generals and their armies. Michael attacks and defeats the dragon, casting the monster out of heaven. The picture illustrates how Christ's atonement for sin stripped Satan of his accusatory power against believers (Rom. 8:33). In addition, when Satan is defeated, God's power is vindicated, those in heaven rejoice, and Satan is filled with wrath.

In 12:13–17 the angry dragon, unable to defeat the Christ and knowing time is short, unleashes its fury on the woman who gave birth to the Son, that is, the church. But the Lord protects the people, lifting them up with eagle's wings. The evil one tries to engulf the church in a stream of lies and delusions, but he cannot deceive her. So the dragon increases his attack on the rest of the women's seed, that is, individual believers. As a result, the church experiences both good and bad—the persecution of Satan and the special protection of God—as it pro-

---

[37]Calkins, *The Social Message of the Book of Revelation*, 117.

claims the gospel far and wide (11:1–10). This time of persecution and protection (between the first and second comings of Christ) is followed by three and a half days—a brief span of time during which the devil intensifies his attack and which is followed by the second coming of Christ for judgment (20:11).

The second vision in this section describes the beast of the sea (13:2–10), one of the agents used by the dragon to attack the church. The beast is a monster of horror rising from the sea, an emblem of the influence of the world insofar as it is opposed to God.[38] This beast, a composite of animals that symbolize four kingdoms in Daniel 7, represents the spirit of the world (1 Cor. 2:12) that opposes and persecutes the church.[39] Its influence can be found everywhere, including the church, the state, and the home. While the saints will be troubled and persecuted by this foe, they will be preserved.

The third vision describes the beast of the earth (13:11–18). This is a difficult paragraph, wherein the details are obscure but the main idea is clear. The beast symbolizes false religion and false philosophy in whatever form it may appear throughout this dispensation. The beast out of the earth is the false prophet (16:13; 19:20), who outwardly resembles the Lamb but is really an agent of the dragon. The false prophet marks each individual who belongs to him. The mark is 666, a symbol of eternal failure, for seven means perfection and wholeness. A mark on the forehead symbolizes the individual's mind, thought, and philosophy of life. A mark on the right hand indicates action, deeds, and enterprise. Those who receive the mark of the beast, then, belong to the army of those who persecute the church with both mind and action.

Comparing the two beasts, we conclude that the first is a monster of horror while the second appears harmless and for that reason is more dangerous than the first. The first is Satan's hand and the second his mind. The first represents the persecuting power of Satan, operating in and through the spirit of this world and its government. The second symbolizes false religions and philosophies of this world. The beast of the sea and the beast of the earth work hand in hand. The spirit of the world as found in anti-Christian government conspires with anti-Christian religion

---

[38]Milligan, *The Book of Revelation*, 887.
[39]Schick, *Revelation: The Last Book of the Bible*, 52.

and attacks Christ and his church. The work of these cohorts is obvious in the crucifixion of Jesus Christ, where the Sanhedrin partnered with Pilate to murder the Messiah. Their attacks continue throughout this dispensation.

The fourth and final vision of this section is the Lamb and the 144,000 (14:1–20). This vision illustrates the ultimate triumph of God and his church. It encourages the believer who may be overwhelmed by the previous scenes of the dragon, the beast of the sea, and the beast out of the earth. The vision is divided into three sections, each beginning with "I saw." (1) John saw a Lamb standing on Mount Zion with the triumphant church in heaven (14:1–5). The congregation numbers 144,000, a complete number without one missing soul. These 144,000 have not accepted Satan's lie; now they enjoy the blessedness of their redemption. (2) John saw the gracious warning of God of the coming judgment and punishment of the wicked (14:6, 8–9), which will precede the second coming of Christ. (3) John witnessed the final and complete judgment of the wicked, symbolized by the image of a harvest that takes place when Christ returns. The Son of Man is seated on the throne of judgment. He directs his angels to swing the sickle of harvest, for the time has come.

The Seven Bowls (Rev. 15:1–16:21)

Throughout history you will find a reoccurring order of events.[40] The church causes the light of Christ to shine forth into the darkness of the world. That activity leads to the persecution of God's people. Behind this ever-present confrontation between the church and the world is a more fundamental conflict, that between God and Satan. God, through the work of Jesus Christ, has won the ultimate victory over Satan and his hosts. Consequently, he will judge and punish those who persecute the righteous.

Before passing judgment, however, God warns the unrighteous. When the trumpets of warning fail to move unbelievers to repentance, God proceeds with bowls of wrath on the unrepentant, who have received the mark of the beast and worship the dragon (9:21; 16:9). The bowls unveil God's righteous indig-

---

[40]Hendriksen, *More Than Conquerors*, 189; *Three Lectures on the Book of Revelation*, 19.

nation and wrath on the deliberate and determined followers of the beast, who blaspheme God amid their suffering.[41] God must not be trifled with.[42]

Several aspects of this vision are noteworthy. (1) Before John reveals the seven angels with their bowls of wrath, he offers a scene of the church triumphant. Drawing on the story of the drowning of Pharaoh's host in the Red Sea (Ex. 14:15ff.), John assures the reader that even after the bowls of wrath are poured out, God will preserve a victorious multitude of saints, playing their harps and singing the song of Moses and the Lamb. The victory over the Egyptians, then, foreshadows the victory of God's people over the beast.

(2) The seven bowls of wrath bear striking resemblance to the plagues in Egypt (Ex. 7–10). It is unnecessary to dwell on particulars of the plagues, for the general effect is most significant: God uses every department of creation to punish the unrepentant.

(3) The vision of the bowls runs parallel in time to the vision of the trumpets. Each covers the entire dispensation from the first to second coming of Christ. This means that for one individual a particular calamity may be a warning trumpet of judgment while for another individual it may be a bowl of wrath. The primary difference between the trumpets and the bowls is the intensity of punishment. The trumpets, for example, destroy one-third of the creatures in the sea, while the bowl of wrath destroys every living thing.

(4) Chapter 15 affirms again that Revelation is not chronological. It begins with a heavenly vision of the church triumphant at the end of the age before returning in time to God's final judgment on the wicked.

(5) The seven bowls are poured out in rapid and uninterrupted succession. As with the seals and trumpets, they are divided into groups of four and three, and those of the first group may be taken together.[43]

(6) Armageddon appears in the narration accompanying the sixth bowl as the location of a great battle. The dragon and its cohorts, the beast of the earth and the beast of the sea or the

[41]Milligan, *The Book of Revelation*, 899.

[42]Schick, *Revelation: The Last Book of the Bible*, 56.

[43]Milligan, *The Book of Revelation*, 896.

false prophet, will confront the people of God in a final battle. The children of God will experience victory through the sudden and dramatic intercession of Christ. Armageddon, then, is a symbol of every battle in which Satan gathers his troops against the church. Then Christ suddenly and dramatically appears to deliver his people and defeat the enemy. Battles at Armageddon may take place throughout the history of the world, though the final one coincides with Satan's day of judgment.

(7) The vision ends with a vivid description of the final judgment: stones falling from heaven. The final fall of Babylon is the crushing blow for those who bear the mark of the beast. All that delights them collapses as the great city, Babylon, is broken into three pieces.

Babylon (Rev. 17:1–19:21)

We have just witnessed God's righteous indignation and wrath on the unrepentant as seven angels each poured out their vials. One of the seven introduces a new section that, as a coherent whole covering the whole history of the world from paradise to the Judgment Day, describes the ultimate victory of Jesus and the destruction of the spiritual forces energizing the convictions and behavior of the unrepentant. The message of this section is one of encouragement: While the forces of evil prevail and persecute the saints, their time of apparent victory is temporary. While the forces of evil appear invulnerable, Babylon, the beast of the earth, and the beast out of the sea or false prophet will be destroyed by Christ, the Lord of Lords, who is the victor. Therefore, the church should take courage until that time of ultimate victory.

The structure of the section is simple. Chapter 17 describes the great harlot, Babylon, and reveals the doom of the beast of the sea; chapter 18 reveals the complete fall of Babylon; chapter 19 unveils the victory over Babylon and the subsequent celestial celebration and marriage of the Lamb to the church. Hence, the future of five characters is described: Babylon, the beast out of the sea, the beast of the earth or false prophet, the church, and the Lamb.

(1) The predominant character in the drama is Babylon, the great harlot (17:5, 18; 19:2–3). John mentioned Babylon on two

previous occasions (14:8; 16:19). Now she receives fuller treatment. Carried away by the Spirit to a desert, John saw a woman sitting on a beast. This is not the radiant woman of 12:1, though both are found in the desert. Instead, the scarlet woman is different, as evidenced by her relationship to the beast. The beast saddled by the scarlet woman is the same beast that aids the dragon in an attack on the radiant women.[44] The enemy of one is there the friend and servant of the other. The scarlet woman is dressed like a prostitute, luring all who behold her. She entices individuals to drink from her golden cup, tempting them to turn from God. She is drunk with the blood of saints spilled during her war against the Lamb (17:6). She influences the whole world from her high elevation and rules it with a firm hand. She is Babylon (17:5, 18; 19:2–3).

The identity of Babylon has been a subject of some debate. Two options seem viable. (a) Babylon represents the worldly city or center of wickedness that allures, tempts, and draws people away from God (Ezek. 27–28). Babylon is the pleasure-mad, arrogant world, with all its seductive luxuries and pleasures, with its anti-Christian philosophy and culture, and with its teeming multitudes that have forsaken God and have lived according to the lusts of the flesh and the desires of the mind.[45] John does not condemn society itself but the kind of society that rebels against God—a society where there is no place for God and no room for redemption by Christ.[46] In the first century, Babylon was Rome. Two generations ago it was Berlin. Today, perhaps, it is Las Vegas or even a university campus. Babylon can be found everywhere throughout the history of the world.[47] It is the center of anti-Christian seduction any time in history.

(b) The second option is that Babylon represents the world in the church,[48] the unspiritual or earthly element that has infiltrated the body of Christ, or even a false church like Jerusalem.[49] Six reasons support this theory: (i) In 2:9 John knows of a community that claims to be a congregation of the living God but is really a

[44]Pieters, *Studies in Revelation*, 246–47.

[45]Hendriksen, *More Than Conquerors*, 200–202.

[46]Unjhem, *Book of Revelation*, 117–18.

[47]Ibid., 119.

[48]Milligan, *The Book of Revelation*, 904.

[49]Cornelis Vanderwaal, *Hal Lindsey and Biblical Prophecy* (St. Catherines, Ont.: Paideia, 1978), 105.

synagogue of Satan; (ii) Revelation 17 echoes Exodus 16 and 23, where Israel is branded a harlot who fails to keep the covenant; (iii) the great city is mentioned in Revelation 11:8, where a political-cultural interpretation is out of the question and suggests that Babylon should not be interpreted as a political-cultural entity in chapters 17 and 18; (iv) the officials of Jerusalem, during his earthly ministry, opposed Jesus and encouraged Rome to crucify him (Acts 2:23; 3:13; 4:10; 5:30; 7:52); (v) when the harlot is destroyed (Rev. 18:20), God squares accounts for what she has done to the prophets and apostles (1 Kings 19:10); (vi) Revelation 18:22–23 echoes Jeremiah 25:10, a passage that deals with Jerusalem.[50]

While the identity of Babylon may be uncertain, its future is not: Babylon will be destroyed (18:21–23). Judgment is the predominant message of this scene. God will not forget her sins, and Babylon will perish. Before final punishment arrives, however, believers are encouraged to refuse fellowship with her sins and to turn away from her allurements and enticements.[51] Those who do not leave but set their hearts on the spirit of the world will suffer with Babylon. When Babylon perishes, kings, merchants, and sailors will mourn, for that on which they have pinned their hopes will have collapsed. This is true with respect to the fall of every Babylon throughout the history of the world, and especially with respect to the final kingdom of the Antichrist at the close of the age. Conversely, the destruction of Babylon leads to rejoicing in heaven by the saints, apostles, and prophets (19:1–10). Heaven celebrates God's victory over the harlot, Babylon. The twenty-four elders, symbolizing the entire church, praise God with four representative cherubim.

(2) The second major character in this section is the beast (17:3). As just mentioned, the beast is that described in 13:2–10. It came out of the sea and earlier assisted the dragon in its attack on the radiant woman and her seed. The beast represents the spirit and empires of the world, who work hand in hand with the seductive woman. Working together, for example, the empires of this world do not need to destroy every church building. They can change some of them into places of worldly amusement.[52]

---

[50]Vanderwaal refers to Benne Holwerda's 1949 Dutch work called *The Church in Final Judgment*, in his *Hal Lindsey and Biblical Prophecy*, 105.

[51]Hendriksen, *More Than Conquerors*, 208.

[52]Ibid., 203.

The beast and the woman associate with one another until the beast turns against the woman (17:16–18). For a time, the world commits adultery with the harlot and drinks of her golden cup. But in the end, the people who constitute the anti-Christian world turn on the whore. Worldly people strip the prostitute and burn her. The lesson is that the same people (those who constitute the beast) who were at one time infatuated with the harlot and all she offered, realize their folly. But instead of repenting, they harden themselves against God and are consequently punished for their own foolishness. The beast, like the harlot, suffers doom. The rider on the white horse captures the beast and throws him into the fiery lake of burning sulfur (19:19–20).

(3) The third character is the beast of the earth or false prophet (13:11–17), who performs miracles on behalf of the beast out of the sea and who had confused many who received his mark and worshiped him. This beast is also captured and punished with eternal destruction (19:20). This completes the destruction of the three forces that supported the unrepentant persecutors of the church. Now, the persecutors and the spiritual forces have all been punished with eternal destruction.

(4) The fourth and final characters are the eternal bride and groom: Jesus Christ and the church. With mixed images, the Messiah is represented as a Lamb (19:7–9), engaged to marry the bride or the church. Throughout this entire dispensation, the church has prepared for her wedding day. Now at its end, after the judgment of the wicked, the groom, accompanied by angels, comes to receive his bride (Matt. 25:31). The wedding feast begins and continues throughout eternity.

Then John receives a view of heaven that takes the reader back to the moments preceding the final judgment. He sees Jesus Christ represented in this scene by a rider on a white horse, prepared for the battle at Armageddon: the final attack on the church and Christ's victory over Satan's vast army. Again, the beast and harlot direct their energies against the true church, those who are chosen and faithful. While they succeed for a short time, the Lamb is victorious. The angel, confident of his victory, invites the birds to gather for a great supper of God, where they can feast on the dead corpses of the people of Babylon. The principal lesson is this: Jesus Christ is King of kings and

Lord of lords (19:16). While the saints may suffer for a while, God is on their side and is faithful to his promises. Christ, the rider on the white horse, triumphs, though one foe remains.

Judgment of Satan and the Wicked (Rev. 20:1–15)

Thus far we have witnessed the final judgment and punishment of the unrepentant who persecute the church, Babylon, the beast of the sea, and the beast out of the earth or the false prophet. Now we witness the overthrow and destruction of the final enemy, Satan, as John portrays the ultimate victory of Christ over every force of evil.[53] The vision illustrates God's judgment of the dead, great and small, according to what they have done during their lifetimes, and their punishment in the lake of fire. Several aspects of this scene merit special attention.

(1) The vision begins with a heavenly angel capturing and binding Satan for a thousand years (vv. 1–3). Allowing Scripture to interpret Scripture, we may conclude that this scene describes the effect of Christ's earthly ministry on Satan (Mark 3:27; Luke 10:17–18). This is consistent with several visions in the Apocalypse that return the reader to the beginning of our current dispensation. This vision highlights Jesus' dominion over the serpent through the crucifixion and resurrection. Through his redemptive work, Christ curtailed the forces of Satan and paved the way for the successful proclamation of the gospel throughout the world.[54] Of course, this does not mean that Satan is neutralized. On the contrary, God permits Satan to influence and impact society within the circle of his imprisonment.

(2) The next scene in this vision (vv. 4–6) moves the viewer from the abyss to heaven. Parallel in time to the thousand-year imprisonment of Satan, this scene describes the millennial reign of Christ, who is assisted by martyrs not receiving the mark of the beast. The scene encourages the true believers, who have witnessed both the persecution of the faithful and the apostasy of those seduced by the limited, but powerful influence of Satan. It teaches that those who experienced the first resurrection of regeneration (Col. 3:1) and refused to receive the mark of the beast reign with Christ (Eph. 2:6). This reign begins for the believer

---

[53]Milligan, *The Book of Revelation*, 913.
[54]Hendriksen, *Three Lectures on the Book of Revelation*, 23.

while on earth but continues in heaven, since the believer's soul, on his or her death, is raised to heaven while the body awaits Christ's return. Finally, the resurrection of the body is secure, for the second death—that is, eternal punishment—has no power over believers.

(3) John does not place the opening scene at any point in human history, nor does he relate the reign of Christ to the Second Coming.[55] John, in an effort to encourage the faithful, takes the believer behind the scene of earthly persecution to witness a sovereign Christ and bound Satan. The vision affirms that Christ is victor and the martyrs are alive.

(4) The Millennium is not the central theme of this vision, even though it has received considerable attention throughout the centuries. Furthermore, the number itself is not difficult to understand. Throughout the Apocalypse numbers have been used symbolically. The use of the number one thousand in this vision is no exception. As amillennialists suggest, John is not describing a special period of time between this age and the eternal reign of Christ.[56] Rather, the number indicates completion or perfection instead of a specific span of time (Ps. 50:10). Amillennialists typically list three reasons in support of their conviction: No other passage of Scripture mentions a thousand-year period; a symbolic interpretation is consistent with the apocalyptic nature of the text; and the historic creeds of Christendom do not mention a literal period between this age and the eternal kingdom.[57]

(5) The third portion of this vision (vv. 7–10) describes the long-awaited destruction of Satan, who is thrown into the lake of burning sulfur with the beast and the false prophet. Before receiving eternal punishment, he is released from captivity. For a short time he is allowed to rally the nations for a concentrated, major attack upon the church. When has or will Satan enjoy his short season? William Milligan believes that the thousand-year reign refers to the earthly ministry of Christ, culminating in his death and resurrection, while the short season refers to the entire dispensation until Christ's second coming.[58]

---

[55]Leon Morris, *The Revelation of St. John* (TNTC; Grand Rapids: Eerdmans, 1969), 234.

[56]Harry Buis, *The Book of Revelation: A Simplified Commentary* (Philadelphia: Presbyterian and Reformed, 1960), 107.

[57]Ibid.

[58]Milligan, *The Book of Revelation*, 913.

William Hendriksen offers an alternative more consistent with what has been described thus far.[59] Reflecting dependence on Jesus' teaching regarding the end of time (Matt. 24:29–30), Hendriksen believes this scene foretells a time of tribulation when the world, functioning as one unit, attempts to destroy the church just before Christ's second coming. John's vision responds to those doubting believers who are suffering tribulation and who may conclude that Satan, not God, is sovereign. It assures them that though the world harnesses all its resources and power against the Lord, the attack will fail to overcome the church. Satan's time is short. God will complete his punishment of the wicked and devour the enemy with fire from heaven, casting the devil into the lake of burning sulphur.

(6) The final scene in this vision (vv. 11–15) describes the general and bodily resurrection of both believers and unbelievers, with a focus on the final judgment and punishment of the unrepentant. This vision is unlike most in the book.[60] It includes some symbolism but, for the most part, means exactly what it conveys. These verses include plain predictive sentences and literal explanations, complementing Jesus' prediction in Matthew 25:31–46. The limited symbolism is not difficult to understand. The great white throne symbolizes the majesty, authority, and holiness of God in judgment. The books represent the omniscience of God the Judge, to whom nothing is unknown and by whom nothing is forgotten;[61] every soul will give an account of his or her role in the universal struggle with evil.[62] The book of life is the roll of the redeemed (Luke 10:20; Phil. 4:3; Rev. 3:5). The lake of fire stands for utter destruction and eternal condemnation.[63]

(7) The vision as a whole (20:1–15) supports a general chronological description of time since the first advent. Complementing the teaching of Jesus as recorded in Matthew 24–25, it begins with the first coming of Christ, during which he bound Satan (Rev. 20:1–3) and raised the dead in Christ to reign with him in heaven (vv. 4–6). It continues with a description of a short

[59]Hendriksen, *Three Lectures on the Book of Revelation*, 26–28.
[60]Pieters, *Studies in Revelation*, 312.
[61]Ibid., 313.
[62]Unjhem, *Book of Revelation*, 110.
[63]Pieters, *Studies in Revelation*, 315.

but intense period of attack upon the church (vv. 7–9), followed by the implied second coming of Christ, the final judgment of every person, and the eternal punishment of the unrepentant and the devil (vv. 10–15).

The New Creation (Rev. 21:1–22:5)

This vision, which includes the final angelic appearance (21:9), continues the chronological sequence of major events that began in 20:1 with the incarnation and redemption of Christ (20:1–6) and concluded with universal judgment (20:11–15). John now receives a vision of what God has prepared for those who love him (1 Cor. 2:9–10). The vision highlights three permanent and eternal realities: the new heaven and earth, the new Jerusalem, and the marriage of the Lamb.

(1) The scene of a new heaven and earth (21:1–8), enriched by the holy city and a garden similar to Eden, bears remarkable similarities to its predecessor as described in the first book of the Bible.[64] In Genesis God created the heaven and the earth; in Revelation we read of a new heaven and earth (21:1). In Genesis the luminaries are called into being; in Revelation the glory of the Lord lights the city. In Genesis we read of the cunning power of Satan; in Revelation the devil is bound and hurled into the lake of fire (20:10). In Genesis we read of paradise lost; in Revelation paradise is restored. Genesis describes the divorce of humankind as Adam and Eve run from God; in Revelation the redeemed enjoy the intimate fellowship of marriage to the Lamb. In Genesis nature threatens the security and hurts humanity; in Revelation nature sustains and comforts people. In Genesis the tree of life is protected by an angel lest anyone eat its fruit; Revelation restores humanity's access to the fruit (22:14). This obvious correlation between the first and last books of the Bible illustrates the fulfillment of the first messianic prophecy (Gen. 3:15) and God's faithfulness to the covenant (Rev. 21:3).

Significant debate has taken place on the relationship of the new heaven and earth to the current universe. The Greek term for "new" (*kainos*) and 2 Peter 3:12–13 suggest that the new heaven and earth may be a rejuvenated and transformed version of the old.[65] Perhaps this planet is the final and eternal home

---

[64]Hendriksen, *More Than Conquerors*, 236–37.
[65]Ibid., 239.

of God's people, but the text does not limit the reader to such a conclusion. Rather, it assures the believer that God will provide an eternal dwelling place that is beautiful, safe, and secure.[66] The serenity and peace of this place will not be disturbed by the troubled sea (Isa. 57:20), for the new heaven and earth will not have a sea, from which evil raises its ugly head (Rev. 13:1).[67]

(2) The majority of the vision deals with the unveiling of the holy city, the new Jerusalem, the bride of the Lamb (21:2). John's vivid and detailed description of the holy city has led some to miss an important truth: The new Jerusalem is not a place but a people![68] It is not the final home of the redeemed; it is the redeemed! The new Jerusalem is a symbol of the bride, the church. It is a real and precious community of individuals who have fellowship with God. The city (Ps. 48; Isa. 26:1; 40:9) portrays the ideal condition of Christ's flock, enjoying its victory in Christ over both sin and death.[69] Of course, the new Jerusalem is not a remote possibility in the distant future. The city portrays a real encounter with the living Christ within the fellowship of the church here and now though fragmented and sporadic.[70] This analogy should quell the complacency of Laodicean congregations throughout the ages.[71]

Refraining from a detailed dissection of the vision, several broad strokes of the artist's rendering of the holy city accent additional truths.[72] (a) The holy city descends from heaven, indicating its gracious origin.[73] (b) The name "Jerusalem" reflects continuity between the old and new covenants, between the ancient sanctuary and its eternal successor. At the same time, the adjectives "new" and "holy" distinguish it from the present dispensation.[74] (c) The holy city does not require natural or artificial light, since the glory of God gives it light and the Lamb is its lamp (21:11, 23; 22:5). (d) The city is without a sanctuary, for the Lord God and the Lamb are its temple (21:22). As a result,

[66]Pieters, Studies in Revelation, 331.

[67]Morris, The Revelation of St. John, 243.

[68]Milligan, The Book of Revelation, 918.

[69]Unjhem, Book of Revelation, 110.

[70]Ibid., 111.

[71]Unjhem, Book of Revelation, 110.

[72]See Hendriksen, More Than Conquerors, 243–50.

[73]Kuyper, The Revelation of St. John, 310.

[74]Morris, The Revelation of St. John, 243.

believers have direct and immediate fellowship with God (Jer. 31:33; John 4:23–24; Heb. 8:8). (e) The city and its inhabitants are secure and safe (John 10:28), for the city is protected by a high wall (Rev. 21:12, 17–18). (f) The city with its twelve foundations (21:14, 19–20) is built on the foundation of the apostles (Eph. 2:20). (g) Twelve gates, each bearing the name of a tribe of Israel (Rev. 21:12–13, 21, 25, 27), provide abundant opportunity for entrance for the true Israel, the redeemed church (7:14), while prohibiting entrance by those associated with the harlot. (h) The throne of God and the Lamb are in the city (22:3–4), as God reigns with love and the citizens obey with joy. (i) The size of the city is too large for imagination because it includes citizens from every nation (21:24).

(3) The new heaven and earth with its holy city is the stage on which the world witnesses the marriage of the Lamb, who is mentioned seven times in the final two chapters of Revelation. Before the arrival of the new Jerusalem, the company of believers is described as a bride (Eph. 5:32), but not as a wife. Now in this vision she is described as the wife of the Lamb (Rev. 21:9). The transition is seemingly deferred until the sanctified are separated for the holy city.[75] Now God's children, the bride, will no longer be enticed into sin, for the unbelievers will find their place in the fiery lake of burning sulfur (21:8).[76]

The marriage of Christ to the church illustrates the complete and perfect fulfillment of the covenant promise found throughout Scripture (Gen. 17:7; Jer. 31:33; Rom. 4:22; 2 Cor. 6:16). The divine marriage pronouncement from the throne proclaims, "Now the dwelling of God is with men, and he will live with them. They will be his people, and God himself will be with them and be their God" (Rev. 21:3). The marriage of the Lamb and the new Jerusalem provides intimate and abiding fellowship with God.

Conclusion (Rev. 22:6–21)

We have come to the end of the Apocalypse of John. The visions conclude (22:5) with a picture of the final and complete triumph of the church over all her enemies. Jesus Christ, the Victor,

---

[75]Kuyper, *The Revelation of St. John*, 321.
[76]Ibid., 318.

has conquered death, Hades, the dragon, the beast, the false prophet, and those who worship the beast. Jesus Christ, the Lamb, marries the church, and together they enjoy fellowship in the new heaven and the new earth. While the fulfillment of these visions is yet to come, Christ now reigns victorious, so that nothing will separate Christians from the love of God (Rom. 8:35, 38–39).[77] The sovereign Christ assures believers that nothing will come about in life by fate or chance but by God's fatherly hand.[78] Because of these truths, the children of God may be patient in adversity, thankful for each blessing, and confident about the future.[79] All things will work together for the ultimate good of each believer (Rom. 8:28).

The conclusion (Rev. 22:6–21) offers a closing statement rather than a new vision. Several elements are instructive. (1) John is again overcome with wonder (cf. 1:17) as the angel states that all he has heard and seen, culminating in the return of Christ, is imminent. This announcement drives John to the feet of the herald (22:8). He realizes that the time is near and the eternal issues are fixed. Jesus will return and bring his reward with him.

(2) John does not dilute that feeling of the nearness of the end that earlier Christians had felt (1:3, 7; 3:11; 22:12, 20). His prologue assures his readers that the time is near; his epilogue echoes that assurance. In the phrase "the time is near," John contrasts two worlds: this world of time and the heavenly world beyond. Heavenly realities have penetrated the temporal order through the first coming of Christ and, consequently, have diminished the significance of time.[80] Quantitatively, this world may have a long course to run, but it is short because it is of little importance in comparison with the eternal realities that are now present.

(3) The book closes with a call to repentance (v. 11) and an invitation (v. 17). Christians may repent and recover their former enthusiasm, be encouraged to stand firm when confronted by times of suffering, and be inspired by the book's visions of heavenly victory with the Lamb.[81] "Blessed are those who wash their robes, that they may have the right to the tree of life and may go through the gates into the city" (v. 14).

---

[77]Harrington suggests that the entire book of Revelation is a commentary on that Pauline truth. See his *Understanding the Apocalypse*, 59.

[78]Heidelberg Catechism Question and Answer 27.

[79]Ibid., Question and Answer 28.

[80]Harrington, *Understanding the Apocalypse*, 268.

[81]Pheme Perkins, *Reading the New Testament* (New York: Paulist, 1978), 327.

(4) The book concludes with a warning for any person who would add or delete any portion of the Apocalypse, whose genuineness has been attested by the angel. The warning affirms that the book is not only apocalyptic but prophetic, that is, a word from the Lord rather than the produce of human genius.

(5) The book opened with an epistolary formula (1:4) and closes with a type of final greeting customary in letters.[82] The formula is like those of the Pauline letters but is without exact parallel. The significance of the epistolary bookends is that the book of Revelation is presented as a letter to local Christian congregations, which would be read during weekly services.

(6) The conclusion confirms the optimistic view of human history reflected throughout the book. Jesus Christ is the "Alpha and the Omega, the First and the Last, the Beginning and the End" (v. 13). John's visions have illustrated that history is not haphazard but the realization of God's plan.[83] This optimistic view of history shows us a God of love and of power, who triumphs sovereignly over all his and our enemies. Human history, as we know it, will culminate when Satan suffers eternal defeat and the bridegroom embraces his bride. Then the church will enjoy eternal joy and peace with Jesus. "Come, Lord Jesus."

CONCLUDING OBSERVATIONS

The careful reader has noticed that my idealist approach to Revelation includes little interaction with the three interpretations included in this work. While this omission is by design, the concept of the Counterpoint series, of which this volume is a part, is that each work include some healthy sparring with others in the ring. To that end, I conclude with a defense of the idealistic viewpoint of Revelation as it relates to other perspectives presented in this work.

Before the bell rings, however, I note that my interpretation is not purely idealistic. I waffle from the party line in my comments on Revelation 20–21, convinced that this section complements Jesus' teaching in Matthew 24–25, which presents a general chronological sequence of events culminating in the second coming of Christ. Some idealists are sure to criticize this

---

[82]Harrington, *Understanding the Apocalypse*, 272.
[83]Hendriksen, *Three Lectures on the Book of Revelation*, 30.

exception, preferring a thematic interpretation that excludes any futurist prophetic conclusions.

Why should the modern evangelical Christian adopt an idealistic approach to the Apocalypse of John? The best reason is that the idealist viewpoint stands on a strong hermeneutical foundation. After reading the variety of approaches included in this volume, the reader will most likely conclude that the interpretation of each author has been determined by his hermeneutical presuppositions. In other words, each of the readings of Revelation was determined, not by the text, but by the presuppositions brought to the text. This is a difficult pill to swallow for any evangelical scholar who prefers exegesis over eisegesis, but the various interpretations before you force its acknowledgment. This being the case, the essential issue facing the interpreter of Revelation is the validity of his or her hermeneutical presuppositions. I am convinced, for several reasons, that the idealist approach stands on a stronger hermeneutical foundation than the other approaches represented in this volume.

(1) The idealist acknowledges the apocalyptic nature of Revelation. While granting that the book contains both epistolary and prophetic elements, the idealist believes that John employs the genre of apocalyptic literature to carry his message to the reader. Granted, there are some discrepancies between Revelation and typical first-century apocalyptic literature, such as pseudonymity. But, in spite of a handful of minor inconsistencies, most evangelical scholars conclude that the book is apocalyptic.[84]

Thus, Thomas is correct when he states that the idealist does not treat Revelation as a book of prophecy. The idealist acknowledges that the book does contain some predictions of particular events, such as the second coming of Christ, as well as some epistolary instruction, such as that found in its letters to the churches. This acknowledgment, however, does not mean that the idealist denies the reality of specific biblical prophecy. The Bible is filled with prophecies that were fulfilled at a particular time and place, most notably, those concerning the Mes-

---

[84]The classic dispensationalist disagrees with this presupposition, as in Thomas, who speaks of the book's "alleged apocalyptic genre." Thomas's statement naturally prompts a question from the nonclassic dispensationalist: If the Apocalypse of John is not apocalyptic, what is?

siah. The idealist, however, does not believe that the interpreter should expect to find many specific prophecies in the Apocalypse of John.

(2) The idealist not only acknowledges but also interprets the text as apocalyptic literature. Gentry clearly states the implication of this conviction: "Revelation is a highly figurative book that we cannot approach with a simple straightforward literalism." While nearly every evangelical scholar agrees that Revelation is to some degree apocalyptic, not everyone interprets Revelation as such. The idealist, however, begins with the presupposition that since the book is apocalyptic, every episode or vision is symbolic until proven otherwise.

What are the grounds for a nonliteral interpretation of Revelation? The answer is simple: good hermeneutics. Just as the student of Scripture, recognizing the genre of a particular passage, refuses a literal interpretation of parables or of poetic literature, so that same student, recognizing the unique genre of Revelation, does not interpret Revelation from a literal perspective. In fact, acknowledging Revelation as apocalyptic, the idealist interpreter prefers a nonliteral approach to every verse in the book. For the idealist there must be good reason to refrain from a symbolic interpretation of the text.

(3) The heart and soul of the idealist approach is that Revelation is an apocalyptic book that presents spiritual precepts through symbols, rather than a book of predictive prophecy fulfilled in specific events or persons in human history. Revelation does not so much forecast specific historical events as it does set forth timeless truths concerning the battle between good and evil, which continues through the church age. When we find an event to which, or a person to whom, the prophecy is fairly applicable, we may consider it fulfilled in such an event or person—but not exhausted. This idealist approach does not mean that an event occurs repeatedly throughout history, but that the spiritual truth is timeless, finding several fulfillments throughout this dispensation.

This thematic approach to prophecy finds historical precedent in the Old Testament. Gentry correctly notes that the prophet of Scripture employed figurative language for one of two purposes: "to majestically relate spiritual truths or to dramatically symbolize historical events." The idealist presupposes that since the prophecy of John is delivered in apocalyptic terminology, the purpose of Revelation is to relate spiritual truths rather than predict specific events that would be fulfilled in human history. Idealists, therefore, disassociate linkage between a symbol and an historic event, believing that symbols are multivalent in meaning and without specific historical referent.

My colleagues may question this presupposition, but then I must ask, "On what basis can we conclude that John employed symbols and visions to correlate with definite events that would unfold in human history?" I doubt whether any scholar would push "what soon must take place" (1:1) to such a narrow conclusion. In the idealist approach, then, the interpreter assumes that the apocalyptic episode conveys a timeless truth or idea. In short, the interpretation is idea rather than event orientated. This does not mean that the idealist denies the prophetic element of Revelation. Rather, the idealist affirms that the prophetic element in Revelation is not as event orientated as the nonidealist may assume.

This explains, in part, why the idealist does not interact with the preterist, the progressive dispensationalist, and classical dispensationalist. Each of those approaches to Revelation interprets the text as if its primary purpose is to predict the unfolding of future events; the interpreter identifies the fulfillment of each episode of Revelation with a particular event or person in either the first, last, or both centuries. The idealist interpreter is not interested in expending energy on such an endeavor. Instead, he or she seeks to understand the *idea*, the spiritual truth, or the theme conveyed by the vision. In short, the hermeneutical presupposition of the idealist is clearly distinct from that held in common by each of the three other approaches presented in this volume.

This distinction lends itself to what some may perceive as an elitist or disinterested attitude on the part of the idealist toward those discussions that debate the identification of a figure of speech, while missing the significance of the entire episode in which it is found. The idealist allows each person to connect the truth or idea conveyed through a symbol in Revelation with any event throughout human history. In so doing, the idealist finds many points of agreement with the three alternative approaches represented in this volume, especially that of the preterist, while remaining free of debate that limits the application of a symbol to one particular event or person.

(4) The idealist approach employs good hermeneutical principles. I have already mentioned the principle of identifying the genre before interpreting literature. Additional principles are also affirmed by an idealist reading of Revelation. The idealist, discouraged by a long history of mistaken interpretations of Revelation, insists that the clear teachings of Scripture take precedent over that which is not clear. The idealist does not expect a unique or new teaching to surface in the Apocalypse; rather, he or she expects that the truths contained therein will be taught elsewhere in Scripture. The idealist, affirming the fundamental purpose of Scripture, believes that Revelation is not a historical treatise about the first or last centuries of the church but rather the inspired word of God given for teaching, rebuking, correcting, and training a church that seeks to "shine like stars in the universe" in the midst of a "crooked and depraved generation" (see Phil. 2:15; 2 Tim. 3:16).

(5) Finally, the idealist approach avoids the pitfalls that have plagued interpreters of Revelation for centuries. The history of the interpretation of Revelation should teach one lesson: Beware of attempting to correlate apocalyptic imagery with actual events in human history. Religious libraries are filled with the books of sincere Christian authors identifying the anti-Christ and predicting the date of the end of the world. How many misinterpretations must we endure before we understand that the hermeneutical presuppositions that generate such interpretations are at fault? The presuppositions that govern many approaches to Revelation are bound to produce conflicting interpretations. The idealist, however, cognizant of a long history of disagreement over the meaning of this book, intentionally walks away from a time-bound and event-orientated perspective that, in the past, has only proven to confuse and divide Christians.

Chapter Three

A PROGRESSIVE DISPENSATIONALIST VIEW OF REVELATION

C. Marvin Pate

A PROGRESSIVE DISPENSATIONALIST VIEW OF REVELATION

C. Marvin Pate

I. INTRODUCTION AND THE VISION OF THE RISEN JESUS (REV. 1:1–20)

The opening chapter of Revelation consists of an introduction (vv. 1–8) and a vision of the risen Jesus (vv. 9–20). The introduction calls attention to the mixed genre of the book: It is an apocalypse (vv. 1–3) and a letter (vv. 4–8), written by a prophet (v. 3). As an apocalyptic piece, John's work unfolds God's plan for the end times, especially as it is related to the second coming of Jesus Christ. As a letter, the Apocalypse begins with the typical epistolary format of the day: author—John (v. 4); recipients—the seven churches of Asia (v. 4); salutation—greetings and blessings from the Father (the one "who is . . . was . . . and . . . is to come"), the Holy Spirit (the "seven spirits"), and the Son (vv. 4–8). The vision of the risen Jesus (vv. 9–20) combines descriptions of the heavenly Son of Man and God, the Ancient of Days (cf. Dan. 7:13–14 and Rev. 7:9–10, 13, respectively). The implication of such a combination for John is clear: Jesus is God.

For the progressive dispensationalist, the hermeneutical key to Revelation (and for that matter, the New Testament in general) is the "already/not yet" eschatological tension (see the introduction of this book for the background of such a concept).

That is to say, with the first coming of Jesus Christ the age to come already dawned, but it is not yet complete; it awaits the Parousia for its consummation. Two key verses in Revelation 1 signal this time frame: 1:1 (cf. v. 3) and 1:19. Following is a brief discussion of those critical passages.

(1) In 1:1 John asserts that God revealed to Jesus Christ,[1] and then to himself, the things that "must soon take place" (*ha dei genesthai en tachei*; see 1:3; 4:1; 22:6–7; cf. Dan. 2:28–29, 45). There is a question as to whether the words *en tachei* mean that the end-time events will occur soon (i.e., in John's lifetime), or that, when they do begin, they will transpire with rapidity. The latter of these options allows for an indeterminate period between the apostle's day and the fulfillment of his prophecies. But in light of the subsequent claim in verse 3 regarding these events, "the time is near," the former alternative is to be preferred.

But even here the period of fulfillment need not be limited to the writer's day. A clue to John's meaning may be found in the word "time" in verse 3 (Gk. *kairos*), for, as Oscar Cullmann[2] has shown, such a term indicates that the early church believed that Jesus' death and resurrection inaugurated the last days (see, e.g., 1 Cor. 10:11; Heb. 1:2; 1 John 2:18). This is the "already" aspect of eschatological events. Yet these signs of the times were expected to continue their course within history (however short or long that may be) until the Parousia, that is, until the second coming of Christ (cf. Mark 13:7/Matt. 24:6/Luke 21:9; 2 Thess. 2:1–12). This is the "not yet" aspect of eschatological events.

The point to be gleaned from this consideration is that the early church did not seem to be preoccupied with the specific timing of the completion of these end-time matters. For it, the first coming of Christ was imbued with eschatological meaning, which was more than sufficient to sustain hope until the Parousia. As it turned out, the second coming of Christ was obviously delayed, but such postponement did not seem to dramatically unsettle the church. For the early Christians, the Parousia was an epilogue, albeit an important one, to the first coming of Christ.

(2) If we have rightly interpreted Revelation 1:1, 3, it sheds light on what many consider is the key verse of the book—1:19.

---

[1]The phrase, "revelation of Jesus Christ," is most probably a subjective genitive. That is, the revelation that God reveals to Christ is what Christ discloses to John.

[2]Oscar Cullmann, *Christ and Time: The Primitive Christian Conception of Time and History*, trans. Floyd V. Filson (Philadelphia: Westminster, 1950).

The threefold clause "what you have seen, what is now and what will take place later" is correctly understood as significant for grasping the chronological outline of the Apocalypse. Many take it to refer to the past (the vision of the risen Christ, chap. 1), the present (the seven churches, chaps. 2–3), and the future (the Great Tribulation, the Parousia, the temporary messianic kingdom, and the eternal state, chaps. 4–22). Others, however, perceive a twofold division in verse 19—John is told to write what he saw (either the vision of the Son of Man in chap. 1 or, as we prefer, the vision of the whole book, cf. 1:19 with 1:11), which consists of the things that are (present) and the things that will be (future). This is how the RSV understands the verse: "Now write what you see, what is and what is to take place hereafter."

We would add the following observation to this discussion: What John refers to in verse 19 is his apocalyptic vision of the nature of reality—this age (the present) and the age to come (the future). If this suggestion is accurate, then we do indeed find in verse 19 the interpretive key to the book of Revelation. Chapters 2–3 describe the seven churches, which exist on earth in this present age. Chapters 4–5, in their vivid description of the death and resurrection of Jesus, portray the reality that the age to come has already dawned, but only in heaven. Chapters 6–18, then, depict the transition from this age to the age to come on earth, with the Great Tribulation (or the messianic woes) marking the turning point. Chapters 19–22 present the full arrival of the age to come on earth, initiated by the Parousia and manifested in the messianic reign of Christ then revealed to all.

On this reading of 1:19, since John's tribulation (1:9) belongs to the trials of this age (chaps. 1–3), it does not seem to be understood by him as equivalent to that Great Tribulation that will mark the end of this age and the beginning of the age to come on earth (chaps. 6–18). This observation is in keeping with the pretribulational approach to Revelation. Such a view of 1:19 also provides important backing for the premillennial understanding of the messianic kingdom—while the age to come has dawned in heaven (chaps. 4–18), it has not yet appeared on earth (chaps. 19–22).

II. LETTERS TO THE SEVEN CHURCHES (REV. 2:1–3:22)

Two matters require discussion in order to understand John's letters to the seven churches in the ancient Roman province of Asia: their genre and their interpretation. The second consideration also touches on the nature of the trials encountered by the churches at Smyrna, Pergamum, and especially Philadelphia.

(1) Regarding the genre of the seven letters, David E. Aune has convincingly demonstrated that these correspondences are essentially salvation-judgment oracles reminiscent of the Old Testament prophetic tradition.[3] Accordingly, the structure of John's letters can be delineated into four components. (a) Each begins with the commissioning formula—the command to write to the specific church, with an accompanying description of the Son of Man befitting the respective needs of the congregations (2:1, 8, 12, 18; 3:1, 7, 14). (b) The salvation-judgment oracle forms the heart of each of the letters. Like the Old Testament prophet, the risen Jesus variously praises and/or criticizes each of the seven churches according to their individual situations. Both praise and criticism are directed to the churches at Ephesus (2:2–6), Pergamum (2:13–16), Thyatira (2:19–25), and Sardis (3:1–4). Only praise is offered to the churches at Smyrna (2:9–10) and Philadelphia (3:8–11), while the church at Laodicea receives exclusively criticism (3:15–20). (c) The next component is the call for attention, that is, the challenge to hear and obey the words of the Lord through the Spirit (2:7, 11, 17, 29; 3:6, 13, 22). (d) The final component exhorts the churches to overcome and thus receive eschatological blessings from God (2:7, 11, 17, 26–28; 3:5, 12, 21).

Understanding these letters to be prophetic oracles aids one's interpretation of them, particularly with regard to their time frame. The preterist viewpoint tends to see the fulfillment of these prophecies as occurring mostly in the past (primarily the first century A.D.). On the other hand, a number of classical dispensationalists believe these letters correspond to the unfolding of the church's history (with Laodicea representing the apostasy of the church immediately before the return of Christ).[4] The progressive dispensationalist, however, follows the "already/not yet" hermeneutic in grasping the time frame of these oracles: There is a sense in which the fulfillment of the prophecies both

---

[3]David E. Aune, *Prophecy in Early Christianity and the Ancient Mediterranean World* (Grand Rapids: Eerdmans, 1983), 274–79.

[4]Though it should be said that other classical dispensationalists root these letters to the seven churches in the first century but also see them as all operative throughout the history of the church until the return of Christ.

occurred in the past (particularly with regard to the Roman imperial cult of the first century) and will continue to be fulfilled until the Parousia, the climax of history. What George Ladd says of the fulfillment of prophecy in general in the Apocalypse also applies specifically to the seven churches:

> The Old Testament prophets blended the near and the distant perspective so as to form a single canvas. Biblical prophecy is not primarily three-dimensional but two; it has height and breadth but is little concerned about depth, i.e., the chronology of future events. There is in biblical prophecy a tension between the immediate and the distant future. It is true that the early church lived in expectancy of the return of the Lord, and it is the nature of biblical prophecy to make it possible for every generation to live in expectancy of the end.[5]

In what follows we focus on the already/not yet aspect of the prophetic oracles to the seven churches.

Regarding the already aspect, the situation that forms the historical backdrop to the seven letters is most probably, as Colin J. Hemer has carefully shown, Caesar worship.[6] We provide here the contours of his research in itemized fashion. (1) With Emperor Domitian (A.D. 81–96), the cult of Caesar worship reached its pinnacle in the first century. Numismatic evidence provides us with clear illustrations of his claim to deity; for example, coins bear his title "lord and god" and the image of his deified son, seated on a globe with his hands stretched out to seven stars (cf. Rev. 1:20).

(2) Jews, ironically, were exempt from imperial worship, a privilege extending back to Julius Caesar.

(3) The ensuing resentment of Jews toward Christians in the aftermath of the fall of Jerusalem in A.D. 70[7] did not bode well for Jewish Christians. The synagogues devised a way to expel the latter from their midst by introducing the curse of the "*minîm*" (lit., "heretics," meaning "the Nazarenes" [followers of

---

[5]George Eldon Ladd, *A Commentary on the Revelation of John* (Grand Rapids: Eerdmans, 1972), 22.

[6]Colin J. Hemer, *The Letters to the Seven Churches of Asia in Their Local Setting* (JSNTSS. 11; Sheffield: Univ. of Sheffield Press, 1986).

[7]Christians fled Jerusalem in A.D. 68 in response to a prophetic oracle warning of the impending destruction of the city by the Romans and therefore did not lend their support to the Jewish Revolt (Euseb., *HE*, 3.3).

Jesus]) into the Eighteen Benedictions,[8] which were recited in the synagogues (ca. A.D. 90). Thus exposed and excommunicated, Jewish Christians were no longer perceived by the Roman government as under the umbrella of Judaism and, therefore, faced the cruel dilemma of either forsaking Christ (if they were to be readmitted to the synagogues) or worshiping Caesar. The problem seems to have been exacerbated by those Jews who provided their local Roman officials with lists of Christians who were no longer associated with their congregations (cf. Pliny's "Letter to Trajan," A.D. 112).

This politico-historical background sheds light on the theological problem that John addresses in the seven letters. In effect, these prophetic oracles can be seen as praise and/or warnings to the churches for resisting or not withstanding, respectively, the temptation to succumb to Caesar worship. Accordingly, we now summarize that background as reflected in Revelation 2–3. The Nicolaitans (2:6, 15) and the teaching of Balaam (2:14)—both names mean "to overcome the people"— seem to allude to those in the churches who said it was permissible to worship Caesar. The teachings of Jezebel (2:20–22) may well be included in this category, especially against the backdrop of the union of Caesar worship and pagan idolatry, which permeated the trade guilds of that day. It is in the face of such temptation that the risen Jesus challenges the churches to be faithful to him (2:4–6, 8–10, 12–16, 20–25; 3:1–5, 7–12, 14–21). Special praise is offered to those who suffered to the point of death for obeying Christ, not Caesar (2:8–10, 12–13), while, on the other hand, judgment is pronounced on those Jews who expelled Jewish Christians out of their synagogues, thus exposing them to the imperial cult (2:9; 3:5, 9).

In our estimation, the exclusively futurist approach to Revelation has, in general, neglected the preceding historical backdrop in interpreting chapters 2–3, probably because it does not want to attribute significance to Caesar worship for the under-

---

[8]That "benediction" reads, "For the renegades let there be no hope, and may the arrogant kingdom soon be rooted out in our days, and the Nazarenes and the minîm ['heretics'] perish as in a moment and be blotted out from the book of life and with the righteous may they not be inscribed. Blessed art thou, O Lord, who humblest the arrogant" (quoted in C. K. Barrett, *The New Testament Background: Selected Documents* [New York: Harper & Row, 1961], 167). The Nazarenes are the minîm and are probably to be identified as Jewish Christians.

standing of Revelation 6–18. To do so would be apparently to diminish the futurity of the events described in those chapters, especially the assumption that John looked forward to the day of a revived Roman empire under the rulership of the Antichrist, who will oppose Christ and Israel.[9]

To acknowledge Caesar worship to be the operative background of chapters 2–3 and of chapters 6–18 need not, however, restrict the events of those chapters to the past, as the preterist approach tends to do. This is particularly the case for grasping the time frame of the Great Tribulation, which, to many, is the thematic tie that binds chapters 2–3 and 6–18 together. Dale C. Allison well captures the preterist viewpoint on the subject:

> The Apocalypse was almost certainly composed during a time of severe affliction. The book is addressed to those "who share . . . in Jesus the tribulation and the kingdom and the patient endurance" (1:9). "Tribulation" and "suffering" characterize the present experience of the readers (2:9–10, 13; cf. 2:3; 12:17; 13:7). References to witnesses who have died for the faith are numerous (6:9–11; 12:11; 17:6; 18:24; 20:4; cf. 13:7).
>
> The supposition that the seer, like some Jews and Christians before him, understood his own tribulation to be the great, messianic tribulation is also well founded. *Thlipsis* characterizes the present, and in Revelation this word is a technical term for the final affliction (7:14; cf. 1:9; 2:9, 10, 22). Further, the multitude of Rev. 7:9–17, which has come out of the great tribulation (7:14), includes, without question, those Christians who have recently shed their blood as witnesses of Jesus. John may, admittedly, draw a distinction between the present tribulation and its intensification immediately before the end (3:10). But there is no cleavage between the two periods. The one stands as the climax of the other.[10]

---

[9]This approach to seeing a revived Roman empire in Rev. 6–18 has been enormously popular in America because of the writings of, among others, Hal Lindsey, *The Late Great Planet Earth* (Grand Rapids: Zondervan, 1970). For a critique of this perspective, see C. Marvin Pate and Calvin B. Haines Jr., *Doomsday Delusions. What's Wrong With Predictions About the End of the World* (Downers Grove, Ill.: InterVarsity, 1995).

[10]Dale C. Allison, *The End of the Ages Has Come: An Early Interpretation of the Passion and Resurrection of Jesus* (Philadelphia: Fortress, 1985), 70–71. These sentiments would also be shared by the idealist school of thought and, for that matter, the amillennial perspective.

Allison rightly recognizes 3:10 to be a key text in this discussion, especially with regard to the issue of whether or not the church will go through the Great Tribulation. His statement tacitly admits to a distinction between the trials of John's day (chaps. 2–3) and the Great Tribulation to come (chaps. 6–19). Furthermore, if it could be shown that John's promise to the church at Philadelphia involved sparing it from the coming Great Tribulation, then 3:10 can be understood as setting a precedent for pretribulation deliverance. After all is said, however, the grammatical issue of whether the Greek phrase *tēresō ek* means "will keep [you] from" (the pretribulation view) or "will keep [you] through" (the midtribulation or posttribulation views) is indecisive.[11]

Yet we should like to offer a suggestion heretofore undetected by interpreters of this passage. Revelation 3:10 is an example of "sacral law," a divine pronouncement in which the punishment matches the crime or the reward matches the required behavior.[12] Thus the verse should be understood to mean, "Because you patiently kept my word even to the point of suffering, I will prevent you from the afflictions of the great trial that are about to come over all the earth [the Great Tribulation]." But to say that Christ will allow the Christians at Philadelphia to go through the messianic woes and experience death but nevertheless have their souls delivered afterwards (which is the posttribulation view) does not correctly correlate the reward with their obedient behavior. It is better, therefore, to take the promise as indicating that because the believers at Philadelphia already suffered for their faith, they will therefore be spared any more in the future (i.e., the Great Tribulation; cf. 2:10, 13). If this interpretation is accurate, then the scales seem to tip toward the pretribulation view of this passage, and the distinction between the trials of John's day and the messianic woes to come remains.

---

[11]For helpful discussions of this issue, though from differing perspectives, see Robert L. Thomas, *Revelation 1–7: An Exegetical Commentary* (Chicago: Moody, 1992), 283–88 (as well his contribution in the present work), and Douglas J. Moo, "The Case for the Posttribulation Rapture Position," in *The Rapture: Pre-, Mid-, or Post-Tribulational: Essays by Reiter, Feinberg, Archer, and Moo* (Grand Rapids: Zondervan, 1984), 169–211.

[12]Aune applies this literary form of speech to Revelation 3:10, but makes no connection between it and the pretribulation view, *Prophecy*, 279.

III. THE THRONE ROOM OF GOD AND CHRIST
(REV. 4–5)

In good Jewish apocalyptic fashion, John is raptured to heaven to receive a vision of the throne room of God (cf. Rev. 4:1 with Ezek. 1; *1 Enoch* 14; *4 Ezra* 14; *3 Enoch*).[13] Revelation 4–5 is John's description of the divine heavenly court, using the imagery of concentric circles: (1) the throne of God and Christ is the center circle (4:3; 5:6); (2) the four living creatures (cf. Ezek. 1:5–25) comprise the next circle (Rev. 4:6–9); (3) the twenty-four elders and their thrones (probably a special class of angels) form the next one (4:4, 10–11); (4) an innumerable heavenly host makes up the last circle around the throne (5:11–13). The nearly identical doxologies to God (4:7–11) and to Christ (5:11–14) indicate that the two are equal in divine status.

Ironically, Christ is portrayed as the Lion-Lamb. The former image equates him with the Davidic Messiah (cf. 5:5 with Gen. 49:9; Isa. 11:1, 10) while the latter symbol portrays him as the paschal lamb/suffering servant (cf. Rev. 5:6 with Ex. 12:5–6; Isa. 53:7; John 1:29, 36; Acts 8:32; 1 Peter 1:19). Together, the two metaphors depict Jesus as the suffering Messiah. As such, he alone is qualified to open the seven-sealed scroll, that is, the divine plan for the future of the world, which is the culmination of salvation history. Beyond this, two key concepts pertinent to Revelation 4–5 require brief discussion: the clash in cultural backgrounds presupposed by John's vision of the heavenly throne, and the time frame assumed for Christ's exaltation to the throne.

(1) The historical-cultural background is important to the progressive dispensationalist in interpreting the sacred text. This hermeneutical principle is significant for the understanding of Revelation 4–5 for, as more recent commentators recognize, one probably meets in these chapters a historical-cultural clash between Judaic-Christianity and the Greco-Roman imperial cult. We previously noted that John's vision of the heavenly throne of God was rooted in Jewish apocalypticism, which itself developed from the Old Testament prophetic tradition. That background, as it merges with Christianity, surfaces in Revelation 4–5 in a number of symbols: (a) the heavenly court of Yahweh/Christ (see 1 Kings 22:19; Ps. 89:7; Isa. 24:23); (b) mystic experience as the

---

[13]Revelation 4:1 most likely does not allude to the rapture.

mode for being transported to the divine throne (Ezek. 1; 1 Enoch 14; 4 Ezra 14); (c) the revelation in heaven of the things that will transpire on earth in the end times (Dan. 2:29, 45; 4 Ezra 7:14, 83; 13:18; 2 Baruch 21:12; 1QS 11:5–8); (d) the Lion-Lamb and its respective imagery of the Davidic Messiah/pascal lamb, which becomes the pattern that the people of God in Revelation must follow—first suffering, then glory (cf. Rev. 7; 14).

As David E. Aune has shown, Revelation 4–5 also draws on the imperial ceremonial court.[14] The following points of contact with that milieu emerge in the symbolism of chapters 4–5. (a) Greco-Roman kings were considered to be divine, their courtrooms often artistically expressed in terms of being cosmic, which itself was portrayed in concentric circles. (b) Their attendants were often associated with astrology (seven planetary spheres [cf. Rev. 4:5], twenty-four [the doubling of the twelve signs of the Zodiac] devotees [cf. 4:4, 10; 5:6–10]). (c) These attendants sang hymns of worship to the divine king (cf. 4:8–11; 5:9–14). (d) The king dispensed justice over his empire, symbolized by a scroll (cf. 5:1–8). These considerations, along with the competing claims for the respective deities throughout Revelation between John and the imperial cult of the first century (god, son of god, lord's day, savior of the world) suggest that the two cultures clash in the imagery employed in Revelation 4–5.

(2) Related to the first matter, the time frame assumed by John for Christ's exaltation to the throne requires explanation. The classical dispensationalist relegates the events of Revelation 4–5 to the distant future. The progressive dispensationalist, however, perceives the overlapping of the two ages to be operative in John's vision of the exaltation of Christ to the throne of God. On the one hand, with the death, resurrection, and ascension of Christ, the age to come has dawned in heaven. This is nothing less than the beginning of the fulfillment of the reign of the Davidic Messiah (cf. Rev. 5:5–10a with the usage of Ps. 110:1 in Acts 2:32–36; 1 Cor. 15:25; Heb. 1:13). On the other hand, Christ's Davidic-like kingdom has not yet descended to earth (cf. Rev. 5:10b with 20:1–6). Chapters 6–19 detail the process by which that messianic kingdom will manifest itself on earth. Thus, at the

---

[14]David E. Aune, "The Influence of Roman Imperial Court Ceremonial on the Apocalypse of John," *Papers of the Chicago Society of Biblical Research* 28 (1983): 1–26.

time of the events of Revelation 4–5, the age to come had not yet been completed.[15]

IV. THE MESSIANIC WOES (REV. 6–18)

In early Judaism the messianic woes referred to the time of Great Tribulation and sorrow that would come upon God's people immediately prior to the coming of the Messiah. The concept is foreshadowed in the Old Testament, in association with the Day of the Lord (see, e.g., Isa. 24:17–23; Dan. 12:1; Joel 2:1–11, 28–32; Amos 5:16–20; Zeph. 1:14–2:3), and developed in Jewish apocalypticism (4 Ezra 7:37; Jub. 23:11; 24:3; 2 Apocalypse of Baruch 55:6; 1 Enoch 80:4–5) and in the New Testament (Matt. 24/Mark 13/Luke 21; 2 Thess. 2; Rev. 6–18).

The term "messianic woes," however, does not occur until the writing of the Talmud (e.g., *b. Shabbath* 118a; *b. Pesaḥim* 118a). A number of events were often associated with these woes: wars, earthquakes, famines, the persecution of God's people, the apostasy of believers, and cosmic disturbances.[16] Even a casual reading of Revelation 6–18 indicates that the subject being addressed is the messianic woes or the signs of the times, which will occur immediately prior to the appearance of the Messiah. Two matters serve as our guide in summarizing these chapters from a progressive dispensational point of view: (1) the time frame of the woes, and (2) the identification of the tribulation saints. We will focus on these two issues because they generate lively debate regarding their interpretation. The first consideration will receive the bulk of our attention in this section.

A. The Time Frame of Revelation 6–18

As to the time frame of Revelation 6–18, preterists interpret the messianic woes described therein as having already occurred in John's day. Futurists, on the other hand, especially traditional dispensationalists, hold that these events will not be accom-

---

[15]For a good illustration of the progressive dispensationalist's application of Ps. 110:1 to Jesus' resurrection, see Bock and Blaising, *Progressive Dispensationalism*, 177–78.

[16]The classic study on the subject of Jewish apocalypticism, including a discussion of the messianic woes, is that by David S. Russell, *The Method and Message of Jewish Apocalyptic 200 B.C.–.A.D. 100* (Philadelphia: Westminster, 1964).

plished until the time immediately preceding the Parousia. In contrast to these two schools of thought, idealists argue that the imagery of chapters 6–18 couches the ongoing battle between God and Satan and should not be pinned down to any one chronological period. In a way, the progressive dispensational point of view represents an eclectic approach, combining what it perceives to be the best in the aforementioned interpretations.

In good hermeneutical fashion, the progressive dispensationalist approach begins its treatment of chapters 6–18 by examining their historical-cultural background, which undeniably is to be located in the first century A.D., especially the conflict between Caesar and Christ. But it views the reality of that conflict as also operative throughout the history of God's people. In the end, however, progressive dispensationalists believe that the final fulfillment of these chapters awaits the time of Christ's return. In other words, this approach interprets chapters 6–18 through the lens of the already/not yet eschatological tension. In what follows, we divide this hermeneutic into its two constituent parts: (1) the already aspect—the fulfillment of the prophecies of Revelation 6–18 in John's day; (2) the not yet aspect—the final accomplishment of thoese prophecies in the period immediately prior to the Parousia.

1. The Partial Fulfillment of Revelation 6–18 in John's Day

In support of the thesis that the events described in chapters 6–18 experienced partial fulfillment in the first century, three pieces of evidence can be enlisted: (a) the last days, which chapters 6–18 presuppose, began with the first coming of Christ; (b) the parallel structure between the first half of Jesus' Olivet Discourse (Matt. 24/Mark 13/Luke 21) and the seal judgments of Revelation 6, which pertains to the events leading up to the fall of Jerusalem in A.D. 70; (c) historical allusions to the first-century conflict between Caesar and Christ in Revelation 6–18, which serve as the backdrop for the final fulfillment of those prophecies in the distant future beyond John's day. This hermeneutic of partial fulfillment leading to a final accomplishment should not surprise the reader, for it is the same pattern one finds in connection with Old Testament prophecy.

(a) **The last days and the first coming of Christ**. The New Testament clearly states that the age to come or the last days dawned with the first coming of Christ (Acts 2:16–21; 1 Tim. 4:1; Heb. 1:2; 1 John 2:18). A generation ago, C. H. Dodd expanded on this truth by pointing out that the early church (especially as it is depicted in the book of Acts) attributed eschatological significance to the life, death, and resurrection of Jesus Christ in a number of ways: (1) In Jesus the messianic age dawned (Acts 2:16; 3:18, 24) through his ministry, death, and resurrection (2:23–33). (ii) By his resurrection, Jesus has been exalted to the right hand of God as messianic head of the new people of God (2:33–36; 3:13). (iii) The Holy Spirit is the sign of the presence of the eschaton (the final age) as well as the proof that Jesus currently reigns in heaven in power and glory (2:23). (iv) The messianic age will shortly reach its consummation in the return of Christ (3:21). (v) An invitation is always extended for people to receive Christ and the life of the age to come (2:38–39).[17]

Gordon D. Fee captures the resulting eschatological tension that characterizes the Christian between the first and second comings of Jesus Christ:

> The absolutely essential framework of the self-understanding of primitive Christianity is an eschatological one. Christians had come to believe that, in the event of Christ, the new (coming) age had dawned, and that, especially through Christ's death and resurrection and the subsequent gift of the Spirit, God had set the future in motion, to be consummated by yet another coming (parousia) of Christ. Theirs was therefore an essentially eschatological existence. They lived "between the times" of the beginning and the consummation of the end. Already God had secured their ... salvation; already they were the people of the future, living the life of the future in the present age—and enjoying its benefits. But they still awaited the glorious consummation of this salvation. Thus they lived in an essential tension between the "already" and the "not-yet."[18]

(b) **The parallel structure in Revelation 6 and the Olivet Discourse.** The fact that the last days began with the first coming of Christ permits one to see the prophetic events depicted in

---

[17]C. H. Dodd, *The Apostolic Preaching and Its Developments* (New York: Harper, 1944), 38–45.

[18]Gordon D. Fee, *1 and 2 Timothy, Titus* (Peabody, Mass.: Hendrickson, 1988), 19.

Revelation 6–18 as having partially occurred in the first century A.D. This is confirmed by the parallel structure that exists between the signs of the times as delineated in the first half of the Olivet Discourse and the seal judgments of Revelation 6.[19] This pattern serves to portray Jesus' generation—extending from the time of his life to the fall of Jerusalem in A.D. 70—as the backdrop for the Parousia. In effect, according to the Olivet Discourse, the fall of Jerusalem (albeit in judgment form) is a part of the "already" aspect of the age to come, while the return of Christ constitutes its "not yet" aspect. We proceed now to a discussion of the already aspect, especially relative to the fall of Jerusalem as presented in the Olivet Discourse and Revelation 6.

It is a commonplace among Gospel scholars today to view the Olivet Discourse of Jesus as portraying the Parousia against the background of the fall of Jerusalem. For example, in his magisterial commentary on Luke, Joseph A. Fitzmyer writes of Luke 21:

> The Lucan discourse looks back at the catastrophe on Jerusalem (A.D. 70) in a microcosmic view; it sees the crisis that the earthly coming of Jesus brought into the lives of his own generation, but sees it now as a harbinger of the crisis which Jesus and his message, and above all his coming as the Son of Man, will bring to "all who dwell upon the entire face of the earth" (21:35). Both of the events are examples for Luke of God's judgment. . . . As Jerusalem met its fate, so will all who dwell upon the face of the earth.[20]

Two of the key phrases in the Olivet Discourse highlighting the connection between the fall of Jerusalem and the Parousia are "the beginning of birth pains" and "the end is still to come" (Matt. 24:6–8/Mark 13:7–8; cf. Luke 21:9). These phrases convey the idea that the signs of the times *began* with Jesus and his generation, especially the fall of Jerusalem, but will not be complete until the return of Christ.

In objection to this view, some may wish to say that Jesus' statement, "This generation will certainly not pass away until all these things have happened" (Matt. 24:34/Mark 13:30/Luke

---

[19]The following section is taken from Pate and Haines, *Doomsday Delusions*, 34–57. Used by permission of InterVarsity Press.

[20]Joseph A. Fitzmyer, *The Gospel According to Luke X-XXIV* (AB; New York: Doubleday, 1983), 1329.

21:32), better fits the Parousia than the fall of Jerusalem in A.D. 70. A. L. Moore, however, refutes this plausible contention, especially concerning Mark 13:30, by appealing to two points, one grammatical and the other contextual.[21] Grammatically, the words "all these things" (*tauta panta*) refer back to the "these things" mentioned in verse 29, which refer to the events preceding the end, *not* the end itself. In effect, verses 29–30 speak of the signs of the times that will lead up to the fall of Jerusalem in A.D. 70 (vv. 14–23), not the Parousia.[22] This argument is confirmed by the contextual evidence, that is, the structure of the Markan Olivet Discourse (Mark 13). Moore outlines the passage like this:

vv. 1–4   Introduction; the question raised in v. 4, which leads to a discourse on the end and its date, and the signs of the end and their dates

vv. 5–23   The signs of the end, framed at either end by warnings against the seduction of false messiahs and prophets with the fictitious claim (vv. 5–6 and 21–23)

vv. 24–27 The end itself

vv. 28–31 Regarding the time of the signs of the end and their significance for perceiving the time of the end itself

vv. 32–37 Regarding the time of the end event.[23]

From this structure we can detect that a parallel theme emerges—the signs of the times seem to be separated from the Parousia:

Signs of the Times	*Parousia*
1. vv. 5–23	vv. 24–27
2. vv. 28–31	vv. 32–37

Moore's conclusion seems justified: "Whereas the signs will occur within the immediate future (though not necessarily exhausted by that immediate future), the end itself is not so delimited."[24] For grammatical and contextual reasons, then,

[21]A. L. Moore, *The Parousia in the New Testament* (NovTSup 13; Leiden: E. J. Brill, 1966), 132–36.

[22]Ibid., 132–33.

[23]Ibid., 134.

[24]Ibid., 134–35.

"these things" seem to refer to the events leading up to the fall of Jerusalem in A.D. 70, not the Parousia.

The aforementioned pattern—that the fall of Jerusalem serves as the historical backdrop for the Parousia—also seems to fit the book of Revelation.[25] Recognizing this enables one to associate the signs of the times describing the fall of Jerusalem in the Olivet Discourse with the judgments delineated in the Apocalypse, especially the seal judgments of Revelation 6, the prototype of the trumpet and bowl judgments. R. H. Charles notes the following connections:

Matthew 24:6–7, 9a, 29	Mark 13:7–9a, 24–25	Luke 21:9–12a, 25–26	Revelation 6:2–17; 7:1
1. Wars	1. Wars	1. Wars	Seal 1. Wars
2. International strife	2. International strife	2. International strife	Seal 2. International strife
3. Famines	3. Earthquakes	3. Earthquakes	Seal 3. Famine
4. Earthquakes	4. Famines	4. Famines	Seal 4. Pestilence (Death and Hades)
5. Persecutions	5. Persecutions	5. Pestilence	Seal 5. Persecutions
6. Eclipses of the sun and moon; falling of the stars; shaking of the powers of heaven	6. Eclipses of the sun and moon; falling of the stars; shaking of the powers of heaven	6. Persecutions	Seal 6. (6:12–7:3) Earthquakes, eclipse of the sun, ensanguining of the moon[26]

---

[25]See, for example, the works by J. Massyngberde Ford, *Revelation* (AB; New York: Doubleday, 1975), especially her exposition of Revelation 6 and 17; Alan James Beagley, *The "Sitz im Leben" of the Apocalypse With Particular Reference to the Role of the Church's Enemies* (New York: Walter de Gruyter, 1987), especially chap. 2; Kenneth L. Gentry Jr., *Before Jerusalem Fell: Dating the Book of Revelation* (Tyler, Tex.: Institute for Christian Economics, 1989).

[26]R. H. Charles, *A Critical and Exegetical Commentary on the Revelation of St. John* (ICC; Edinburgh: T. & T. Clark, 1920), 1:158; cf. Louis A. Vos, *The Synoptic Traditions in the Apocalypse* (Kampen: Kok, 1965), 181–92.

The conclusion to be drawn from these comparisons is that the three Gospels and the Apocalypse view the signs of the times as having already begun in Jesus' generation, particularly with the fall of Jerusalem in A.D. 70. The task that lies before us, therefore, is to root briefly the preceding signs of the times in, and around, the events surrounding the fall of Jerusalem. We will reserve discussion of the figure of the Antichrist (cf. Rev. 6:2 with Mark 13:5–6, 21–23 and par.) for our third piece of evidence to follow—the historical allusions in Revelation to the first century A.D.

(i) *Wars (cf. Matt. 24:6–7/Mark 13:7–8/Luke 21:9–10; cf. Rev. 6:3–4)*. In the Olivet Discourse, Jesus acknowledged the certainty of war but added that that was not necessarily the sign that the end had totally arrived. It, like other signs of the times, was only the beginning of "birth pains" or the signs of the times (see Mark 13:7–8 and par.). Many interpreters believe that Jesus' reference to the increase of wars here and in Revelation 6:3–4 (the second horseman) alludes to the first century. The peace that Caesar Augustus (31 B.C.–A.D. 14) established (*pax Romana*) throughout the Roman Empire was short-lived. Wars broke out in Britain, Germany, Armenia, and Parthia under Emperor Claudius (between A.D. 41 and 54). The period following Nero's death (A.D. 69) saw three emperors, Otho, Galba, and Vitellius, quickly rise and fall, amidst civil upheavals and political chaos. So devastating was the period following Nero's death that it threatened to reduce the Roman empire to rubble. The peril Rome faced at that time was well known by that generation. Josephus could write of the Roman civil wars, "I have omitted to give an exact account of them, because they are well known by all, and they are described by a great number of Greek and Roman authors" (*War* 4.9.2; cf. Tacitus *Histories* 1.2–3; Seutonius *Lives*, "Vespasian" 1).

Especially relevant to the end-time sign of wars and rumors of wars was the Jewish revolt against Rome, which culminated in the fall of Jerusalem (A.D. 66–70). The Jewish war against Rome witnessed the deaths of thousands and thousands of Jews in Judea and the enslavement of thousands more. Josephus estimates that as many as 1,100,000 Jews were killed at that time (though he undoubtedly exaggerated the figure). Titus, the Roman general, razed the city to the ground. Josephus writes of this:

Now, as soon as the army had no more people to slay or to plunder, because there remained none to be objects of their fury (for they would not have spared any, had there remained any other such work to be done) Caesar gave orders that they should not demolish the entire city and temple, but should leave as many of the towers standing as were of the greatest eminency; that is, Phasaelus, and Hippicus, and Mariamne, and so much of the wall as enclosed the city on the west side. This wall was spared, in order to afford a camp for such as were to lie in garrison; as were the towers also spared, in order to demonstrate to posterity what kind of city it was, and how well fortified, which the Roman valor had subdued; but for all the rest of the wall, it was so thoroughly laid even with the ground by those that dug it up to the foundation, that there was left nothing to make those that came thither believe it had ever been inhabited. This was the end which Jerusalem came to by the madness of those that were for innovations; a city otherwise of great magnificence, and of mighty fame among all mankind. (*War* 7.1.1)

For Josephus, the destruction of Jerusalem was beyond comparison. He observes:

Whereas the war which the Jews made with the Romans has been the greatest of all those, not only that have been in our times, but, in a manner, of those that ever were heard of; both of those wherein cities have fought against cities, or nations against nations.... Accordingly it appears to me, that the misfortunes of all men, from the beginning of the world, if they be compared to these of the Jews, are not so considerable as they were. (*War*, preface to 1 and 4)

Jesus' prophecy about the city had come true (Matt. 24:15/Mark 13:14/Luke 19:41–44; 21:20–24; Rev. 6:3–4; 11:1–2 [cf. v. 8]; 17–18).

(ii) *Famines (Matt. 24:7/Mark 13:8/Luke 21:11; cf. Rev. 6:5–6).* The inevitable consequence of war is famine, nowhere so starkly depicted as in Revelation 6:5–6 (cf. vv. 7–8), with its description of the third horseman. It would have been easy for the seer of the Apocalypse to envision war and famine. During Claudius's reign, famine occurred in Rome in A.D. 42, and food shortage was reported in Judea in 45–46, in Greece in 49, and in Rome again in 51. The reference to the pair of scales and the inflated prices for food in 6:5–6 cannot help but recall the severe famine that occurred in Jerusalem during its siege by the Roman army. During that time the inhabitants of Jerusalem had to weigh out their food and drink because of the scarcity of those necessities. So severe was it that even the love of a mother for her child ceased. Josephus records the story about Mary, a woman from Perea, who was among the Jews starving in Jerusalem during its siege. She seized her child, an infant at her breast, slew it, and roasted it for food for herself (*War* 6.3.4; cf. 6.5.1; Luke 21:23). Note also this from Josephus concerning the role of famine during the Jewish war against Rome:

> But the famine was too hard for all other passions, and it is destructive to nothing so much as to modesty; for what was otherwise worthy of reverence, was in this case despised; inasmuch that children pulled the very morsels that their fathers were eating, out of their very mouths, and what was still more to be pitied, so did the mothers do as to their infants. (*War* 5.10.5)

The fall of Jerusalem and the resulting famine may also explain the ironic statement in Revelation 6:6, "and do not damage the oil and the wine." The command to spare the oil and the wine is possibly an allusion to General Titus's order that even during the ransacking of Jerusalem, olive trees (for oil) and grapevines (for wine) were to be spared. If so, the fall of Jerusalem serves as the perfect backdrop for the third seal judgment (6:5–6), as it does for the Olivet Discourse prophecy about the eventuality of famines. Indeed, Jesus' statement that such horrors were but the beginning of the end (Mark 13:7), the initiation of the messianic woes (13:8), points in that direction (cf. Rev. 6:7–8 with the fourth seal judgment).

(iii) *Persecution (Matt. 24:9–10/Mark 13:9–19/Luke 21:12–19; cf. Rev. 6:9–11)*. There are three interlocking destinies delineated in the Olivet Discourse and the fifth seal judgment of Revelation: the persecution of Jesus' disciples, Jesus' crucifixion, and the destruction of Jerusalem. The apparent connection to be made from this is that Israel's crucifixion of Jesus and subsequent persecution of his disciples brought about divine destruction on Jerusalem.

The Olivet Discourse ominously predicts that Jesus' disciples will be persecuted (Matt. 24:9–10/Mark 13:9–19/Luke 21:12–19). Luke's second volume, Acts, records the fulfillment of Jesus' prediction, describing the persecutions of Peter and John (Acts 4:1–12; cf. 12:3–19), Stephen (6:8–7:60), James (12:1–2), Paul (16:22–30; 21:27–23:35), and many other Jewish Christians (8:1–4). In being delivered up to the Jewish and Roman authorities, the disciples were repeating the destiny of Jesus (notably, his crucifixion). Allison has carefully demonstrated that such affliction was understood by early Christians as the beginning of the messianic woes, a time of unparalleled persecution of God's people that was expected to precede immediately the arrival of the kingdom of God.[27]

Later church tradition understood that the fall of Jerusalem in A.D. 70 came about as a result of divine judgment because of the Jewish persecution of Jesus' followers. For example, Eusebius, the fourth-century church historian, refers to the belief of many that God judged Jerusalem because it killed the half-brother of Jesus, James the Just (*Eccl. Hist.* 2.23). Even Josephus attributed Jerusalem's fall to divine judgment. Writing of the burning and destruction of the temple in late August/early September A.D. 70, he writes that the fire was not ultimately ignited by the Romans: "The flames . . . owed their origin and cause to God's own people" (*War* 6.4.5).

The same threefold intertwined destinies surface in Revelation 6:9–11, the fifth seal judgment. That the martyrs described therein are Christians is plain. Corresponding descriptions of these saints occur in 7:9–17 and 14:1–5. Their exemplar in suffering for righteousness is Jesus, the Lamb that was slain (5:6–14). But who were the perpetrators of such injustice and violence on the people of God? Revelation 6:10 provides a clue: It was "the inhabitants of the earth" (cf. 3:10; 11:10). While the phrase can mean "the inhabitants of the world," the more likely meaning of this phrase is "the inhabitants of the land [Palestine]." Alan J. Beagley describes these "earth-dwellers" as they are portrayed in the Apocalypse:

> Rev. 6:10 makes it clear that they have been involved in the persecution and slaughter of those who have

---

[27]See Allison, *The End of the Ages Has Come.* For specific treatment of the Luke-Acts correlations from a similar perspective, see J. Bradley Chance, *Jerusalem, the Temple, and the New Age in Luke-Acts* (Macon, Ga.: Mercer Univ. Press, 1988), 120–21.

preached the word of God and who have remained faithful in their witness, and it is against these persecutors in particular that the martyrs cry out to God for vengeance. Then again, it is the "earth-dwellers" who are named specifically as the victims of the three "woes" which are associated with the fifth, sixth and seventh trumpets (8:13). The same term is also used of those who have in some way suffered through the ministry of the "two witnesses" and who rejoice and exchange gifts at the death of the witnesses (Rev. 11:10). It is this same group of people also who give allegiance to the beast from the sea, and they are further characterized as those whose names were "not written before the foundation of the world in the book of life of the lamb that was slain" (13:18). Finally, in chapter 17 the "earth-dwellers" are associated with the harlot, "Babylon," and with the scarlet beast on which she rides: they have become drunk with the wine of the harlot's fornication (v 2) and they are overawed at the beast and its apparent permanence (v 8).[28]

Beagley's interpretation is that the inhabitants of Jerusalem are being described. Others concur. Philip Carrington, for example, sees in the phrase "the earth-dwellers,"

> an indication that the Seer is thinking of a judgment which is to fall on Jerusalem, since there is in the martyrs' cry the first clear echo of the words of Jesus; for he says that there shall come upon you all the Righteous Blood which is being shed upon the Land from the Blood of Righteous Abel to the Blood of Zacharias son of Barachias, whom ye murdered between the Naos and the Altar; verily, I say unto you all these shall come upon this generation (Matt. xxiii.35). Not only is the symbol of blood revenge the same, but it points out what later study will confirm; it is the land of Israel, and in particular the Temple at Jerusalem which is to suffer. And we must remember that there is a hint of the same idea in the Four Seals; for the Four Judgments in Ezekiel, to which they correspond, were all to come upon Jerusalem.[29]

---

[28]Beagley, The "Sitz im Leben" of the Apocalypse, 36.

[29]Philip Carrington, The Meaning of the Revelation (London: SPCK, 1931), 131–32. It should be noted, however, that the parallelism of the (lit.) "earth dwellers" and

(iv) *Cosmic disturbances (Matt. 24:29/Mark 13:24–25/Luke 21:11, 25–26; cf. Rev. 6:12–17).* The Old Testament associated cosmic disturbances with the coming of divine judgment, especially the Day of the Lord (Isa. 34:4; Ezek. 32:7; Joel 3:3–4; Hab. 2:6, 21). That Jesus should use such apocalyptic imagery to describe the fall of Jerusalem (see esp. Luke 21:11) was not unusual. Josephus did the same: "Many of those that were worn away by the famine, and their mouths almost closed, when they saw the fire of the holy house, they exerted their utmost strength, and broke out into groans and outcries again. Perea did also return the echo ... and augmented the force of the entire noise" (*War* 6.5.1). Elsewhere, Josephus blames the inhabitants of Jerusalem for not recognizing God's judgment on the city and not believing the clear portents that signaled the coming desolation. So it was when a star, looking like a sword, stood over the city, and a comet lasted for a year (*War* 6.5.3).

The sixth seal judgment of the Apocalypse (6:12–17) seems to also utilize apocalyptic language to rehearse cosmic disturbances in the first century. The opening of the sixth seal (6:12–17) introduces several spectacular physical phenomena that strike terror into people of every social rank, so that they seek to hide from God and the Lamb. Beagley believes that refers to various earthquakes in the first century, three being referred to by Tacitus (*Annals* 12.43, 58; 14.27)—in A.D. 51, 53, and 60—and others during the seventh decade (mentioned by Seneca, *Naturales Quaestiones* 6.1; 7.28). The darkening of the sun perhaps refers to solar eclipses that occurred between A.D. 49 and 52, or to phenomena associated with the eruption of Vesuvius in 79. Beagley also suggests that the islands being moved from their places (Rev. 6:14) is connected with "the sudden formation of new islands" (e.g., Thera and Terasia; cf. Seneca *Naturales Quaestiones* 6.2, 6). Beagley also calls attention to the connection between Revelation 6:16 and Luke 23:30, both of which allude to the destruction of Jerusalem in A.D. 70.[30]

"the whole inhabited earth" recorded in Rev. 3:10, as Thomas notes below (see his footnote 24), poses a problem for restricting this judgment to the land of Israel. This difficulty would be ameliorated if the judgment in Jerusalem in A.D. 70 presumed in the above references serves as the backdrop for the future judgment of the whole world.

[30]Beagley, *The "Sitz im Leben" of the Apocalypse*, 44–45.

Thus, from a comparison of the first half of the Olivet Discourse and the seal judgments of Revelation 6, one can easily see that the signs of the times began in Jesus' generation, particularly with the fall of Jerusalem.

(c) **Historical allusions to the Caesar-Christ conflict.** Another clue that the events of Revelation 6–18 were partially fulfilled in the first century is the historical allusions to the Caesar-Christ conflict that abound in these chapters. In drawing on this conflict, the apostle John conveys the twofold idea that the spirit of Antichrist had already entered the human scene (cf. Matt. 24:4–5, 11–12, 23–26/Mark 13:5–6/Luke 21:8; 2 Thess. 2; 1 John 4:3; Rev. 6:2) along with the apostasy he was expected to generate (cf. Rev. 13:15–18 with Matt. 24:10–13/Mark 13:20–23/Luke 21:34–36). In what follows, we will focus our attention on the imperial cult, especially the era of Nero (A.D. 54–68), as it forms the historical backdrop to Revelation 6:2; 13:1–18; 17:8–13.

Probably the best understanding of the first horseman of the Apocalypse (6:2) is that it refers to the Antichrist.[31] The symbols of the white horse and the bow and crown serve as a parody of Christ (19:11–19). A popular interpretation of this seal judgment is that it describes the ancient Parthians, using apocalyptic language. The Parthians were expert horsemen and archers, and they posed a constant threat to the Roman empire in the first century. They were always poised to cross the Euphrates River, and in A.D. 62 their military leader, Vologesus, did attack some Roman legions. The Parthians rode white horses, and their founder, Seleucus, was named Nikator, "the victor."[32]

Furthermore, if, as a number of scholars feel, the beast of 13:3 (cf. 17:11), who received a mortal wound in the head but was revived, draws on the *Nero redivivus* (revived) story, then the Parthian background of 6:2 is strengthened. Although Nero's first five years as emperor were relatively good, it was downhill after that. He perpetrated one monstrosity after another, including the murders of foes, friends and family, sodomy, tyranny, and persecution of Christians (beginning in A.D. 64). Indeed, the title "beast" was a fitting one for him (13:1). So unpopular was

---

[31]See the convincing defense of this view by Vos, *The Synoptic Traditions in the Apocalypse*, 187–92.

[32]See the discussion by Ford, *Revelation*, 106–7.

Nero that toward the end of his reign (A.D. 67–68), there were open revolts against his authority in Gaul and Spain. Eventually, the Praetorian Guard and the Senate proclaimed him to be a public enemy and approved Galba as his successor.

Nero fled and reportedly committed suicide by thrusting a sword through his throat on June 9, A.D. 68. However, the rumor spread that he had not died but escaped to Parthia and would return with the Parthian army to regain his throne—hence the story of *Nero redivivus*. This fearful expectation of the return of Nero, a type of the Antichrist, leading the Parthian cavalry riding on white horses with bows and arrows, going forth to conquer, makes good sense of the first horseman of the Apocalypse. In similar fashion, *Sibylline Oracles* 4:119–27, a first-century Jewish writing, provides a combined description of the *Nero redivivus* story and the destruction of Jerusalem by the Roman general, Titus, in A.D. 70:

> And then from Italy a great king, like a fugitive slave, shall flee unseen, unheard of, over the passage of the Euphrates; when he shall dare even the hateful pollution of a mother's murder, and many other things beside, venturing so far with wicked hand. And many for the throne of Rome shall dye the ground with their blood, when he has run away beyond the Parthian land. And a Roman leader [Titus] shall come to Syria, who shall burn down Solyma's temple with fire, and therewith slay many men, and shall waste the great land of the Jews with its broad way.

Examining 13:1–18 through the Neronian backdrop provides a clearer perspective on these otherwise baffling verses. Nero's infamous character merits the title of "beast" applied to him by the seer of the Apocalypse (v. 1). Revelation 13:1–6 gives the generic background of the beast, which is the Roman empire of the first century. The seven heads correspond to the seven hills of Rome, while the ten horns allude to the Caesars of the first century, however one may number them (v. 1).[33] The blasphemous worship demanded by the beast reminds one of the imperial cult of the first century, and the war the beast wages on the

---

[33]Ford provides a thorough discussion of the debate as to whether one should begin with Julius Caesar (47–44 B.C.) or Caesar Augustus (31 B.C.–A.D. 14), as well as related matters on the identification of the ten kings (*Revelation*, 210–17, 289–93).

saints cannot help but recall the intense persecutions Nero, and later Domitian, inflicted on Christians because they did not worship Caesar.

Besides this generic background, there may also be specific allusions in this text to Nero himself, the precursor of the Antichrist. We have already noted his beastly character (v. 1) and his alleged recovery (v. 3). Nero's persecution of Christians from November A.D. 64 to June A.D. 68 could account, in part, for the forty-two months (or three and one-half years) of oppression mentioned in 13:5. The reference in verse 10 to those who kill with the sword being killed by the sword reminds one simultaneously of Nero's persecution of Christians and his own apparent suicide by the sword. The reference in 13:11–15 to the beast of the land securing worship for the beast from the sea (Rome was across the sea from the place of the writing of the Apocalypse [Asia Minor]) reminds one of the local priests of the imperial cult in Asia Minor, whose task was to compel the people to offer a sacrifice to Caesar and proclaim him as lord.

Megalomaniac that he was, Nero had coins minted on which he was called "almighty god" and "savior." Nero's portrait also appears on coins as the god Apollo playing a lyre. While earlier emperors were proclaimed deities upon their deaths, Nero abandoned all reserve and demanded divine honors while still alive (as did also Caligula before him, A.D. 37–41). Those who worshiped the emperor received a certificate or mark of approval (Gk. *charagma*, the same word used in 13:16). Related to this, in the reign of Emperor Decius (A.D. 249–251), those who did not possess the certificate of sacrifice to Caesar could not pursue trades, a prohibition that conceivably goes back to Nero, reminding one of 13:17. Finally, in the number 666 (13:18) one can detect the apocalyptic seer's usage of *gematria*, a mathematic cryptogram that assigns numerical values to letters of the alphabet. More than one scholar has seen a possible referent of this number in *Neron Kaiser*. The Hebrew numerical valuation for *NRWN QSR* is as follows: $N = 50$, $R = 200$, $W = 6$, $N = 50$, $Q = 100$, $S = 60$, and $R = 200$, all of which add up to 666.[34]

The Neronian background also throws light on 17:8–13. The same metaphors rooted in the Roman empire occur here—seven

---

[34]See Gentry's convenient summary of the issue, *The Beast of Revelation* (Tyler, Tex.: Institute for Christian Economics, 1989), chap. 3.

heads, seven hills, and ten horns, Caesars with blasphemous names demanding worship. The added detail concerns the identification of the beast who "was and is not, and is about to come up out of the abyss" (v. 8, NASB). More specific information about this personage is supplied in verses 10–11. According to Charles, the fifth king "who was and is to come" is Nero (in particular, the story of *Nero redivivus*). Moreover, notes Charles, the king "who is," is Vespasian (A.D. 69–79, discounting the short and ineffective reigns of Galba [68–69], Otha [69] and Vitellius [69]). The other king who has not yet come, and when he comes, must remain a little while, is, according to Charles, Titus (79–81), who died after a short reign.[35]

Utilizing this historical framework also helps to uncover the meaning of 17:1–7. The apostle John describes there a harlot, full of blasphemous names, sitting on the beast. A number of commentators, rightly in our estimation, identify the harlot with unfaithful Israel, especially Jerusalem.[36] The description in verse 6 of the harlot's killing of the martyrs is distinctly reminiscent of Jesus' accusations against Jerusalem (Matt. 23:29–39). The city's idolatry also recalls Israel's past unfaithfulness to God, in this instance probably manifested in first-century Judaism's privileged religious status before Rome. Early Jewish Christians, however, did not share this status. Expelled from the synagogues, they were thereby forced to face Caesar worship.[37] When John speaks of the beast turning on the harlot and destroying her (vv. 16–18), he in all probability alludes to the divine judgment that befell Jerusalem for cooperating with the imperial cult. The destruction of Jerusalem in A.D. 70 also seems to be drawn upon in 11:2, where it is said that the outer court of the temple "has been given to the Gentiles. They will trample on the holy city" (cf. Luke 21:24).

In connection with this discussion of 17:1–13 we may recall 13:15–18, and in particular one further detail in that text—the mark of the beast on the worshiper's right hand and/or forehead may well be a parody of the Jewish phylacteries in Jesus'

---

[35]Charles, *The Revelation of John*, 2:69–70.

[36]E.g., Ford, *Revelation*, 285–88; Beagley, *The "Sitz im Leben" of the Apocalypse*, 92–102.

[37]See Everett Ferguson's discussion of this topic, *Backgrounds of Early Christianity* (Grand Rapids: Eerdmans, 1987), 342–43.

day. Based on Deuteronomy 6:8, Jewish males adopted the custom of tying leather boxes containing portions of the Ten Commandments to their arms and heads during their times of prayer. Seen against this backdrop, the exposure of the mark of the beast can be understood as pointing a guilty finger at those Jews in the first century who belied their commitment to monotheism by cooperating with imperial Rome. This poignantly explains why the Apocalypse refers to such people as those "who say they are Jews and are not, but are a synagogue of Satan" (2:9, 24; cf. 1:7; 17:3). Their rejection of Jesus and his followers on the one hand and their acceptance, or at least condoning, of Caesar worship on the other, according to the seer of the Apocalypse, was nothing less than eschatological apostasy.

2. The Culmination of Revelation 6–18 at the Parousia

Although historical allusions to John's day can be detected in the seal judgments of Revelation 6, as well as throughout chapters 6–18 (e.g., cf. chap. 11, and also possibly chaps. 17–18 with the fall of Jerusalem; or note the imperial cult echoes in chaps. 13 and 18), the progressive dispensationalist believes that the ultimate fulfillment of the prophetic events contained in these chapters awaits the time of the Parousia. The most significant evidence supporting this perspective is the relationship that exists between the three sets of judgment delineated in Revelation 6–18: seals (chap. 6), trumpets (chaps. 8–9), and bowls (chaps. 15–16).

If one interprets these judgments as parallel, then it is possible to conclude that they were all accomplished in the first century, particularly in and around the circumstances of the fall of Jerusalem. On this reading, the cosmic and catastrophic language employed to describe these demonstrations of divine wrath was but an apocalyptic way to depict the historical realities to which they correlated.[38] If, however, the three judgments encompassing the messianic woes are sequential and therefore

---

[38]For a good illustration of this perspective, see Gentry, *Before Jerusalem Fell*, along with his contribution in the present work. It should also be noted that posttribulationists in the premillennial camp often view the three judgments as parallel, but still regard them as futuristic in orientation and therefore largely unfulfilled as of yet. See, for example, Moo, "The Case for the Posttribulation Rapture Position," 203–5.

intensifying in effect, then it is less likely that the totality of these events correspond to the first century. On the contrary, they point to a future era for their ultimate fulfillment.

At least six pieces of evidence seem to establish the view that the judgments of Revelation 6–18 are sequential, not parallel. (1) The three sets of judgment appear to be linear, that is, the seals lead to the trumpets lead to the bowl judgments. In other words, the seventh seal (8:1–5) unfolds in the seven trumpets (8:6–11:15) and the seventh trumpet (11:15ff.) unfolds in the seven bowls (chaps. 16–18), which, in turn, culminate in the Parousia (chap. 19).

(2) The intensification of language used in describing the judgments makes it difficult to root the trumpet and bowl portents in history. Two examples illustrate this point: (a) Only a part of earth and humanity are affected in the seal and trumpet judgments whereas the entire earth and humanity are affected in the bowl judgments. (b) The bowl judgments are labeled the "last plagues" because with them God's wrath is completed (15:1; 16:17); not so for the seal and trumpet judgments. This seems to militate against classifying the first half of the messianic woes as the period of divine wrath; rather, the second half seems to be reserved for that feature.

(3) Related to the last point, the intensification of language depicting the judgments corresponds to the Jewish apocalyptic concept that the Great Tribulation should be compared to "birth pains" (cf. Matt. 24:8 and par.). Johnson writes of this:

> The seals closely parallel the signs of the approaching end times spoken of in Jesus' Olivet Discourse (Matt. 24:1–35; Mark 13:1–37; Luke 21:5–33). In these passages the events of the last days fall into three periods: (1) the period of false Christs, wars, famines, pestilences, earthquakes, and death, called "the beginning of birth pains" (Matt. 24:8); (2) the period of the Great Tribulation (Matt. 24:21; NIV, "great distress") and, (3) finally, the period "immediately after the distress of those days," when the sun, moon, and stars will be affected and Christ will return (Matt. 24:29–30). This parallel to major parts of Revelation is too striking to be ignored. Thus the seals would correspond to the "beginning of birth pains" found in the Olivet Discourse. The events are similar to those occurring under the trumpets (8:2–11:19) and bowls

(15:1–16:21) but they should not be confused with those later and more severe judgments. In Jewish apocalyptic literature (cf. 2 Baruch 25–30), the Great Tribulation precedes the age to come and is divided into twelve parts of various trials lasting possibly a week of seven weeks, or forty-nine years.[39]

(4) The successive nature of the judgments in Revelation 6–18 fits the spiral structure evident elsewhere in Johannine literature (e.g., 1 John).

(5) There is a difference in sequence and content of the events described in each series of judgments.

(6) The reference to those not sealed in 9:4 (fifth trumpet) presupposes the sealing of 7:1–8, and hence, linear development.

An objection, however, is often raised against a chronological reading of the judgments, thus arguing for their parallel structure—namely, interconnections among the judgments point to their simultaneous unfolding. Most notable in this regard is the similarity among the sixth-seventh seal, the seventh trumpet (11:15ff.), and the seventh bowl (16:17ff.), which all appear to depict events associated with the second coming of Christ.

That there is partial recapitulation or some overlapping in the judgments on this point is probable. But that the three judgments are parallel and therefore identical is improbable, as Johnson argues, because of a number of considerations: (1) The sixth seal unfolds into the period of wrath poured out on the worshipers of the beast but does not actually advance to the event of the Parousia (6:12–17). (2) The seventh seal introduces the trumpet judgments, which run their course, and the seventh trumpet seems to bring one into the kingdom of Christ (11:15–18). (3) The seventh bowl then brings one to the culmination point in the return of Christ (chaps. 16–17). (4) Interludes come between the sixth and seventh seals and between the sixth and seventh trumpets but not between the sixth and seventh bowls, which would be expected if the trumpets were strictly parallel to the bowls.[40]

All of this to say that the sequential nature of the judgments seems to allow for their partial fulfillment in history (e.g., the

---

[39]Alan F. Johnson, "Revelation," in *The Expositor's Bible Commentary*, ed. Frank E. Gaebelein(Grand Rapids: Zondervan, 1981), 12:472.

[40]The reader is referred to Johnson's discussion of this point, "Revelation," 12:491.

seal judgments), but only at the end of history will they be fully accomplished (the trumpet and bowl judgments). But who do progressive dispensationalists believe will undergo the Great Tribulation? To that issue we now briefly turn.

B. The Identification of the Tribulation Saints

The question of who will experience the Great Tribulation as detailed in Revelation 6–18 largely depends on the identification of the 144,000 sealed servants of God (7:1–8). Two main interpretations have been proposed. The first is that the number and tribal identification are to be taken literally with reference to the nation of Israel. Consequently, it is Israel that undergoes the Great Tribulation, not the church (the pretribulational view). The other view suggests that the language must be interpreted symbolically, so that John is referring to the church, the new Israel. Thus the church will go through the Great Tribulation (the posttribulational view). After addressing this issue, we will add two other comments in order to round out the discussion: the relationship between the 144,000 sealed servants (7:1–8) and the innumerable multitude (7:9–17), and the Great Tribulation and the overlapping of the two ages.

(1) With regard to the matter of the identification of the 144,000, the second view (the church is the new Israel) appeals to those New Testament references that seem to apply the language once used of Israel to the church (Matt. 19:28; Rom. 2:29; 4:11; 9:6–8; Gal. 3:29; 6:16; Phil. 3:3; James 1:1; 1 Peter 1:1; 2:4, 9; Rev. 1:6; 2:9; 3:9; 18:4). But alongside this line of witnesses must also be placed other testimony in the New Testament that serves to distinguish Israel from the church: (a) There is no clear-cut example of the church being called ".Israel" in the New Testament or in the church fathers before A.D. 160.[41] (b) The most natural meaning for the term "Israel" in both Old and New Testament is the physical descendants of the patriarchs.[42] (c) A distinction between ethnic Israel and the church is amply attested to in Romans 9–11.[43] (d) Moving from the exegetical data

---

[41]See Peter Richardson, *Israel in the Apostolic Church* (SNTSMS; Cambridge: Cambridge Univ. Press, 1969), 74–84, 206.

[42]On this point, see Thomas, *Revelation 1–7*, 476–77.

[43]For support for this statement, see C. Marvin Pate, *The End of the Age Has Come: The Theology of Paul* (Grand Rapids: Zondervan, 1995), 196–98.

to the level of theological consideration, it seems that the purpose of the Great Tribulation is to win the nation of Israel to its Messiah. In aligning himself with the first view (the literal interpretation of Israel), Paul Benware states the point succinctly:

> The primary purpose of preparing Israel for her Messiah and His kingdom is evidenced in a number of passages. For example, this period is viewed as the "time of Jacob's trouble" (Jer. 30:7 KJV). Whereas this does not mean that other nations will not be involved, it does suggest that Israel is the focus of this tribulation period. Other passages show that the Tribulation has a definite Jewish character (e.g., Dt. 4:30; Da. 12:1; Eze. 20:37; Zec. 13:8–9; Matt. 24:15–20). The important focus of this period is the coming of salvation to Israel and, consequently, to the Gentiles as well (e.g., Da. 9:24; Eze. 36:25–36; 37:1–14; 39:21–29; Jer. 31:31–34; Mal. 4:4–6; Ro. 11:25–28; Rev. 7:4–14).[44]

While the evidence does not permit dogmatism, it does seem that the reference to the 144,000 chosen out of the twelve tribes of Israel indicates that racial Jews are in John's mind, specifically Jewish Christians converted during the Great Tribulation.

(2) A related matter in this discussion is the question of the relationship between the 144,000 (7:1–8) and the innumerable multitude that endures the Great Tribulation (7:9–17). Are they the same group of people? Assuming the symbolic interpretation of the 144,000, posttribulationists equate the two groups with the church. Pretribulationists, however, see significant differences between the groups: The first is numbered, the second is innumerable; the first is limited to Jews, the second refers to every nation; the first is preserved from martyrdom for a longer period of time (see 12:13; 14:1–5) than the second. These differences would seem to outweigh the similarities between the two groups. Given this distinction, it is possible to view the 144,000 as a select group of Jews who are converted to Christ during the Great Tribulation, which, in turn, evangelizes the Gentile nations—the innumerable multitude.

Support for the preceding interpretation comes from those Old Testament passages that speak prophetically of Gentiles as

---

[44]Paul N. Benware, *Understanding End-Times Prophecy: A Comprehensive Approach* (Chicago: Moody, 1995), 167.

joining Israel in worshiping God at the temple in Jerusalem during the end times (e.g., Isa. 2:2; 49:6; 56:6–8; Zech. 14:16). Such a perspective continues in the New Testament with Paul, who may well have understood his collection from the Gentiles for the poor in Jerusalem as the beginning fulfillment of those Old Testament prophecies (see Rom. 15:23–33; 1 Cor. 16; 2 Cor. 8–9). A similar notion probably informs Revelation 7.

(3) The final comment we offer with respect to the endurance of the Great Tribulation by the saints is that the overlapping of the two ages leaves its imprint on this subject in Revelation. Specifically, John adopts the prevalent Jewish apocalyptic notion that righteous suffering in this age of tribulation ensures heavenly glory in the age to come (e.g., 4 Ezra 4:27; 7:12; 2 Bar. 15:8; 48:50; *The Damascus Rule* 3:18–20/4:13, 17–18). The Jewish perspective of the two ages, however, was consecutive in nature: When Messiah comes, this age will give way to the age to come. But according to John and the New Testament as a whole, those two ages now overlap because of the death and resurrection of Jesus Christ. Consequently Christians, because they are in Jesus, currently and simultaneously participate in the suffering of Christ's cross as well as in his resurrection glory (see Rev. 1:5–9; 12; cf. Rom. 8:17–25; 1 Peter 1:4–9). For John, the fact that the tribulation saints experience Christ's glory is a sign that they live in the overlapping of the two ages. In other words, their present experience of glory is proof that they will ultimately overcome the messianic woes (whether in life or by death). After such a period, their affliction will completely be replaced by heavenly glory.

V. THE RETURN OF CHRIST (REV. 19)

We previously argued, based on the similarities between the first half of the Olivet Discourse and the seal judgments of Revelation 6 (along with the considerations of the beginning of the last days in Christ's generation and allusions in Rev. 6–18 to first-century Caesar worship), that the fall of Jerusalem in A.D. 70 serves as the historical backdrop to the Apocalypse. This does not suggest to the progressive dispensationalist, however, that what we have in this event is the final fulfillment of Revelation 6–18; note the sequential, and therefore intensifying, nature of the trumpet and bowl judgments. These await final accomplishment in the last generation, whenever that may be.

The decision one reaches here has direct bearing on one's interpretation of 19:11–21. The futurist understands this passage to be describing the Parousia, the second coming of Christ at the end of human history, while the preterist view is that the event portrayed there was fully realized at Christ's "coming" in judgment on Jerusalem.[45] While a full-scale treatment of this *crux interpretum* is not possible here, three comments will be offered in support of the traditional view, that 19:11–21 refers to the second coming of Christ in glory at the conclusion of time.

(1) Despite the preterist's attempt to root the *entirety* of the Olivet Discourse in history at the fall of Jerusalem, the best understanding of that tradition is to locate its ultimate fulfillment at the time of the return of Christ. In our opinion, the preterist viewpoint makes a fundamental mistake in interpreting the Olivet Discourse by overlooking the parallel structure within it that itself is informed by the already/not yet tension. This is especially clear in Luke 21, where the author distinguishes between the fall of Jerusalem in A.D. 70 (vv. 8–24) and the return of Christ at the end of history (vv. 25–36). That this chronological separation of the two events is intended by Luke is evidenced by two facts: (a) The fall of Jerusalem had already occurred by his day (see v. 20 and its specific description of that event, as contrasted with the generic presentation of Mark 13:14 and Matt. 24:15); (b) Luke omits the phrase found in Mark 13:19 (cf. Matt. 24:21)—"those will be days of distress unequaled from the beginning . . . until now—and never to be equaled again"— with reference to the fall of Jerusalem. In other words, Luke did not equate the afflictions surrounding that event with the Great Tribulation at the end of time. For Luke (and probably also Mark and Matthew, though less explicitly), the signs of the times already began at the fall of Jerusalem but will not be completed until the return of Christ to end world history.

(2) The preterist viewpoint makes much of the immediacy of the fulfillment of Jesus' promise in Revelation to come quickly,

---

[45]For a good example of this interpretation, the reader is referred to the study by Gary DeMar, *Last Days Madness: Obsession of the Modern Church* (Atlanta: American Vision, 1991), 263–65. DeMar's work defends the thesis that the events delineated in the Olivet Discourse, 2 Thess. 2, and Revelation were all fulfilled at or around the fall of Jerusalem in A.D. 70.

applying it to the fall of Jerusalem (Rev. 1:1, 3; 2:16; 3:11; 11:14; 22:6–7, 10, 12, 20).[46] Put another way, the coming of Jesus Christ as recorded in 19:11–21 refers not to the second coming of Christ at the end of history but to the coming of Christ to judge Jerusalem in A.D. 70. Two problems, however, surface with this theory: (a) Revelation 19:11–21 matches descriptions found elsewhere in the New Testament that refer to the second coming of Christ in glory at the end of history (Matt. 24:30–31/Mark 13:26–27/Luke 21:27–28; 2 Thess. 2:8; Titus 2:13–14; Jude 14–15). Only with great difficulty can these texts be explained in terms other than that of the Parousia.

(b) The preterist interpretation does not take into account the nuance of the word "time" (*kairos*, e.g., Rev. 1:3), which, as Oscar Cullmann has demonstrated, is informed by the already/not yet eschatological tension.[47] This understanding, on the one hand, allows for immediate fulfillment of the prophecy of Jesus in Revelation to come soon while not denying, on the other hand, a future significance to them as well (see our earlier comments on 1:1, 3). That is to say, the preterist position unnecessarily alleviates the tension between the already (the first coming of Jesus) and the not yet (the second coming of Jesus). In effect, this viewpoint is akin to "realized eschatology," the view that says that basically all end-time prophecies of the New Testament were fulfilled in the first century, an interpretation rightly criticized.[48]

(3) The preterist view of 19:11–21 is intimately related to the hypothesis that the identity of the Babylon that is destroyed in chapters 17–18 is Jerusalem, more particularly first-century Judaism, which enjoyed the privileged status from Rome of being a legal religion. As the theory goes, John looks on that benefit as nothing less than an idolatrous compromise with the imperial cult. The description, therefore, of Christ's coming in judgment (19:11–21) is applied to Jerusalem's destruction by the Romans. Revelation 17:16–17, in its portrayal of the beast (Rome) on which the harlot (Jerusalem) sits, turning against her and

---

[46]For defense of this hypothesis, see Gentry, *Before Jerusalem Fell*, 133–45; DeMar, *Last Days Madness*, 263–65; David Chilton, *The Days of Vengeance: An Exposition of the Book of Revelation* (Fort Worth, Tex.: Dominion, 1987), 5–75.

[47]Cullmann, *Christ and Time*.

[48]Often associated with the works of C. H. Dodd, for example, *The Apostolic Preaching and Its Development*. It is commonly perceived by scholars today that Dodd

destroying her, is then understood as the method by which Christ judged Jerusalem.[49] The progressive dispensationalist can accept this hypothesis as plausible. But this does not suggest that there is no futurity to the coming of Christ as depicted in 19:11–21, for reasons we explained under our second comment above.

Furthermore, a careful reading of Revelation 11 seems to indicate that God, even though having permitted the destruction of Jerusalem (see 11:1–2), is not yet finished with Israel/Jerusalem. We suggest that Revelation 11 is informed by the threefold paradigm operative in Romans 11, a pattern that envisions the future restoration of the Jewish nation.

Romans 11 makes the basic point that God still has a plan for the Jews. Paul provides three arguments to that effect. (a) Israel's rejection of Jesus Messiah is partial, not total. Jewish Christians are ample testimony to that fact (11:1–10). (b) Israel's rejection of Messiah serves a merciful purpose—it is the divine means for reaching Gentiles with the gospel (11:11–29). (c) Israel's rejection of Messiah is temporal, not eternal. One day Christ will return, and "all Israel will be saved" (11:25–36).[50]

We submit that the same pattern is at work in Revelation 11. (a) Israel's rejection of Jesus Messiah is partial, not total. Jewish Christians, the remnant, are proof of that (11:1, 3–12). On this reading, Elijah and Moses are God's messengers who will represent the Jewish Christian community at the end of history.

(b) Israel's rejection of Jesus serves a merciful purpose—it is the catalyst for drawing Gentiles to Christ. This plan will be in effect until the end of history, at which time the fullness of the Gentiles will have arrived. The dominance of the Gentiles in the plan of God began with the destruction of Jerusalem in A.D. 70 (cf. Rev. 11:2 with Luke 21:24) and will continue until God has accomplished his purpose with them (Rom. 11:25).

(c) At that culminating point, God will then restore Israel unto himself. This seems to be the sense behind Revelation 11:13. The seven thousand who will be killed in Jerusalem by an earthquake (a minority), leaving the rest of the city (the majority) to

---

overstated his point and that the best way to categorize the New Testament is with the already/not yet eschatological construct.

[49]See the brief treatment by Pate and Haines, *Doomsday Delusions*, 43.

[50]See again Pate, *The End of the Age Has Come*, 196–98. I have also developed this theme relative to Luke's writings in my commentary *Luke* (Moody Gospel Commentary; Chicago: Moody, 1995).

repent and turn to God, constitutes a *reversal* of the Elijah/remnant motif. In the Old Testament during Elijah's day, only he and the faithful seven thousand did not bow the knee to Baal, while the rest of the nation did. But in the end time, the opposite will take place—the witness of Elijah (and Moses, 11:3–12), along with the divine earthquake affirming their message (v. 13), will bring the majority of Jews to faith. This is John's apocalyptic way of saying what Paul had earlier said—all Israel will be saved. That is, the nation as a whole will become the remnant, the ones who are faithful to God. Interestingly enough, the conversion of Jerusalem to Christ happens right before his second coming (11:15–19; cf. 19:11–21).

VI. THE MILLENNIUM (REV. 20)

Much ink has been spilled over the interpretation of Revelation 20:1–6, with three basic viewpoints emerging in the discussion: premillennial, amillennial, and postmillennial.[51] The progressive dispensationalist approach to this text is clearly to be identified with the first of these options. Although believers are spiritually raised with Christ at conversion and currently reign with him from heaven (e.g., Eph. 2:1–10; Col. 3:1–4), not until Christ's second advent will that reign descend to earth. Two objections to this interpretation can be answered here, albeit briefly: that only the martyrs of the Great Tribulation are referred to as reigning with Christ (Rev. 20:4), and that the resurrection mentioned is spiritual, not physical, in nature (vv. 4–6).

(1) Regarding the first objection, it is sometimes said that the ones who will be raised to rule with Christ on the earth during the Millennium are exclusively those believers martyred during the Great Tribulation (v. 4). But, as Robert L. Thomas has observed, there are two insurmountable problems with this view.[52] (a) The resurrection of the martyrs does not occur until later, thus distinguishing them from the general populace of Christians, who also coreign with Christ (v. 4). (b) Elsewhere John promises that the faithful, not just the martyrs, will share Christ's future reign (2:26–28; 3:12, 21; 5:10; cf. 1 Cor. 6:2–3).

---

[51]For a good summary of the millennial views, see Stanley J. Grenz's study, *The Millennial Maze: Sorting Out Evangelical Options* (Downers Grove, Ill.: InterVarsity, 1992).

[52]Thomas, *Revelation 1–7*, 413–14.

(2) Regarding the second objection—that the nature of the resurrection in 20:4–6 is spiritual, not physical—two key factors militate against this perception of the passage.[53] (a) A spiritual resurrection can hardly explain the compensation provided for the martyrs mentioned in verse 4. From John's perspective they are physically dead but spiritually alive. What they need is a bodily resurrection. (b) The best understanding of the verb *ezēsan* ("they lived") in verse 4 is that it refers to a bodily resurrection. Why? (i) The same verb in verse 5 means bodily resurrection. (ii) *Zaō* ("live") frequently in Revelation refers to bodily resurrection (1:18; 2:8; 13:14; 20:5). (iii) Actually, *zaō* in the context of death always refers to physical resurrection in the New Testament (cf. John 11:25; Acts 1:3; 9:41). (iv) John clearly equates "live" with resurrection in Revelation 20:5—the first "resurrection" (*anastasis*, a word used over forty times in the New Testament with reference to physical resurrection).

VII. THE ETERNAL STATE (REV. 21–22)

Throughout our overview of the Apocalypse, it has been demonstrated that the already/not yet eschatological tension governs the progressive dispensationalist's interpretation of that book. Revelation 21–22 and its portrayal of the eternal state will be treated no differently here. The key to grasping the significance of these two chapters, we suggest, is to realize that they envision the future restoration of paradise lost (the not yet aspect, which is to be actualized at the second coming of Christ). If we bring into this discussion the Johannine literature as a whole, however, we discover that these end-times blessings are in the process of being partially fulfilled now (the already aspect, which began with the first coming of Christ). We briefly develop this twofold hypothesis below by providing a chart of the three time frames involved in our thesis, followed by a summary explanation.

Genesis 1–3	*Revelation 21–22*	*Johannine literature*
Beginning of time	End of time (second coming of Christ)	Middle of time (first coming of Christ)

---

[53]See again ibid., 417.

Old creation (1:1)	New creation (21:1)	New creation in Christ (John 1:1–5; 1 John 1:1–5)
Loss of the presence of God (3:23–24)	God's presence among God's people, the new temple (21:2–3, 9–27)	Christ the temple of God (John 2:19–21)
Entrance of death (2:17)	Defeat of death (21:4)	Eternal life (John 11:24–26; 1 John 5:20)
Rivers of paradise (2:10–14)	Water of life (22:1)	Water of life (John 4:14; 7:37–42)
Tree of life (3:24)	Heavenly food of eternal life (22:2–4, 14; cf. 2:17)	Heavenly food of eternal life (John 6:25–59)
Son of God (1:26–28)	Sons of God (21:7)	Sons of God (John 1:12; 3:3–8; 1 John 3:1, 10; 5:2)

Revelation 21–22 envisions the future restoration of at least six paradisical blessings, but which are partially being fulfilled now for believers in Christ. (1) The new creation of the eternal state will restore the old creation marred by the fall of Adam and Eve. But even now, when people place their faith in Christ, they become participants in that new creation. (2) The eternal state will fully recover the presence and fellowship with God that humanity lost in the Garden of Eden. Indeed, Christ, the temple and locus of God's presence, is in the process of restoring that fellowship to believers. (3) The eternal state will witness the defeat of death and the gift of eternal life, which, with the death and resurrection of Christ, has already begun. (4) The water of life expected to flow in the eternal state, symbolic of abiding contentment, is now available in Christ. (5) Similarly, the tree of life with its promise of fulfillment and eternal life is being offered to all in Christ. (6) Sin marred the image of God in the human race, but in the eternal state God will make believers his children, a blessing now being realized in Christ.

CONCLUSION

The Apocalypse is arguably the most controversial book in the Bible. My reading of the approaches represented in this volume (the classical dispensational view will be treated next) leads me to believe that two core issues emerge in Revelation that demand treatment: hermeneutical and theological. I conclude this section by reflecting on those concerns.

(1) Obviously a hermeneutical thicket awaits the interpreter of Revelation. Taking into account the four contributions presented here, it seems clear that the central problem of the discussion is: How are we to understand symbolic literature? Or, more precisely, does the genre of prophetic/apocalyptic require single, dual, or multiple fulfillments?

Interestingly enough, *all* four views apparently base their respective approaches on the cherished Reformation principle of the historical-grammatical hermeneutic, however that hermeneutic works itself out. In concert with this principle, it seems to this writer that, ultimately, the operative criterion for interpreting Revelation is *historical* in nature. That is to say, all four views included in this volume take as their point of departure for understanding Revelation the question of whether or not the book's message has been fulfilled in history. Thus, although they are at the opposite ends of the spectrum, the classical dispensationalist and the preterist approaches appeal to history in order to validate their differing interpretations. Consequently, the former can find little in measurable time and space where the events of Revelation have witnessed fulfillment, whereas the latter discovers amazing correspondences in the first century A.D. for those prophecies. Ironically, both attribute single fulfillment to the symbolism of Revelation.

The progressive dispensationalist sees both perspectives as viable: There is partial fulfillment (the past) as well as final realization (the future) regarding those things in history. Thus the symbolism of Revelation attests to dual fulfillment.

For the idealist, who is not interested in a mere history lesson from the remote past or a moral story set in the distant horizon, the concern is to demonstrate that God is our eternal contemporary and therefore has a word for humanity in the present. As a result, Revelation offers multiple fulfillments of its message—this despite the idealist's apparent ahistorical approach.

Does this consideration that all four views of Revelation appeal to history, but with decidedly different results in order to legitimate their stances, cause a hermeneutical impasse? Not necessarily. The solution to this quandary seems to lie in a suggestion mentioned at the beginning of this study, namely, that the four approaches offered here can be combined to present an interpretive whole for grasping the meaning of the last book in the Bible. Thus, the preterist can teach us about God's powerful dealings with humanity in the past, while the classical dispensationalist reminds us that God's work is not yet finished; only the future will unveil the full scope of the divine plan. Progressives perhaps offer a balanced statement of the previous views, arguing that the past is proof positive that God will complete in the future what he started. Meanwhile, idealists provide a model for applying God's prophetic word to our contemporary and changing situations.

(2) A second key issue generated by Revelation is a theological one—the "delay" of the Parousia. This is the ultimate question raised by Revelation 1:1, 3, with reference to the nearness of the fulfillment of the prophecies of the Apocalypse, along with the predictions of the Olivet Discourse (Matt. 24; Mark 13; Luke 21). Here the question is: How are we to understand Jesus' and John's predictions about the signs of the times culminating in the Second Coming? The liberal theologian has an easy answer to this query—Jesus predicted that such an event would occur during the first generation of Christians (see Mark 13:30 and parallel passages), but he was wrong! His prophecy failed and history has continued unbroken. The evangelical, however, is not satisfied with such a response, and rightly so.

But beyond that, there is no consensus among conservative theologians as to the timing of the fulfillment of those forecasts. The preterist regards them as prophecies largely accomplished in the first Christian centuries, while the classical dispensationalist believes their realization awaits the future. The progressive dispensationalist argues that there was partial actualization of Jesus' statements surrounding the fall of Jerusalem in A.D. 70, which serves as the backdrop for their final fulfillment at the end of history. For the idealist, Jesus' comments were not so much prophecies but rather symbolic statements about the present structure of spiritual reality. How, then, can we proceed through this theological maze?

If my fellow contributors will indulge me for a moment, here is where the "already/not yet" eschatological tension provides an answer for the issue of the delay of the Parousia. As has been carefully, and I think convincingly, argued for the last fifty years by New Testament scholars, the best understanding of the Gospels—the Olivet Discourse included—is that Jesus' utterances about the Kingdom of God were partially fulfilled at his first coming (the already aspect) but remain forthcoming until his return (the not yet aspect). When all is said and done, this is the most viable solution to both the quest for the historical Jesus and the apparent delay of the Second Coming. In other words, just as Jesus promised, the age to come did indeed dawn in his coming, but within the context of this present age. Though sometimes equated with only one school of thought, the situation seems to be more the case that the already/not yet perspective is hospitable to all four viewpoints delineated in this work, not just one.

In conclusion, we summarize our contribution to this volume by relating the already/not yet hermeneutic to the three eschatological hallmarks of dispensationalism. (1) Concerning the distiction between the church and Israel, progressives believe that already the Gentiles have been included into the one people of God, by faith in Christ; but God is not yet finished with Israel, for one day he will restore that nation to himself and Jesus Messiah. (2) Regarding the premillennial stance of progressive dispensationalism, according to Revelation the kingdom of God (the age to come) has dawned in heaven, but it has not yet appeared on earth. That awaits the return of Christ, whose second coming will establish his one-thousand-year reign in Jerusalem. (3) According to progressive dispensationalists, while the signs of the times (messianic woes) were initiated during the first generation of Christians (in connection with the fall of Jerusalem), the Great Tribulation has not yet occurred; that awaits the future, from which the church (but not Israel) will be exempt.

Chapter Four

A CLASSICAL DISPENSATIONALIST VIEW OF REVELATION

Robert L. Thomas

A CLASSICAL DISPENSATIONALIST VIEW OF REVELATION

Robert L. Thomas

PREAMBLE

In presenting a dispensational view on the book of Revelation, I want first to express my respect for two groups. The first is other dispensationalists with whom I differ in interpretational details here and there within the last book of the Bible. The scope of the present discussion allows me to present only my own interpretation.[1] The other group are those who do not embrace a dispensational view, particularly the other three contributors to this work. I respect them and their interpretations and do not want any of the following remarks to be construed as impugning them personally or otherwise.

The following discussion is a *typical* dispensational view. To cover the designated view in this chapter, I must clarify the meaning of "dispensationalism," explore areas of analysis representative of a dispensational view, explain an emphasis on the major issue distinguishing dispensational understanding, and give an overview of Revelation.

---

[1]My own interpretation is explored in my two books, *Revelation 1–7: An Exegetical Commentary* (Chicago: Moody, 1992) and *Revelation 8–22: An Exegetical Commentary* (Chicago: Moody, 1995).

CLARIFICATION OF DISPENSATIONALISM

In recent years some discussions of dispensationalism have sought to distinguish changes in the dispensational system of theology, dividing the system into categories such as "Niagara Premillennialism" (1875–1909), "Scofieldism" (1909–1965), and "Essentialist" (1965–1985), or "Classical" (ca. 1800–c. 1950) and "Revised" (ca. 1950–ca. 1990).[2] These categories are unwarranted in that differences in dispensational interpretation through the years have resulted from closer applications of the grammatical-historical method of exegesis and do not amount to changes in the system, but are rather refinements in or developments of the system.

Progressive dispensationalism, on the other hand, represents a significant change in principles of interpretation,[3] so that the name "dispensationalism" does not apply to that system. Another name suggested for traditional dispensationalism has been "normative dispensationalism,"[4] but this essay will use simply "dispensationalism" to refer to the system as historically known.

SELECTED AREAS TO HIGHLIGHT THE DISPENSATIONAL VIEW

Selectivity is necessary in a work comparing views on Revelation, so the following categories or passages will typify a dispensational approach.

1. Hermeneutical System

The standard hermeneutical approach to Scripture, at least since the Reformation, has been the grammatical-historical approach, sometimes called literal interpretation. Applied to Revelation, this approach results in a dispensational under-

---

[2]Craig Blaising and Darrell Bock, *Progressive Dispensationalism* (Wheaton, Ill.: Victor, 1993), 21–23; idem, eds., *Dispensationalism, Israel, and the Church* (Grand Rapids: Zondervan, 1992), 13–34.

[3]See Robert L. Thomas, "A Critique of Progressive Dispensational Hermeneutics," *When the Trumpet Sounds*, ed. Thomas Ice and Timothy Demy (Eugene, Ore.: Harvest House, 1995), 414–25.

[4]Larry Crutchfield, *The Origins of Dispensationalism: The Darby Factor* (Lanham, Md.: Univ. Press of America, 1992), 23–42.

standing of the book. Some recommend different interpretive principles because of the book's alleged apocalyptic genre, but by its own claim the book is a prophecy and deserves a literal interpretation, just as other prophetic books do.[5] To justify a spiritualizing approach on the basis of the book's many symbols misses a significant distinction between the way God gave the revelation to John and the way readers should interpret that revelation. In 1:1, where John writes, "he signified it"[6] (*esēmanen*), some have misunderstood that as justification for symbolic interpretation throughout the book. Those words, however, tell the means God used to inspire John to write; they do not provide grounds for nonliteral interpretation. Interpreters should understand the revelation to John as they do the rest of the Bible, even though God gave it in an unusual symbolic fashion.

A preterist approach must assume an apocalyptic genre, in which the language only faintly and indirectly reflects actual events. This extreme allegorical interpretation allows for finding fulfillments in the first-century Roman empire prior to the destruction of Jerusalem in A.D. 70. Incidentally, most preterism dates the book's writing in the 60s, thirty years earlier than the generally accepted date of writing.

An idealist approach also must spiritualize the text because of an assumed apocalyptic genre. To those following this method of interpretation, the Apocalypse speaks of the eternal conflict between good and evil and expresses basic principles that God follows throughout history. Applying these principles to any period, usually that of the interpreter himself or herself, the system generalizes the specifics and denies the prophetic character of the book by emphasizing the repetitive cycle that marks each generation. It has no room for particular points in history that mark the fulfillment of specific prophecies.[7]

If it follows the path of its earliest advocates, a progressive dispensational approach will posit both a literal understanding

---

[5] Thomas, *Revelation 1–7*, 23–29.

[6] All Bible translations in this chapter are by the author.

[7] See, e.g., Sam Hamstra Jr. ("An Idealist View of Revelation," in this volume), who illustrates this characteristic in his frequent use of such phrases as "not particular incidents," "the vision as a whole," "rather than analyzing every detail," "no details of particular wars ... in general terms," "resist the temptation to link each trumpet with a particular date or person," "do not symbolize single and separate events," "unnecessary to dwell on particulars," and "refraining from a detailed dissection of the vision."

and additional ones. Referred to as "complementary hermeneutics" or a "historical-grammatical-literary-theological" method,[8] this approach allows an interpreter at least two understandings of the text, one a grammatical-historical and the other a symbolic or allegorical one. Though a definitive work on Revelation by a progressive dispensationalist has yet to appear, one might expect it to combine elements of futurism with elements of idealistic interpretation and even preterism. Such combined systems of hermeneutics also occur among historic premillennialists, a group who are nondispensationalists.[9]

In contrast to each of these, a consistent adherence to grammatical-historical principles leads to a dispensational understanding of Revelation. The rules of grammar and the facts of history result in the following interpretations of texts relevant to that overall view of the book. The handling of the following topics and passages will illustrate the parameters of grammatical-historical or literal interpretation.

2. Continuity with Daniel 2

The words "things that must happen" (ha dei genesthai) in 1:1 summarize the content of the revelation to John. They represent a theme of long-standing interest, one that traces its roots to the Greek version of Daniel 2:28 (cf. also 2:29, 45). In that passage Daniel interprets Nebuchadnezzar's dream about a statue representing four successive world empires. A stone—cut without hands from a mountain—that destroys that statue stands for an everlasting kingdom that will supersede the earlier four empires. Using the king's dream, Daniel was predicting the eventual establishment of God's kingdom on earth.

Jesus drew upon the same excerpt of Daniel 2:28 in the Matthean record of his Olivet Discourse: "they must happen" (dei genesthai, Matt. 24:6; cf. Mark 13:7; Luke 21:9). The predicted "things" were still future at the end of his first advent. They have found and will find no fulfillment during the period from Pentecost to the church's rapture. God's program for Israel will

---

[8]Darrell L. Bock, "The Son of David and the Saints' Task: The Hermeneutics of Initial Fulfillment," BSac 150 (October–December 1993): 447; idem, "Current Messianic Activity and OT Davidic Promise: Dispensationalism, Hermeneutics, and NT Fulfillment," TrinJ 15NS (1994): 71; Blaising and Bock, Progressive Dispensationalism, 64, 77.

[9]Thomas, Revelation 1–7, 32–34.

resume only after events of Daniel's seventy-week prophecy (Dan. 9:24–27) begin to unfold.

Some sixty years after Jesus' Olivet Discourse, John resumes discussion of this long-awaited series of events and devotes most of his book to developing them in greater detail. The same phrase (*ha dei genesthai*) brackets the visional portion of the book, appearing in Revelation 4:1 at the head of the section and in 22:6 at its conclusion. So 4:1–22:5 comprises "the things that must happen," that is, the series of events leading to the establishment of God's kingdom on earth about which Daniel prophesied. In 1:19, a similar phrase, "the things that will happen" (*ha mellei genesthai*), points to the same body of material. That verse furnishes the outline for the book and will be a focus of attention below.

In two of the places where John uses the expression "things that must happen" (1:1 and 22:6), he couples with it the anticipation of an imminent fulfillment through the addition of "soon" (*en tachei*). Shortness of time until Christ returns, another distinctly dispensational perspective, will receive further attention below in connection with "The Twofold Coming of Christ."

3. Continuity with the Davidic Covenant

Further indication of God's resumption of his program for Israel comes in several verses throughout Revelation that deal with Jesus Christ as the fulfillment of the Davidic covenant. The first of these is 1:5, where the three titles for Christ—"the faithful witness," "the firstborn from the dead," "the ruler of the kings of the earth"—hark back to Psalm 89, an inspired exposition of the Davidic covenant of 2 Samuel 7:8–16. Use of the titles early in the book anticipates Christ's future occupancy of David's throne once the kingdom on earth begins (Rev. 20:1–10).

Progressive dispensationalists have mistakenly interpreted the verse as indication of Christ's present occupancy of the Davidic throne, thereby granting to him both a present and a future tenure on that throne.[10] That conclusion illustrates the hermeneutical weakness of the system in assigning the same passage more than one meaning.[11] Christ's presence on a future

---

[10]Blaising and Bock, *Progressive Dispensationalism*, 179, 181, 183.

[11]Assigning multiple meanings is a characteristic of progressive dispensationalism (Thomas, "Critique of Progressive Dispensational Hermeneutics," 420–21).

earthly throne (e.g., 11:15; 20:4) is specific in Revelation. The Old Testament is specific in placing that throne on earth; to rule over the kings of the earth, one must be on earth (Ps. 89:27). To say that his present heavenly throne is the throne of David adds to the text an additional meaning not warranted by grammatical-historical exegesis.

Literal interpretation of 3:21 also sees Christ as the fulfill-ment of the Davidic covenant. This verse speaks of two thrones, the Father's and Christ's. Throughout Revelation, the Father's throne is in heaven (e.g., 4:2) and Christ's is on earth (since it is the throne of David). His authority to grant and deny access to the Davidic kingdom (3:7–8) is further evidence of this.

A progressive dispensational denial of this distinction in thrones cites contextual evidence (2:18, 26–27; 3:7, 12; 5:5) that Christ is presently on David's throne,[12] but in each passage the explanation confuses a reference to Christ's present authority with his personal seating on David's throne. Old Testament cita-tions to prove Christ is presently on David's throne (1 Chron. 28:5; 29:23; 2 Chron. 9:8)[13] are unconvincing, because in each case, the Old Testament context clarifies that "the throne of the LORD" is on earth, not in heaven. The plain fact about Revelation 3:21 is that it distinguishes between two thrones, the Father's and Christ's. To ignore this is to ignore the obvious: One is in heaven, so the other must be on earth in the future.[14]

Revelation 5:5 and 22:16 are other reminders of the book's continuity with Old Testament promises to David that his descendant would someday rule from his throne. "The lion who is of the tribe of Judah, the root of David," appears in the throne-room scene, introducing the seven-sealed book (5:5). The titles "lion of the tribe of Judah" (cf. Gen. 49:9) and "the root of David" (cf. Isa. 11:1, 10) betoken Christ's strength and headship in the final Davidic kingdom. "The root and offspring of David" (Rev. 22:16) cast Christ in his role of both ancestor and descen-

---

[12]Blaising and Bock, *Progressive Dispensationalism*, 183–84.

[13]Ibid., 312–13.

[14]Interestingly, another progressive dispensationalist who thinks Christ is already on David's throne sides with dispensationalists in proposing that he is not yet ruling, basing his theory on the promise in 3:21 that overcomers will rule on that *future* throne with him (Robert L. Saucy, *The Case for Progressive Dispensationalism: The Interface Between Dispensational and Non-Dispensational Theology* [Grand Rapids: Zondervan, 1993], 73, 282–83).

dant of David. In his preincarnate state he began the Davidic economy, and in his incarnate state, at his second coming, he will climax it. He will fulfill all the messianic promises associated with the Davidic line.[15]

Preterist and idealist views of Revelation spiritualize the promises regarding David's descendant and so have no future role for him to play at his second advent.

4. Futurity of Revelation 1:7

Another distinguishing mark of a literal approach to Revelation is its handling of the theme verse of the book, 1:7. The verse is a conflation of Daniel 7:13 and Zechariah 12:10. "Behold, he comes with the clouds" draws from Daniel's vision in which he saw the future coming of the Son of Man to rule the world in an unending kingdom (Dan. 7:14, 27). "Every eye will see him, even those who pierced him, and all the families of the earth will mourn over him" alludes to Zechariah 12:10, 12, 14. The Zechariah context describes the future repentance of Israel in the day when the Lord restores Jerusalem and the nation to its promised supremacy.

Jesus' use of this same conflation in Matthew 24:30 to describe his second coming supplies additional confirmation to Revelation's use of it to anticipate the details surrounding his return to earth to establish his kingdom. It speaks of his *future* coming, not a coming that lies in the past.

A progressive dispensationalist will probably agree with the above, as will an idealist, but at least some preterists refer the verse to the judgment of God against the Jewish nations in A.D. 70.[16] By using several Old Testament references to clouds associated with the judgment of God (e.g., Ps. 18:7–15; 104:3; Isa. 19:1; Joel 2:1–2; Nah. 1:2ff.; Zeph. 1:14–15), they conclude that 1:7 is not a personal coming of Christ but rather a nonpersonal coming of God in judgment.[17]

---

[15]Stephen J. Nichols ("The Dispensational View of the Davidic Kingdom: A Response to Progressive Dispensationalism," *The Master's Seminary Journal* 7/2 [Fall 1996]: 213–39) documents this view of the Davidic throne and kingdom as being a central feature of traditional dispensationalism.

[16]E.g., David Chilton, *The Days of Vengeance: An Exposition of the Book of Revelation* (Ft. Worth, Tex.: Dominion, 1987), 64; Kenneth L. Gentry Jr., *Before Jerusalem Fell: Dating the Book of Revelation* (Tyler, Tex.: Institute for Christian Economics, 1989), 131–32.

[17]E.g., Gentry, *Before Jerusalem Fell*, 123.

This preterist view of 1:7 creates numerous problems, however. It requires the writing of Revelation before A.D. 70, a dating that runs counter to early church tradition (that it was written in the 90s). It also creates several unsolvable interpretive dilemmas within the verse itself, not to mention elsewhere in the book: inconsistency regarding the identity of "those who pierced him," "the tribes of the earth," and "the land [or earth]."[18] Are they limited to Jews and their land, or do they include Romans and the rest of the world? A preterist must contradict himself on these issues to have a past fulfillment of 1:7. They cannot limit "those who pierced him" to Jews only and elsewhere include the Romans as objects of Christ's "cloud coming." They cannot limit "the tribes of the earth [or land]" to Israel only, because in this case Zechariah 12:10ff. would require the mourning to be one of repentance, not of despair (as their interpretation holds). Their acknowledged worldwide scope of Revelation as a whole rules out their limitation of "the land" to Palestine in this verse.

Interpreting 1:7 at face value to speak of Christ's future coming and the events surrounding it fits into the dispensational framework. When he returns, all will see him, especially those of Jewish extraction whose ancestors were so close to the events of his crucifixion. That will generate tears of despair for unredeemed humanity as he judges an unrepentant world with a severity unparalleled in history. Remaining chapters of Revelation elaborate on that punishment.

5. The Threefold Division Based on 1:19

Dispensationalists generally use a literal interpretation of 1:19 as an outline for Revelation. "The things you have seen" refers naturally to John's preliminary vision of the glorified Christ in chapter 1. "The things that will happen after these things" refers naturally to 4:1–22:5, the section framed by *ha dei genesthai* ("things that must happen"; see discussion above). Revelation 2–3 naturally constitutes "the things which are," that is, conditions presently prevailing as typified by seven churches of Asia. In 1:19 John received a commission to write, based on what he had learned of Christ in his initial vision (chap. 1), to seven churches

---

[18]Robert L. Thomas, "Theonomy and the Dating of Revelation," *The Master's Seminary Journal* 5/2 (Fall 1994): 190–92.

whose conditions are typical of churches throughout the age till the church's rapture (chaps. 2–3) about future events on earth connected with Christ's establishment of his kingdom (chaps. 4–22).

Some progressive dispensationalists perhaps agree with that outline,[19] but preterists and idealists are more likely to see the various sections of the book as interminglings of past, present, and future. Some interpreters have taken 1:19 to denote one unbroken division in the book, or two divisions (comprised of chapters 1–3 and 4–22), as well as the three divisions outlined above. Yet the symmetry of the commission in which three relative clauses, each introduced by the same word, connect with each other by the simple conjunction *kai* ("and") argues persuasively for three divisions rather than one or two. Further, the past tense of "you have seen" in 1:19 and the relationship of "the things that will happen after these things" with "the things that must happen after these things" of 4:1 give further corroboration to the threefold division.

The words "will happen" in 1:19 translate a combination of words (*mellei genesthai*) that always expresses imminence. The third division (4:1–22:5) may commence at any moment, terminating the period of "the things that are" (chaps. 2–3).[20]

6. The Jews in 2:9 and 3:9

Two churches in Asia were experiencing persecution at the hands of a group calling themselves "Jews," the one at Smyrna (2:9) and the other at Philadelphia (3:9). In Smyrna pressure took the form of slander that exposed Christians to the penalties of civil law, probably the accusation of political disloyalty to Rome. Jesus denied that the accusers were Jews in the true sense of the word; they have rather allied them with the synagogue of Satan.

Strangely, some have spiritualized the name "Jew" and made it refer to people of all racial backgrounds who claimed they were Jews inwardly. They contend that Christians are "the

---

[19]In a companion chapter of this volume progressive C. Marvin Pate opts for a twofold outline because of his preunderstanding of an "already/not yet" hermeneutical key, through which he interprets the book. This illustrates how one's preunderstanding, if allowed in the hermeneutical process, influences the interpretation of Scripture.

[20]The discussion below, "The Twofold Coming of Christ in 3:10–11," will elaborate on this feature of the book.

Israel of God" (Gal. 6:16) and that real Jews are those who worship by the Spirit of God and glory in Christ Jesus (cf. Phil. 3:3).[21] This mode of identification is void of exegetical support in the New Testament. Besides this, if they called themselves "the Israel of God" in that mystical sense, they would be the church, and why would the church be the principal source of calumny against the church in this city? Why would a person who is not a physical descendant of Abraham claim Jewish lineage and then turn to persecuting fellow-Christians without recanting his claim? Obviously, he would not, so the self-professed "Jews" in Smyrna must have descended physically from Abraham.

The persecution of Christians by those of Jewish physical lineage is a well-known phenomenon in the New Testament (cf. Acts 13:50; 14:2, 5, 19; 17:5; 26:2; 1 Thess. 2:14–15). Jesus denies the title "Jews" to them, however, identifying them instead with the synagogue of Satan, as he did his Jewish opponents in John 8:31–47. The New Testament elsewhere denies the title to Abraham's physical lineage if they are not inwardly Abraham's *spiritual* descendants (cf. Matt. 3:9; Rom. 2:28–29; 2 Cor. 11:22; Phil. 3:4ff.). Only a literal understanding of the term for "Jews" in Revelation 2:9 will suffice, and that is the dispensational view.

A similar scenario ensues in the Philadelphian message (3:9), where the self-claim of the church's persecutors is that "they themselves are Jews." As before, some take this to mean that the ancestral title "Jew" has passed to the Christian church and that the associated racial succession has passed to Christianity.[22] In denying the false claim to the title in 3:9, Christ endorsed no such change. He simply denied that, because of their spiritual state, this particular group of Abraham's descendants deserved that recognition. A true Jew is a Jew who recognizes Jesus as the Messiah; a false Jew is one who rejects Jesus as the Messiah and, in this case, also rejects those who believe in Jesus. This is the literal meaning of the words—the way dispensationalism understands them.

---

[21]E.g., Homer Hailey, *Revelation, an Introduction and Commentary* (Grand Rapids: Baker, 1970), 126.

[22]E.g., James Moffatt, "The Revelation of St. John the Divine," *Expositor's Greek Testament*, ed. W. Robertson Nicoll (Grand Rapids: Eerdmans, n.d.), 5:367.

7. The Twofold Coming of Christ in 3:10–11

Revelation 3:10–11 includes references to two types of action Christ will take when he returns and illustrates references to his coming in five of the other six messages. "I will come soon" extends an encouragement to the persecuted Philadelphian church. "Soon" (*tachy*, which some mistakenly refer to the speed of his coming [i.e., "quickly"]) refers to the timing of his coming. The speed of his coming would provide no consolation to John's readers, but the timing, "soon," does. Revelation and the rest of the New Testament teach an attitude that expects Jesus to return imminently, that is, at any moment. "Imminence" means "ready to take place,"[23] or in a biblical context, no biblical prophecy remains to be fulfilled prior to the predicted happening. The proper Christian perspective accepts the possibility that Jesus' return could occur at any moment. That is the prospect encouraged in "I will come soon," a welcome one for a church under severe persecution because his return would mean relief from suffering.

On the basis of this coming for deliverance, Jesus promised the church to preserve them in a location away from the scene of "the hour of trial" (3:10). In the combination *tērēsō ek* ("I will keep from"), the verb speaks of preservation and the preposition speaks of an outside position. In other words, Christ's promise amounts to a promise of protection in a position outside the time period known as "the hour of trial." A promise to preserve the faithful church as it experienced the hour of trial would have been no promise at all. Though they could remain present on earth and be immune to the wrath of God, they would not be free from the persecutions and martyrdom at the hands of the beast during that period. The latter abuses were also well-known aspects of that future period. For them to escape their present persecution only to fall prey to more severe beast-inflicted sufferings would offer no incentive for persevering any longer. Yet Christ urges them to persevere because of their imminent deliverance from *all* suffering.

The other aspect of Christ's coming surfaces in the words "the hour of trial that is about to come upon the whole inhabited

---

[23]*Merriam-Webster's Collegiate Dictionary*, 10th ed. (Springfield, Mass.: Merriam-Webster, 1993), 580.

earth" (3:10). That refers to the coming of Christ to punish a world in rebellion against God. "The hour of trial" has "the whole inhabited earth" as its object[24] and identifies with the period of judgment on earth described in chapters 4–20. It is the seventieth week of the Daniel 9:24–27 prophecy and the opening phase of the Day of the Lord, and it includes as its last half the Great Tribulation. The Jews know it as the period of "messianic woes." It is a period to test the wicked and hopefully lead them to repentance, but if not, to punish them for failure to repent.

This punitive aspect of Christ's coming is also imminent, as indicated by the words "that is about to" (*tēs mellousēs*). The verb indicates that the coming of "the hour of trial" could happen at any moment. Just as the faithful derive encouragement from Christ's imminent deliverance, the unrepentant face the dread of his imminent judgment, which could begin "in the twinkling of an eye." Townsend concurs: "Both the coming of the hour [of testing] and the coming of the Lord are imminent. . . . There will be preservation outside the imminent hour of testing for the Philadelphian church when the Lord comes."[25]

Other portions in the seven messages confirm these two aspects of Christ's coming. References to his coming for judgment beginning with "the hour of trial" include 2:5, 16; 3:3 (cf. 2:22; 3:16). Someone might object that these are not *personal* comings of Christ, just as the A.D. 70 destruction of Jerusalem was not a personal coming. Yet the other major interpretation of these comings refers them to special comings in judgment against individual churches early in the Christian era and does not see them as personal comings either. In other words, no interpretation of 2:5, 16; 3:3 understands them to be personal comings of Christ.

The advantage of understanding 2:5, 16; 3:3 to be eschatological comings to initiate "the hour of trial" is that his personal coming will *climax* that period of temporal judgments on earth.

---

[24]In his chapter of this volume Pate limits "the inhabitants of the world" in 3:10 to only "the inhabitants of the land [Palestine]." Perhaps he has overlooked the parallelism of the "earthdwellers" in that verse with "the whole inhabited earth." The scope of judgment under the seals, bowls, and trumpets is worldwide, not localized. In his companion chapter of this volume, Gentry locates the wrathful visitations of God in the land of Israel too. That is inadequate to explain the far-reaching consequences of the judgments.

[25]Jeffrey L. Townsend, "The Rapture in Revelation 3:10," *When the Trumpet Sounds*, eds. Thomas Ice and Timothy Demy (Eugene, Ore.: Harvest, House, 1995), 377.

The fact that he personally is the initiator of the seal, trumpet, and bowl judgments (6:1ff.) also favors allowing that these passages do speak of his coming to do the same. Those are characteristics that distinguish the comings from an alleged coming in A.D. 70 and from special comings to individual churches early in the Christian era—proposals that offer no connection to his personal involvement.

Other references to Christ's coming for deliverance include 2:25 and 3:20 (cf. 3:10). His promise provides encouragement for the faithful in the churches who face opposition of one type or another.[26] These receive the promise of preservation in a location away from the earthly scene of "the hour of trial" (3:10). The church at Philadelphia faced severe suffering as the Lord addressed these words to them. To promise them protection from God's judgment and then have them experience "the hour of trial" would have been ridiculous, because it was well known that saints who will live under the end-time regime of the beast will suffer more than any before them, even to the point of martyrdom (e.g., 13:7). For Christ's promise in 3:10 to have any substance, it must mean he will take them away from the scene before it begins (3:11).

Preterism uses the "soonness" of Christ's coming to prove a writing of Revelation in the 60s and fulfillment of much of the book's prophecies by A.D. 70.[27] Placing a time limit on "soon" is, however, unwarranted. Jesus taught against pinpointing the time of his return (e.g., Matt. 24:36, 42, 44; 25:13) as did Paul (e.g., 1 Thess. 5:1–2). He could have returned by 70, but he did not. God has not been pleased to reveal how long it will be. So far "soon" has extended to over 1900 years, but God's people still must anticipate an any-moment return of Christ. In other words, the "soon" teaches an attitude rather than sets a time limit. Nineteen hundred years may not seem to be "soon" for humans, but they must accept God's lesson about expecting Christ's coming to be near.

8. Telescoping of the Seals, Trumpets, and Bowls

Another feature of a dispensational view dictated by grammatical-historical interpretation of Revelation is the structure

---

[26]For a fuller discussion of Christ's coming in Revelation 2–3, see Robert L. Thomas, "The 'Comings' of Christ in Revelation 2–3," *The Master's Seminary Journal* 7/2 (Fall 1996): 153–81.

[27]Gentry, *Before Jerusalem Fell*, 133–45.

of three series: seals, trumpets, and bowls. Strongest evidence points to a telescopic or "dovetailing" relationship under which the seven trumpets comprise the seventh seal and the seven bowls comprise the seventh trumpet. The other main option, a theory of recapitulation, has each of the seven series covering the same period from a different perspective.[28]

A theory of recapitulation is weak because it impairs the organic unity of 4:1–22:5 by separating the trumpets and bowls from the seven-sealed scroll introduced in chapter 5. It also fails to account for the increasing intensity of judgments from seals to trumpets to bowls. A telescopic approach, on the other hand, explains the absence of an immediate outworking of wrath on earth after the opening of the seventh seal (8:1) and blowing of the seventh trumpet (11:15). Further, it explains the mounting intensity of wrath as the account progresses into the period and the storm theophany in conjunction with the seventh member of each series (8:5; 11:19; 16:18). Though each series has a different beginning, all three end simultaneously—that is, with the events of the seventh bowl. That last bowl is the last of the seven last plagues (15:1), a feature that distinguishes it from the nature of the seventh seal and seventh trumpet. The telescoping view allows for this difference.

Telescoping does not fit well with preterism and idealism, because those theories prefer the liberty to "skip around" through history, finding events that fit various parts of Revelation's description—events that are not chronologically sequential, as telescoping requires. For example, preterists cannot fit the seven last plagues (15:1) into the time connected with Christ's second coming; they must connect them with the destruction of Jerusalem in A.D. 70.[29] Idealists cannot handle telescoping for a different reason: They want a given account in Revelation to refer to several different times in history. Typically, they do not want to limit "the great city" of 11:8 to any one location, but to designate all cities that have opposed the Lord through the centuries.[30]

---

[28]For a full discussion of the two views of Revelation's structure, see Robert L. Thomas, *Revelation 8–22*, 525–43. Recapitulation is the structural scheme proposed by Gentry in a companion chapter of this book.

[29]E.g., Chilton, *Days of Vengeance*, 383–84.

[30]Leon Morris, *The Revelation of St. John* (TNTC; Grand Rapids: Eerdmans, 1969), 150; Sam Hamstra Jr., "An Idealist View of Revelation," in his section on "Babylon" in this book.

The telescopic structure of Revelation fits the seven last plagues and "the great city" into the future period just before Christ returns. Some try to combine futurism in the Apocalypse with idealism and find themselves emphasizing the artistic qualities of the text to the point of questioning its logical coherence.[31] But the book is at no point irrational. It appealed to John's reason and that of his initial audience in the seven churches, and it still makes good sense.

A dispensational understanding of Revelation's structure, therefore, sees an ongoing chronological framework represented in the telescoping of the seals, trumpets, and bowls.

9. Correlation of the First Six Seals with the Olivet Discourse

Dispensationalism pays special attention to the way the first six seals of Revelation 6 follow the pattern of Jesus' Olivet Discourse (Matt. 24–25/Mark 13/Luke 21). This correspondence makes sense because Christ is the revealer in both instances. What he revealed by direct teaching in that discourse to the twelve disciples, he revealed in a symbolic mode to John some sixty-five years later, furnishing a more detailed portrayal in the latter. In the discourse he divided the period just before his return into two parts, the beginning of birth pangs (Matt. 24:8) and the Great Tribulation (24:21). He separated the two with the "abomination of desolation" (24:15), implying that the two parts compose the two halves of the seventieth week of the Daniel's prophecy in Daniel 9:24–27. The beginning of birth pangs parallels the first six seals, the first four of them very closely.

The first seal portrays a rider on a white horse, who represents a growing movement of anti-Christian and false Christian forces at work early in the period. Details of the seal's description indicate that this movement will succeed in creating peaceful conditions by uniting the world without bloodshed. This description matches well with Christ's words in Matthew 24:5: "Many will come in my name, saying, 'I am the Christ,' and will deceive many." Their outward success on the world scene will set the stage for the second seal.

The opening of the second seal reveals a rider on a fiery red horse—a picture of war, internal discord, and international and

---

[31]Cf. Thomas, *Revelation 1–7*, 32–35.

civil strife in the world. Here is another set of forces, this time one that receives power to take peace from the earth and generate warlike conditions everywhere. This development corresponds with Jesus' prophecy of Matthew 24:6–7: "You will hear of wars and rumors of wars. .... Nation will rise against nation and kingdom against kingdom." He included with this prediction the phrase from Daniel 2:28 that John has used to designate the contents of Revelation, *dei genesthai* ("they must happen," Matt. 24:6, see "Continuity with Daniel 2," above).

The third seal has a rider on a black horse, representative of famine-inducing forces. Hunger is usually an aftermath of war, so the same will occur following the widespread warfare of the second seal. Jesus had predicted famines in his discourse on the Mount of Olives: "There will be famines" (Matt. 24:7). The sequence of predicted events represented in the seals continues to follow the sequence of Jesus' earlier discourse.

The rider on the pale green horse of the fourth seal brings word about the death of a fourth of the world's population through the sword, worsening famine, and pestilence and by the beasts of the earth. Jesus added pestilence to his list of coming threats in Luke's account of the Olivet Discourse (Luke 21:11), so the parallelism between the two prophecies continues. The fourfold cause of death under the forces of the pale green horse will take a huge toll of the world's population. This is still a continuation of "the beginning of birth pangs."

The next in the opening of consecutive seals (6:9–11) is different in character from the first four. The prayers of the martyrs for judgment against their persecutors assure God's vengeance against earth's rebels. The earthlings have already tasted a measure of judgment under the first four seals, but the worst for them is yet to come when God answers prayers of the faithful in the form of seven trumpets, which compose the seventh seal. The indirect hint of hardship yet to come for Christ's followers is latent in this seal, a feature that Jesus spoke about next in his Olivet Discourse: "Then they will deliver you to affliction and they will kill you, and you will be hated by all the nations for the sake of my name. And then many will be caused to stumble and will betray one another and hate one another" (Matt. 24:9–10). This too will occur during "the beginning of birth pangs."

The sixth seal tells of a great earthquake and widespread heavenly disturbances. These create international panic among the population, but are not identical with similar phenomena that Jesus predicted at the end of the seven-year period (Matt. 24:29). In this case, people have opportunity to flee and hide, something they will be unable to do at Christ's second advent. This manifestation of divine wrath comes just before the abomination of desolation of 24:15 as part of "the beginning of birth pangs" (24:7) and includes "great signs from heaven," as Jesus taught earlier (Luke 21:11).

Demonstrating the futurity of these six seals, of course, depends on how one interprets the Olivet Discourse. Was Jesus speaking only of events prior to the destruction of Jerusalem, as the preterist holds?[32] That is hardly feasible in light of the remainder of the discourse, which refers to the future abomination of desolation (Matt. 24:15) and the future return of Christ (24:29–31). If Jesus spoke of events that were still future when John wrote Revelation in the 90s, events that apparently will come shortly before the abomination of desolation, then the time frame of the first six seals fits into the same period. It is clear from verses introductory to Matthew 24 that Jesus was prophesying about events that did not occur during the lifetime of those who were listening to him. He told them along with others just prior to this, "*You* shall in no way see me from now until *you* say, 'Blessed is the one who comes in the name of the Lord'" (23:39, italics added). Jerusalem did not so repent during the first century nor have they done so since then. Jesus must therefore have had his second advent in mind.

10. The Wrath of God in 6:16–17

Another significant characteristic of a dispensational view relates to the mention of God's wrath in 6:16–17. The words from earth's unrepentant population, terrified by the cataclysmic upheavals of the sixth-seal judgment, recognize the outpouring of God's wrath in the happenings they are witnessing. They go even further in their identification of the events as part of "the great day of their wrath" (6:17), none other than "the day of the LORD" spoken of so frequently in the Old Testament as a concomitant of the

---

[32]As indicated in Kenneth Gentry's companion chapter in this volume, the preterist finds no reference to Christ's second advent in Matthew 24. Nor does Gentry—though stating his belief in a second advent—find a reference to Christ's second coming anywhere in the book of Revelation.

Messiah's coming in judgment (e.g., Joel 2:11, 30–31; cf. Isa. 2:10–11, 19–21; 13:9–13; 34:4, 8; Ezek. 32:7–8; Hos. 10:8).

Jesus had earlier identified this day with the Great Tribulation in particular and the whole of Daniel's seventieth week in general (cf. Matt. 24:21 with Jer. 30:7; Dan. 12:1; Joel 2:2). It will be a period of prolonged agony, comparable to a woman's labor before giving birth (Isa. 13:8; 26:17–19; 66:7–9; Jer. 30:6–8; Mic. 4:9–10; cf. Matt. 24:8; 1 Thess. 5:3). The Messiah's personal return will climax that period of human torment (Matt. 24:29–30). The series of tribulation visitations and Armageddon are inseparable parts of "the day of the LORD."

The terror-stricken earthlings' analysis in Revelation 6:16–17 is correct: The arrival of the first-seal judgment is also the arrival of the day of the Lord. When in response to the sixth seal they say that the day "has come" (*ēlthen*), they are reflecting on what preceded the sixth seal (i.e., the first five seals). The severity of the sixth seal awakens them to the cause of other catastrophes that have preceded. They realize, perhaps for the first time, that the day of the Lord is in progress and that the wrath of God and of the Lamb has produced these miseries. The verb they use (*ēlthen*) cannot anticipate miseries yet future. It must refer to those already in progress.

Preterists and idealists can hardly subscribe to this kind of future specificity in the prophecy. The former finds a fulfillment in the A.D. 70 destruction of Jerusalem,[33] and the latter in any time the citizens in a fallen order "attempt to hide themselves from God in, beneath, and behind the broken pieces of their fallen world."[34] Preterism denies the continuing futurity of fulfillment, and idealism its specificity.

11. A Literal Understanding of the 144,000

A literal interpretation of the 144,000 servants of God in Revelation 7:3–8 sees them as ethnic Israel, physical descendants of Abraham, Isaac, and Jacob. Dispensationalists and probably progressive dispensationalists accept this meaning. Preterists and idealists, along with others of a covenantal orientation,

---

[33]Gentry, *Before Jerusalem Fell*, 130.

[34]M. Robert Mulholland Jr., *Revelation: Holy Living in an Unholy World* (Grand Rapids: Zondervan, 1990), 179.

interpret "Israel" in a nonliteral or symbolic sense, identifying the 144,000 as "spiritual Israel" or the church.[35] The best support they can muster for that identification is a number of New Testament passages that, so they claim, call the church "Israel." They also cite a variety of theological and logical reasons why the 144,000 must equate with the Christian community. The New Testament passages they use do not prove their point because the same questionable interpretation accompanies the other texts as is involved in this one. The theological and logical reasons fall short too, lacking a biblical rationale to support them.

The fact is, no clear-cut example of the church being called Israel exists in the New Testament, the first example in history appearing in about A.D. 160. The most-often cited text, Galatians 6:16, interpreted correctly, does not call the church "Israel"; the "Israel of God" in that verse is a group of Christian Jews within the church. The identification of the church with Israel in Revelation 7 creates a strange typological necessity for dividing the church into twelve tribes to coincide with the listings of 7:5–8. Such necessity is misconceived and violates seriously the context of Revelation 7.

The natural understanding and the normal usage of "Israel" in the New Testament identifies these as the Israel of the Old Testament, as physical descendants of Abraham, Isaac, and Jacob. It also explains their division into twelve tribes in 7:5–8, tribal distinctions lost insofar as human records are concerned but still fixed in the mind of God. It also provides for distinguishing them from the group introduced in 7:9, an innumerable multitude from all racial backgrounds. A number of possible objections to this position are philosophically feasible, but crumble under the scrutiny of biblical revelation.

Israel has not and will not lose her distinctive national identity before God, despite human proposals to the contrary. These 144,000 are not the entirety of the faithful remnant of Israel, but are a group of them charged with the special task of witnessing for Christ during the world's darkest hour. They eventually will suffer martyrdom for faithfulness to their task.

---

[35]In his companion chapter of this volume, Kenneth Gentry is an exception to this generality in that he identifies the 144,000 as Christian Jews, though he conceives of them as part of the church, not as separate from the church. Another preterist, David Chilton, seemingly equates the 144,000 with the church as a whole (*The Days of Vengeance*, 206–8).

12. A Literal Temple in 11:1ff.

Figurative interpretations of the temple in 11:1 have identified it as the church because the New Testament sometimes calls the church "the temple of God" (1 Cor. 3:16; 2 Cor. 6:16; Eph. 2:21; 1 Peter 3:5). This meaning appeals to idealists who have no room in their system for a future temple in Jerusalem for Jewish worship. Yet this understanding of the temple encounters serious obstacles, the most notable of which is, if the temple is the church, who are the worshipers who are measured along with the sanctuary and the altar? It entails an impossible combination of nonliteral interpretation with what is clearly literal. It is inconsistent and self-contradictory.

The only way out of this hopeless entanglement is to recognize a literal temple in Jerusalem to be rebuilt during the period just before Christ returns, allowing for a distinction between the temple and its worshipers. This coincides well with the future repentance of Israel and a reinstitution of Israel's national life that are taught in the broader context of Revelation.

One preterist interpreter agrees with the reference to a literal temple up to a certain point, arguing that 11:2 refers to the Herodian temple that was destroyed in A.D. 70.[36] Yet he contends that the same Greek word for "temple" (*naos*) has a figurative meaning in 11:1. His is a strange mixture of figurative and literal in consecutive verses, a mixture that he recognizes and tries to defend, but unconvincingly. He refers the temple and the altar to literal structures early in his discussion and to the spiritual temple of the church a few pages later.[37] His main problem lies in making it a literal temple of the past rather than one that belongs to the future.

The instructions for John to measure the temple, the altar, and the worshipers in 11:1 and not to measure the court outside in 11:2 lead into a divulging of information about the ministry of two witnesses in Jerusalem of the future in 11:3–13. A literal understanding of the passage fits the dispensational teaching of a future restoration of the Jewish nation.

13. Identity of the Woman in 12:1ff.

Revelation 12:1 illustrates how grammatical-historical (or "literal") interpretation recognizes figures of speech when the

---

[36]Gentry, *Before Jerusalem Fell*, 165–74.
[37]Ibid., 174; cf. Thomas, "Theonomy and the Dating of Revelation," 195–97.

author intended figurative language. The text designates "a woman clothed with the sun, and the moon was under her feet, and upon her head was a crown of twelve stars" as a "great sign in heaven." With that signal, the interpreter begins searching for keys to what the symbols mean and does not try to force the meaning of a literal woman.

Descriptions of the Virgin Mary in Isaiah 7:10–11, 14 and Matthew 1:18, 23 have inclined some toward that identification of the woman, but the symbolic language along with other factors contradicts the "Mary" interpretation. Various elements of the symbolism show a connection with Genesis 37:9–10, where the sun in Joseph's dream stood for Jacob, the moon for Rachel, and the eleven stars for the eleven sons of Israel (Joseph accounts for the missing star, i.e., eleven rather than twelve). Figures of Israel as a travailing woman in the Old Testament bolster this interpretation (Isa. 26:17–18; 66:7ff.; Jer. 4:31; 13:21; Mic. 4:10; 5:3) as does the reference to Israel's ark of the covenant in the verse just prior to Revelation 12:1 (11:19). The "Jewishness" of the context finds further support in references to the twelve tribes of Israel in 7:5–8 and 21:12 and to the temple and Jerusalem in 11:1–13. All these details point to identifying the woman as a symbol for national Israel.

To add to that symbolic meaning the idea that the woman also stands for the people of God in the New Testament is unjustified, however, because it merges members of the body of Christ with the physical descendants of Abraham. No one has proven that alleged continuity in Scripture. In fact, should such exist, it would contradict the ethnic identity of Israel that clearly exists in the pages of the Apocalypse. The distinctiveness of Israel has already surfaced in discussions of 2:9; 3:9; 7:4–8. Besides, it would be impossible to regard the Jewish Messiah of 12:5 as a child of the Christian community, as he clearly is of the Jewish community.

Chapter 12 tells of the ongoing animosity of Satan toward Israel in general and toward her Messiah in particular. Most of the chapter anticipates a final showdown to come during the fulfillment of Daniel's seventy-week prophecy (Dan. 9:24–27), when Satan will be cast from heaven and will exercise his wrath against the woman and "the rest of her seed" (probably the 144,000). The account refers to the last half of that week several different ways, as "a thousand two hundred and sixty days"

(12:6), "a time and times and half a time" (12:14), and "forty-two months" (13:5). Chapter 13 continues the description of that clash as the dragon (Satan) raises the beast from the sea and the beast from the earth to persecute and martyr "the rest" of the woman's seed (13:7, 15).

14. The Beast of 13:1ff.

The characteristic dispensational view of Revelation also identifies the beast out of the sea in 13:1 with a future false-Christ type of figure, who will rise to world rulership just before Christ returns. The beast's description lends itself somewhat to seeing it as an aggregate of world empires, but the unified personal qualities of the beast determine that he must be a personal figure who heads such an empire. His number is that of a man (13:18). He is identified with one of his slain heads (13:3, 6), who is a travesty of the slain Lamb. Both have followers with their leader's name on their foreheads (13:16–17; 14:1). Both have horns (5:6; 13:1). Both rise after being slain (13:3, 8) to new life and authority over the whole world (1:5; 7:9; 13:7; 17:12). Because chapter 13 continues the description of chapter 12, this beast has to be a malevolent person who will embody satanic forces in controlling the final world empire—probably a revived form of the Roman empire of the past—in the role of a counterfeit Christ, who will deceive earth's inhabitants.

An alternative to this literal interpretation of the text's symbolism has offered the Roman empire as the beast's identity, a view that usually connects the seven hills of 17:9 with the Roman empire. Rome, of course, was the immediate oppressor in John's exile on Patmos. The Rome view identifies the wounded head as Nero Caesar (13:3) and explains the number 666 in 13:18 as the number of his name.[38] A problem with this approach is that no phase of the Roman empire of the past can fully satisfy the textual criteria regarding the beast. More obviously, the beast is not just an empire, as the description of 13:3–

---

[38]In his chapter on the progressive dispensational reading of Revelation, Pate comes close to the preterist understanding of the beast, which finds fulfillment of the prophecy by Nero in the 60s. As indicated in my main discussion and elsewhere in this chapter, this creates a hopeless dilemma, particularly regarding the date the book of Revelation was written.

8 clearly shows; rather, it is a created person. Besides this, he belongs to the future, not to the past.[39]

A dispensational understanding of the beast allows also for John's allusions to Daniel 7 in his description of the beast. The seven heads represent seven consecutive world empires: Egypt, Assyria, Babylon, Medo-Persia, Greece, Rome, and the empire of the beast, of which Daniel's four beasts include Babylon, Medo-Persia, Greece, and Rome. The seven kings of 17:10 represent these empires. The ten horns, the same as those of Daniel's fourth beast (Dan. 7:7, 24), portray ten kings who will act as simultaneous subrulers under the beast's authority (cf. 17:12).

Preterists and idealists generally deny the futurity of the beast and attempt explanations relating him to the past or present.

15. The Futurity of Babylon in Revelation 17–18

The identity of Babylon, mentioned first in 14:8 and then discussed fully in 16:19 and 17:1–18:24, has been a puzzle for interpreters. Preterists incline to see the name as a code word for Jerusalem.[40] This goes with their problematic dating of the book before the fall of Jerusalem in A.D. 70. Besides having no ground for assuming symbolism in the name, the view lacks contextual foundation.

A common explanation of "Babylon" views it as a way Christians had of disguising references they made to Rome.[41] Supposedly Peter used Babylon in this sense in 1 Peter 5:13, and others, including John in these passages, followed him. This use of the name, however, is purely speculative, having only two extrabiblical works to support it (*Sibylline Oracles* 5.143, 159, 434; *Apocalypse of Baruch* 11:1; 67:7), both written in the second century long after the writing of Revelation and therefore reflecting a Christian usage later than John's time. Couple this with the probability that Peter in his first letter referred to Babylon on the Euphrates rather than to Rome, and the "Rome" identification is weak. A correct interpretation of the "seven hills" in 17:9

---

[39] Incidentally, explaining 666 as the number of Nero Caesar's name is also fraught with problems.

[40] Chilton, *Days of Vengeance*, 362; Joseph R. Balyeat, *Babylon, the Great City of Revelation* (Sevierville, Tenn.: Onward, 1991), 69–142.

[41] E.g., Henry Barclay Swete, *The Apocalypse of St. John* (Grand Rapids: Eerdmans, n.d.), 183.

identifies them with kingdoms, not a topographical feature of the city of Rome.

John used city names in Revelation 1–3, all in a nonfigurative sense. When he does use a city name figuratively, he makes that clear (see 11:8). The best solution is faithfulness to literal interpretation—that is, identifying Babylon as the city on the Euphrates River. In fact, Revelation mentions that river twice, both times in a literal sense (9:14; 16:12). The imposing influence of that city and its dominance in world affairs are major considerations during the period just before Christ returns to judge her. Literal Babylon's visibility may be minimal at a given time in history, but the city could rise to world prominence very quickly.

In its treatment of Babylon, progressive dispensationalism joins forces with the idealist in recommending "multilayered" meanings of the text. It suggests that Babylon may stand for both Rome and a rebuilt Babylon and that its references may refer to "the sweep of history."[42] In fact, it observes that the world empire's center is always shifting, so Babylon conceivably could stand for any city. This reading of the text furnishes another illustration of an interpretive weakness and departure from grammatical-historical interpretation, which limits each passage to a single meaning. Babylon either refers only to a world capital of the future or it does not. It cannot include past, present, and future, or else Scripture loses its specificity. This is not to say that Scripture is void of applications to every age, but simply to point out that a single and exclusive interpretation limits those applications.[43]

Progressives use a "special case" rationale to justify interpreting the Apocalypse by principles different from the rest of

---

[42]Blaising and Bock, *Progressive Dispensationalism*, 93–96. The "layered" approach to interpreting Revelation comes close to that of amillennialist Poythress, who proposes four levels of communication in the symbolism of Revelation (Vern S. Poythress, "Genre and Hermeneutics in Rev 20:1–6," *JETS* 36 [1993]: 41–43). In another chapter in this volume, progressive dispensationalist Pate combines his progressive dispensationalism with the preterist approach when he identifies the harlot Babylon with Jerusalem. This further illustrates progressive dispensationalism's freedom in assigning "multilayered" meanings to a single text.

[43]Another similarity of progressive dispensationalism to idealism appears in the way it denies that specific identification of the locusts of Rev. 9:1–10 is possible. It says that they are symbols for "moving destructive forces on the earth connected with Satan" (Blaising and Bock, *Progressive Dispensationalism*, 92).

the Bible, appealing to its apocalyptic genre as a basis for relying more heavily on symbolism.[44] Their failure to appreciate the book's primary character as a prophecy brings an uncalled-for vagueness and a sort of "shotgun" approach to the book. Their conclusion about a threefold meaning of Babylon in Revelation illustrates this. They make Babylon representative in regard to the genealogical relationship of world empires, a future worldwide rebellion against God, and the evils of Babylon and the present.[45] This diversification of interpretations blunts the pointed focus of the prophecy on the future.

Preterism reflects its departure from literal interpretation in its handling of 17:9–11. Using the "seven hills" to prove the Roman empire is in view,[46] it concludes that the seven kings of 17:9 (17:10 in English versions) are seven consecutive Roman emperors, the sixth of whom is Nero Caesar.[47] As pointed out above, however, the seven hills refer to the scope and nature of the beast's power, not to the physical layout of a city. Even stranger is preterism's futile attempt to explain why John talks about Rome in a chapter devoted to discussing Jerusalem, which that system takes to be the meaning of Babylon. Its theory of an alliance between Jerusalem and Rome against Christianity belies the fact of Rome's prolonged siege and destruction of Jerusalem between the late 60s and 70. Its theory meets further complications in juggling the Roman emperors to make Nero Caesar the sixth of them.

The key to explaining 17:9 is to see the seven heads and mountains as seven successive empires, with the seven kings of verse 10 as seven kings who are both heads and personifications of those empires. This agrees with the common connotation of a mountain or hill in the Bible and with another biblical practice of equating kingdoms with the kings that rule them (Dan. 7:17, 23). As in the listing of empires above under "The Beast of 13:1ff.," Rome is the sixth of those seven empires—"one is" (17:10)—but the seven mountains or hills have no reference to the city's topography. Of the seven kings (i.e., seven kingdoms), five have fallen (17:10): Egypt, Assyria, Babylon, Persia, and

[44]Ibid., 90–91.
[45]Ibid., 95–96.
[46]Gentry, *Before Jerusalem Fell*, 149–51.
[47]Ibid., 151–59.

Greece. "One is," from John's perspective the empire existing during his lifetime (Rome). "The other has not yet come" because it is the empire of the beast yet future.

Tracing John's explanation into verse 11, one learns how the beast "who was and is not" can be the eighth as well as one of the seven. The focus returns to the king rather than his kingdom. He can be the eighth and still be one of the seven by virtue of the healing of his death wound (13:3, 12, 14).[48]

In other words, the interpreter who is faithful to grammatical-historical principles of interpretation finds a purely futuristic reference in 17:9–11 in particular and chapters 17–18 in general.

16. The Millennial Kingdom of 20:1–10

Dispensationalism and progressive dispensationalism part ways abruptly from preterist and idealist interpretations of Revelation in dealing with 20:1–10. The former two understand the verses to speak of a future kingdom on earth, in contrast with the latter two, which envision a past or present fulfillment of the passage. This categorizes the former as premillennial in their outlook and the latter as postmillennial or amillennial, because of the timing of Christ's second coming relative to the millennium in 20:1–10. "Premillennial" means he comes before, "postmillennial" means after, and "amillennial" means there is or will be no specific thousand-year period as such.

Grammatical-historical exegesis of chapter 20 dictates that the kingdom portrayed therein will be future. Several considerations provide cumulative weight to this conclusion. (1) The verses constitute the fourth and fifth scenes of the seventh bowl judgment (16:17), which is the last of the seven last plagues (15:1). The judgment consists of eight scenes, each introduced by "and I saw" (*kai eidon*): the second coming of Christ (19:11–16), the summons of the birds to a human feast (19:17–18), the slaughter of Christ's human opponents (19:19–21), Satan's imprisonment (20:1–3), Satan's release and final defeat (20:4–10), the setting of the Great White Throne (20:11), the sentencing to the lake of fire (20:12–15), the sketch of the new Jerusalem (21:1–8). For these to be the "last" in the series of God's last judgments, they all must be future.

---

[48]For a more detailed explanation of 17:9–11, see Thomas, *Revelation 8–22*, 295–98.

(2) One of these judgment scenes entails the binding of Satan during the Millennium (20:1–3). A perusal of the scenes reveals they are chronologically arranged, placing the binding after the second coming of Christ. Furthermore, Satan's binding and imprisonment incapacitate him completely for a thousand years, necessitating a future fulfillment. The only way one could locate his binding during the present is to limit it to a curtailing of his activities,[49] but his penalty involves more than that. Not only is he in prison, the abyss, but chains such as are necessary to contain a spiritual being keep him under absolute control. His activities cease completely. Such a total cessation is unknown in history until Christ returns. But even if he were bound during the era until Christ returns, what would his release after the thousand years mean (20:7)?[50] It would coincide with the return of Christ and have no meaning at all.

(3) The relation of Satan's consignment to the lake of fire *after* the Millennium (20:7–10) and that of the beast and false prophet *before* the Millennium (19:20) require the Millennium to be future. Christ assigns the beast and false prophet to that doom in conjunction with his second advent (19:11–20). When he assigns Satan there, it is after the passage of a thousand years (20:7), and he joins the beast and false prophet who are *already*

---

[49]If someone were to propose that Satan is bound and in prison but that his demons are still on the loose, producing their havoc of evil during present era, that explanation would meet at least two objections: (1) Most obvious, 1 Peter 5:8 indicates Satan is, during the present age, roaming around like a lion seeking someone to devour. That nullifies the notion that he is currently in prison. (2) Demons without a leader cannot equal the damage that Satan's organized kingdom can inflict when their leader is available to give direction. His kingdom cannot stand without a leader any better than it can if it were divided against itself (cf. Matt. 12:26). Scripture does not specify the location and/or activity of demons while Satan is in prison, but presumably they will not be able to conduct organized campaigns of evil without him available to direct them.

[50]Elsewhere in this volume, Hamstra has suggested that the release of Satan after the one thousand years leads to the Great Tribulation, symbolized by the battle of Gog and Magog in 20:7–10. Yet those verses are inappropriate to describe the Great Tribulation, a period that begins with the abomination of desolation (Matt. 24:15, 21). These verses do not mention the abomination of desolation or unparalleled distress on earth, nor do they speak of a period of a significant length such as will comprise the Great Tribulation. They rather refer to a single great confrontation in which Satan and his forces meet their defeat as the result of a fiery judgment from heaven. The verses contain no mention of a personal coming of Christ; they refer

there (20:10). The text is explicit that the Millennium follows the return of Christ.

(4) Two occurrences of the verb *ezēsan* ("they lived," "they came to life") in 20:4–5 offer compelling evidence of the Millennium's futurity. In verse 4 that word depicts the resurrection of martyrs, who will reign with Christ for a thousand years. According to verse 5, the resurrection of the rest of the dead does not come until a thousand years later. Two resurrections separated by a thousand years must be future, because except for Christ's resurrection, no one has yet risen from the dead and remained alive. Efforts to circumvent this obvious teaching of the text have included suggestions that the resurrection of verse 4 is a spiritual one or is a coded apocalyptic symbol for the martyrs' reward. These falter under careful exegetical scrutiny, however. How can the same word in consecutive verses used conspicuously in the same sense denote different kinds of "resurrections"? Of course, it cannot.

In light of strong proof of the Millennium's futurity, it is not surprising to find even nonpremillenarians admitting they must resort to other Scriptures or theological systems that allegedly support their nonpremillennial views of 20:1–10.[51] They cannot derive their meaning from this central text on the subject. Insofar as the rest of Revelation is concerned, the kingdom is always

---

only to direct punishment from heaven and the relegation of Satan to the lake of fire to which the beast and the false prophet will have been committed a thousand years earlier. A better perspective has the personal return of Christ coinciding with the beginning—not the end—of Satan's imprisonment as the chronological sequence of 19:11–20:3 dictates. For discussion of why the eight scenes mentioned in "(1)" above must be chronological, see Thomas, *Revelation 8–22*, 579–81.

[51]E.g., Chilton, *Days of Vengeance*, 493; William Hendriksen, *More Than Conquerors: An Interpretation of the Book of Revelation* (Grand Rapids: Baker, 1944), 222–26; Michael Wilcock, *The Message of Revelation* (Downers Grove, Ill.: InterVarsity, 1975), 181–82. George Ladd's statement is relevant: "Unless there is some reason intrinsic within the text itself which requires a symbolic interpretation, or unless there are other Scriptures which interpret a parallel prophecy in a symbolic sense, we are required to employ a natural, literal interpretation" (*Crucial Questions About the Kingdom of God* [Grand Rapids: Eerdmans, 1954], 141). The first part of Ladd's statement is valid, that is, "unless there is some reason within the text itself which requires a symbolic interpretation." The other part is not, that is, "unless there are other Scriptures which interpret a parallel prophecy in a symbolic sense." Inclusion of that latter hermeneutical principle is what distinguishes Ladd's historic premillennialism from literal interpretation and dispensationalism.

future. The kingdom of 1:9 is future; overcomers will rule the nations of earth with Christ in the future (2:26–27) and will join him sitting on David's future throne (3:21); the reign of the redeemed on earth in 5:10 is future. That is the consistent picture throughout the book.

Defining the nature of that future kingdom is where progressive dispensationalism departs from literal hermeneutics, however. True to the text of 20:1–10, dispensationalism understands the preeminence of Israel in the future kingdom. "The beloved city" in 20:9 is Jerusalem, the center of Jewish activity and the focus of world attention in the promised kingdom according to Old Testament promises (e.g., Isa. 2:2–4; 52:9–10; 56:7; 60:9, 14–15; 62:3; 66:18). At the end of the Millennium that city will be Satan's prime objective with his rebel army, because Israel will be leader among the nations.

Another indication of Israel's preeminence are the occurrences in 20:4, 6 of the name "Christ" unaccompanied by "Jesus" or any other name. The only other uses of that name alone in Revelation (11:15; 12:10) are in passages that allude to Psalm 2, the first two verses of which read, "Why do the nations rage and the people devise a vain thing? The kings of the earth take their stand, and the rulers take counsel together against the LORD and against his Anointed." "Christ" transliterates the Greek term that means "Anointed," another name for the Jewish "Messiah." His future rule will fulfill God's promises to Israel. In the broader context of the whole book, allusions to his assumption of the Davidic throne (see above under "Continuity with the Davidic Covenant") and citations of the book's theme verse (see above under "Futurity of Revelation 1:7") bring further confirmation that this will be a kingdom of Israelite preeminence.

Progressive dispensationalists, however, indicate that they reject Jewish supremacy in the kingdom:

> A Jew who becomes a Christian today does not lose his or her relationship to Israel's future promises. Jewish Christians will join the Old Testament remnant of faith in the inheritance of Israel. Gentile Christians will be joined by saved Gentiles of earlier dispensations. All together, Jews and Gentiles, will share the same blessings of the Spirit, as testified to by the relationship of Jew and Gentile in the church of this dispensation. The result will be that all peoples will be reconciled in peace, their ethnic

and national differences being no cause for hostility. Earlier forms of dispensationalism, for all their emphasis on a future for Israel, excluded Jewish Christians from that future, postulating the church as a different people-group from Israel and Gentiles.[52]

These words apparently advocate an equality by which all the redeemed share equally in the same kingdom roles, with no distinction between Israel and the body of Christ.

This would mean that Israel will no longer be a special people and special recipients of the Old Testament promises made to them. Progressive dispensationalism broadens the promises to Israel to include those outside Israel and, in so doing, neglects the ongoing uniqueness of Abraham's descendants in God's plan. That approximates closely or even matches the picture of the Millennium painted by the nondispensational system of historic premillennialism, a picture that subordinates the role of Israel.[53] Historic premillennialism subordinates Israel by contending that Christ removed Israel's national prerogatives at his first advent—that is, a sort of demotion for national Israel. The progressive system subordinates that role by making non-Israelites recipients of the same promises that God gave to Israel—that is, a sort of promotion for non-Israelite believers. The result of both is the same. National Israel is no longer the special people of God. Needless to say, that representation of Israel's future role (or lack of it) results from a spiritualizing of the text, not only of 20:1–10 and the rest of the book, but also much of the Old and New Testaments.

Dispensationalism retains Israel's unique position at the forefront during the millennial kingdom because that is the position that grammatical-historical interpretation gives her.

17. The New Creation of 21:1ff.

Almost all evangelical viewpoints on Revelation allow for a new creation to follow the present creation. They include those which have no room for a future Millennium on earth, such as

[52]Blaising and Bock, *Progressive Dispensationalism*, 50.

[53]George Eldon Ladd, *A Commentary on the Revelation of John* (Grand Rapids: Eerdmans, 1972), 260–61; idem, *Crucial Questions*, 159–69; cf. John F. Walvoord, *The Revelation of Jesus Christ* (Chicago: Moody, 1966), 283.

the preterist and the idealist. A dispensationalist view accepts the new creation too, but places it after the future temporal kingdom of a thousand years on earth. Revelation 21:1–22:5 provides the most extensive biblical revelation about the new heaven and the new earth (cf. also Ps. 102:25–26; Isa. 24:23; 26:2; 51:6, 16; 54:11–12; 60:11, 19; 65:17; 66:22).

That new creation will be the scene of Christ's eternal kingdom, which will follow his temporal kingdom on the present earth. John's overview of the new creation constitutes the eighth and last scene of the seventh bowl judgment in 21:1–8. Though the bulk of the scene tells of future bliss and not judgment (21:1–7), the last verse (21:8) describes exclusion from the new creation because of God's relegation of the rebels to the lake of fire (cf. 20:12–15). An extensive elaboration regarding the new Jerusalem, the wonder of the new creation, follows in 21:9–22:5.

Some preterists doubt the future reference of 21:1ff., preferring to interpret it as a picture of the present age of the Christian church.[54] That view imposes a symbolic view of the language that violates the obvious chronological progression in Revelation's framework. At the same time, of course, it taxes beyond limits the grammatical-historical system of interpretation.

Progressive dispensationalism also argues for symbolism in Revelation's description of the new creation, but not to the extreme of the preterists.[55] It justifies a nonliteral interpretation on the basis of the book's apocalyptic imagery. It does not go so far as denying it is a prophecy of future reality, but questions the literality of specific features of the new Jerusalem. For example, because no oysters large enough to produce pearls of sufficient size exist, 21:21 cannot be literal because it says the twelve gates of the city will be pearls.[56] Also, because not enough gold is available to pave all the streets of such a large city, the same verse cannot be literal.[57] Yet these are paltry reasons for denying literality; the resources available to an infinite God to create such a city are beyond present comprehension. Far more materials are

---

[54]Chilton, *Days of Vengeance*, 538–45; see also Gentry's chapter in this volume.

[55]David L. Turner, "The New Jerusalem in Revelation 21:1–22:5: Consummation of a Biblical Continuum," *Dispensationalism, Israel, and the Church*, ed. Craig A. Blaising and Darrell L. Bock (Grand Rapids: Zondervan, 1992), 265, 275–78.

[56]Ibid., 277.

[57]Ibid.

available to him than humans of the present era can possibly comprehend.

Proper hermeneutics allow for the material existence of the new Jerusalem and do not explain it merely as a new level of ethics.[58] Dispensationalism allows for the material reality of the new creation as well as its ethical perfection, but acknowledges that its description is an accommodation to finite minds. The new heaven and the new earth will exceed human comprehension, because no human has yet experienced it. Unquestionably, the tangible aspects of the city's architecture have symbolic meaning, but that does not deny their materiality. An infinite God will create this city, illumined by his glory. An advanced preview found in this portion of Revelation is as much as humans can grasp in this life.

Another progressive theme attempts to eliminate Israel's distinctiveness in the eternal kingdom by positing just one people of God. This interpretation is strangely oblivious to the separate roles of Israel and the church as indicated in 21:12, 14. "Gates," representative of the twelve tribes of Israel, and "foundations," representative of the twelve apostles, serve a city in different ways. Turner acknowledges a difference in roles in suggesting that the gates are a symbol of access to salvation through Israel's covenants and the Messiah and the foundations are a symbol of the church's confession of the Lamb. But he turns immediately and refers to "the transdispensational continuity of Israel and the church as *the one people of God.*"[59]

Turner may or may not be correct about what the separate roles are; humanity will not fully understand the symbolism of the gates and foundations of the city until they arrive in the city. But separation of roles is a clear depiction of the continuing uniqueness of Israel and of the separateness of the church from Israel in God's plan. That distinctiveness of Israel is evident throughout the rest of the Bible, beginning in Genesis 12; and the church is separate from Israel throughout the New Testament. This will not change in Christ's eternal kingdom.

---

[58]Contra ibid., 278. Turner aligns his concept of the new Jerusalem with that of George Ladd (*The Presence of the Future* [Grand Rapids: Eerdmans, 1974], 62–64), well known for his nondispensational, historic premillennial eschatology.

[59]Ibid., 288 [italics added].

THE MAJOR ISSUE: HERMENEUTICAL SYSTEMS

Selected areas of discussion have illustrated the dispensational approach to Revelation and demonstrated the critical importance of one's hermeneutical system. The proposal has been that the system leading to dispensational conclusions is the grammatical-historical, sometimes called the literal. But recent discussions have raised questions about the nature of this time-honored system.

Perhaps all four views represented in this volume would claim to apply the method of grammatical-historical interpretation to Revelation. A comparison of the four interpretations reveals a good bit of diversity regarding what this type of interpretation is. It apparently is a label that has a changing meaning for some. Blaising speaks of "historical-grammatical"—the same as "grammatical-historical"—as a label that has "adaptability to the literary and historical developments in hermeneutics," such as the inclusion of the interpreter's preunderstanding in the interpretive process.[60] His "developments" are acknowledged changes in the hermeneutical process since an analysis of grammatical-historical interpretation in such time-honored works as the nineteenth-century definitive description of the method by Milton Terry.[61] Recent proposed changes in hermeneutical theory have resulted in the use of "grammatical-historical" to connote something different from what it once did.

On the basis of this change in meaning of "grammatical-historical," Blaising ventures his opinion that "the old divisions of spiritual versus literal interpretation have been left behind"

---

[60]Craig A. Blaising, "Dispensationalism: The Search for Definition," *Dispensationalism, Israel, and the Church*, 30–32. Pate's description of his hermeneutical key to Revelation illustrates how preunderstanding affects interpretation (see n. 19 above). In his chapter of the present volume, he identifies that key as "the 'already/not yet' eschatological tension" (see "I. Introduction and the Vision of the Risen Jesus [1:1–20]"). That theological presupposition leads him to find fulfillments of prophecy throughout the course of history until the Parousia. The difference between the method of progressives and grammatical-historical interpretation is that the latter consciously attempts to exclude any preunderstanding from the interpretive process and limits itself to one fulfillment of a given prophecy. See Robert L. Thomas, "Current Hermeneutical Trends: Toward Explanation or Obfuscation," *JETS* 39 (June 1996): 249–55.

[61]Milton S. Terry, *Biblical Hermeneutics: A Treatise ont he Interpretation of the Old and New Testaments*, 2d ed. (Grand Rapids: Zondervan, 1974).

among evangelicals.[62] To be correct, he should have said "the old divisions" have been left behind for those who have embraced a new definition of grammatical-historical interpretation. Contrary to his statement, a substantial group of evangelicals still adhere to the time-honored definition as set forth in such works as Terry's.

Blaising and Bock confirm that progressive dispensationalism has emerged as a new system because of its new approach to hermeneutics, which at times they call "historical-grammatical," but at others "historical-grammatical-literary-theological."[63] In referring to changes in hermeneutics, they write, "These are developments which have led to what is now called 'progressive dispensationalism.'"[64] They speak as though all evangelicals have endorsed the changes, but that is not accurate. Some still follow grammatical-historical principles as historically construed.

One traditional principle often violated by the "revised" grammatical-historical approach is that of limiting a given passage to a single meaning. Terry stated it thus:

> A fundamental principle in grammatico-historical exposition is that the words and sentences can have but one significance in one and the same connection. The moment we neglect this principle we drift out upon a sea of uncertainty and conjecture.[65]

Another hermeneutical text states: "But here we must remember the old adage: 'Interpretation is one, application is many.' This means that there is only one meaning to a passage of Scripture which is determined by careful study."[66] Progressive dispensationalism's proclivity toward assigning multiple meanings has shown itself in earlier discussion in this essay (see sections on "Continuity with the Davidic Covenant" and "The Futurity of Babylon in Revelation 17–18"). This sets the system in opposition to traditional grammatical-historical interpretation and thereby distinguishes it from dispensationalism.

---

[62]Blaising, "Dispensationalism: The Search for Definition," 32.

[63]Blaising and Bock, *Progressive Dispensationalism*, 37, 77.

[64]Ibid., 11.

[65]Terry, *Biblical Hermeneutics*, 205.

[66]Bernard Ramm, *Protestant Biblical Interpretation: A Textbook of Hermeneutics*, 3d rev. ed. (Grand Rapids: Baker, 1970), 113.

Amillennialist Poythress distinguishes between historical-grammatical interpretation and those who have not advanced beyond a "flat level" form of literal interpretation.[67] He has apparently preempted the "historical-grammatical" label for a type of hermeneutics that is not limited to a single meaning for each text, and has applied new terminology, "flat interpretation," to traditional grammatical-historical hermeneutics.[68] He recommends finding a spiritualized meaning of some Old Testament texts in addition to the meaning the original author intended and the original audience understood. That way of defining grammatical-historical interpretation significantly confuses the nature of the method. The above series of illustrations from Revelation have illustrated traditional grammatical-historical interpretation, without whatever innuendoes current hermeneutical trends may have brought in under that same label.

Preterism follows a mixture of hermeneutical principles—sometimes literal, sometimes symbolic. For example, Gentry advocates the principle of the symbolic use of numbers in Revelation whenever the number is a large rounded number—for example, 1,000, 144,000, 200,000,000—but he thinks smaller numbers (such as seven) are literal.[69] Also, at one point he allows that the 144,000 may represent the church as a whole, but just ten pages later he identifies them as saved people of Jewish lineage only.[70] That type of interpretive vacillation is the only way one can arrive at a preterist view.

The idealist approach to Revelation does not treat the book as a prophecy. It rather conceives of it more as a philosophy of history. The world constantly witnesses cycles in the conflict between the forces of God and the forces of evil, so one can find recurring fulfillments of the same passages. That viewpoint, however, calls into question the specificity of biblical prophecy. A true prophet was one who received vindication when specific historic happenings fulfilled his prophecies (Jer. 28:9). If a prophecy is so general that it can have numerous "fulfillments," it is hardly fitting to call that work prophecy. Yet Revelation is

---

[67]Vern S. Poythress, *Understanding Dispensationalists*, 2d ed. (Phillipsburg, N.J.: Presbyterian and Reformed, 1994), 82–96.

[68]Ibid., 91, 95–96.

[69]Gentry, *Before Jerusalem Fell*, 162–63.

[70]Ibid., 223–24, 233.

prophecy; it predicts events to occur at particular junctures in the future and not on a repetitive cycle.

Inattention to hermeneutical methodology has led some to combine futuristic interpretations in Revelation with idealist and preterist ones. Such attempts generally parallel suggestions that the writer has expressed a logically impossible combination. An example is Mounce's approving citation of the opinion that "a perfectly logical apocalypse" is an oxymoron.[71] Consistent application of traditional grammatical-historical interpretation alleviates the necessity for such an extreme opinion about Revelation, however. As the following summary will show, the literal sense of the book makes perfectly good sense and is logical and rational in the way it presents God's plan for the future.

AN OVERVIEW OF REVELATION

1. Preparation of the Prophet (1:1–20)

Prologue (1:1–8). Revelation begins with an introductory chapter, which includes a prologue (1:1–8) and John's commission to write (1:9–20). In anticipation of what is to follow, the prologue supplies the book's title, which is "the revelation of Jesus Christ," and information about that revelation, including channels for communicating it, its content, its time of fulfillment, and the method for communicating it. The chain of communication begins with God, who gave the revelation to Jesus Christ to show to God's servants, at times using an angel to communicate data to John, the prophetic writer.

The content of the revelation consists of "things that must happen" (v. 1).[72] The time of fulfillment of the revelation is

---

[71]Robert H. Mounce, *The Book of Revelation* (NICNT; Grand Rapids: Eerdmans, 1977), 178. Pate in his contribution to the present book illustrates a logically impossible combination by merging preterism and futurism. He must assign two dates for the writing of the book, one during Nero's reign and one during Domitian's (in his chapter on "Introduction to Revelation," see section on the date of Revelation). This arises from his effort to find a fulfillment before the destruction of Jerusalem as well as allowing for a Domitian background long after A.D. 70. Unless John wrote Revelation in two stages separated by thirty years, an unlikely possibility, the combination is impossible. This is one of the difficulties with Pate's "eclectic approach" to Revelation.

[72]The long anticipation of these events is the subject of the discussion under "Continuity with Daniel 2."

"soon."[73] The coming of Christ to deliver his church and inflict wrath upon the world was at John's writing, and continues to be today, imminent. The method of communicating the revelation is through dramatic representations, using many symbolic pictures. John received these dramatizations and recorded them so that readers could interpret them, using the usual grammatical-historical rules of interpretation.[74] The prologue also stresses the blessing accompanying the public reading and obedient compliance with the ethical standards expressed in the remainder of the book.

Another feature of the prologue is its epistolary address to seven churches located in the first-century Roman province of Asia. It comes from the three members of the Trinity, the Father, the Holy Spirit, and Jesus Christ, the last of whom receives a special description in three titles selected from Psalm 89. That psalm provides an exposition of God's covenant with David, that one of his descendants would eventually sit on his throne on earth forever. Jesus Christ, being that descendant, takes center stage throughout the book, not only as the principal revealer to John but also as the ultimate fulfiller of the promises to David.[75]

The final part of the prologue furnishes the theme for the book, a theme built on two Old Testament verses that predict the Messiah's return to establish his kingdom on earth.[76]

John's commission to write (1:9–20). The latter phase of the prophet's preparation is the commission given him to write. Christ appears to John in a glorified state symbolic of future events of the prophecy and tells him to write what he sees (1:11, present tense). John proceeds to do that, penning various details about the figure who stands before him. After completing that description, he receives a further command to write what he has seen (past tense, i.e., the vision of the glorified Christ), what current conditions are (i.e., conditions as reflected in the seven messages of chapters 2–3), and what will occur after the current conditions (i.e., beyond the epoch represented by the seven churches).[77]

---

[73]See the material under the heading "The Twofold Coming of Christ in 3:10–11."

[74]See the section "The Major Issue: Hermeneutical Systems."

[75]See "Continuity with the Davidic Covenant."

[76]See "Futurity of Revelation 1:7."

[77]See "The Threefold Division Based on 1:19."

2. Preparation of the People (2:1–3:22)

Seven messages conveyed through seven moral representatives of the seven churches follow in the next two chapters.
The design of these is to prepare churches in seven cities to
observe certain ethical standards. The persuasive motivation for
compliance comes from the severity of predicted judgments to
be described after completion of the seven messages.

Spiritual conditions in the churches varied. Ephesus was a
church of loveless orthodoxy. Smyrnan Christians were faithful
in facing persecution and martyrdom. Pergamum was a church
that practiced indiscriminate tolerance. The Thyatirans were
compromisers in the bad sense. In Sardis professing Christians
were complacent. Because of their faithfulness to the Lord,
Philadelphian believers received Christ's promise of deliverance
from their enemies and from the coming hour of trial. Laodicean
Christianity was deficient because of its lukewarmness.

Christ urged the faithful in these churches to persevere in
the face of opposition and offered the promise of his imminent
coming to deliver them. To the disobedient he threatened imminent punishment through the judgments about to be portrayed
(beginning in ch. 4).[78]

Obviously, Christ did not return during the lives of the generation to whom John wrote, but the nature of the seven
churches makes them representative not only of the rest of the
churches of their time, but also of the entire age until Christ
comes. The churches beginning with Ephesus and ending with
Laodicea do not represent successive periods of church history,
but they represent conditions existing simultaneously in various
churches throughout the world at any given time. Whatever a
church's state, its anticipation should be that Christ will return at
any moment. The seven messages prepare the churches to
respond to a description of what Christ's anticipated coming will
mean to them and the rest of the world.

3. Publication of the Prophecy (4:1–22:5)

With the prophet prepared to deliver and the people prepared
to receive the prophecy, the account begins a delineation of the

---

[78]The above discussion of "The Twofold Coming of Christ in 3:10–11" furnishes additional details regarding incentives derived from his coming.

prophecy's substance in chapter 4. The whole prophecy builds around a scroll with seven seals. The scroll's source is the heavenly throne room, where the Father (4:1–11) and the Lamb (5:1–14) are centers of attention. Chapter 4 sets the tone for the judgmental activities to follow, with a description of the throne and him who sits upon it and of the activities around that throne. At this point John signals a beginning of predictions of the future with his reference to "things that must happen after these things" in 4:1.[79]

The Lamb enters the scene in chapter 5, following the appearance of the seven-sealed scroll. In addition to being the slain Lamb, he is also the Lion of the tribe of Judah and the root of David. Through his sacrificial death he is worthy to open the scroll and, as a mighty lion-like descendant of David, impose the judgments foretold in the scroll. This relieves John's earlier frustration over the nonexistence of anyone worthy to receive and open the scroll. Because of his worthiness the Lamb receives universal tribute.

The seven-sealed scroll opened (6:1–22:5). The scroll's content begins to unfold after descriptions of the grandeur of and activities in the throne room end. Description of that content progresses with the opening of the seals, the blowing of the trumpets, and the pouring out of the bowls. Several *intercalations* spread themselves among the *events* of the three series.

Chapter 6 tells *events* following the Lamb's opening of the first six seals and the types and degrees of divine wrath of which they consist. They include peaceful conquests by anti-Christian forces, worldwide warfare, famine, death to one-quarter of earth's population via four means, penal consequences because of martyrs' prayers, and cosmic upheavals that strike terror among earth's inhabitants. By the time of the last seal, world citizens will realize they are experiencing the promised wrath of God that begins the prophesied day of the Lord.[80]

The futurity of the first six seals receives confirmation from Jesus' teaching about sixty years earlier in his Olivet Discourse. The parallelism of the seals with his sequence of future events there described provides a more detailed understanding of what this opening period of the day of the Lord will be like.[81]

---

[79] See discussions of "Continuity with the Davidic Covenant" and "The Three-fold Division Based on 1:19."

[80] See "The Wrath of God in 6:16–17."

[81] See "Correlation of the First Six Seals with the Olivet Discourse" for more details.

Jesus' labeling of that period as "the beginning of birth pangs" facilitates fixing its time. It will come before "the abomination of desolation" that marks the middle of Daniel's seventieth week, so it will transpire during the first three and one-half years of that seven-year period.

At chapter 7 an *intercalation* injects a pause in the book's chronological movement. Postponement of the seventh seal allows for a picture of two groups that will exist midway through the seven years. One group is entirely of Jewish lineage—144,000 in number and faithful to the Lamb.[82] They are on earth with a mission to accomplish. To protect them from the effects of God's wrath directed against unbelievers, they receive a seal that exempts them from judgments falling on the rest of humankind. They will witness for Christ during the last half of the "week" of years, when persecution intensifies in response to an intensification of God's wrath against a rebellious world. The witnesses have protection from God's wrath, but not from the beast's animosity.

The other group in chapter 7, coming from all racial backgrounds, are innumerable. They are loyal followers of the Lamb who, by midweek, will have gone to heaven. They have come from the world before "the great tribulation" begins and, along with other heavenly beings, are thankful worshipers of him.

The seven trumpets sounded (8:1–22:5). Chronological sequence of *events* resumes in chapters 8–9, with the opening of the seventh seal and the blowing of the first six trumpets. Scripture references with "the seven-sealed scroll opened" section above reflect the inclusion of the seven trumpets as part of that scroll, because the opening of the seventh seal in 8:1 results in no earthly activity other than those trumpets.[83] The substance of that seal begins with the first-trumpet visitation in 8:7 and continues with the next five. The period of their fulfillment is the last half of Daniel's seventieth week.

The trumpet judgments are of greater intensity than the seals. For instance, the death toll under the fourth seal is one-fourth of the world's people, but under the sixth trumpet it is one-third. That coincides with the label given this period by Jesus in his Olivet Discourse: "the great tribulation." The mis-

---

[82] See "A Literal Understanding of the 144,000."

[83] See "Telescoping of the Seals, Trumpets, and Bowls."

ery following "the abomination of desolation" in the middle of the week will be unparalleled in human history. That is the period of the trumpets. As the end of the seventieth week draws nearer, the visitations of God's wrath will intensify.

The first six trumpets include the burning of a third of earth's vegetation, destruction of a third of sea life, poisoning of a third of freshwater sources, darkening of a third of heavenly bodies, a demonic locust plague causing aggravated human pain, and death of a third of earth's inhabitants through a demonic-army invasion.

An *intercalation* brings another pause in chronological movement after the sixth trumpet, one that allows first a dramatic announcement of the end of delay (10:1–11). That announcement of a strong angel brings an aura of apprehension because of the emphatic way it anticipates the nearness of God's kingdom on earth. That will happen in conjunction with the sounding of the remaining trumpet.

The pause in chronological progress includes also a "measurement" of Jerusalem's temple and its worshipers (11:1–14). It predicts not only a rebuilding of the temple for Jewish worship,[84] but also a future conflict between the beast from the sea and God's two witnesses during the last half of the seventieth week. Their witness will prosper for a while, but toward the end they will experience martyrdom. God's consequent judgment against Jerusalem for her ill-treatment of his witnesses will cause widespread death, but will also bring revival among those who remain alive—possibly a reference to a future repentance of Israel at Christ's second advent.

The seven bowls poured out (11:15–22:5). Again, note the inclusiveness of Scripture references above, with both the seven seals and the seven trumpets. As the seventh seal contains the seven trumpets, so the seventh trumpet contains the seven bowls. That is why the sounding of the seventh trumpet in 11:15 results in no immediate description of earthly activity. In fact, the book's sequential movement does not resume until the pouring out of the seven bowls in chapters 15–16. So, just as the seals extend their purview all the way to 22:5, so do the trumpets.

The first of three "bowl" *intercalations* halts temporal progress following the seventh trumpet, allowing for a sequence

---

[84]See "A Literal Temple in 11:1ff."

of visions to set the stage for the seven bowls and introduce personnel and antagonistic forces at work under the bowl judgments. The introduction's first part dwells on a long-standing hostility between the devil and the people of Israel.[85] It had its beginning with the fall of Satan and his angels and manifested itself throughout the Old Testament period in his many attempts to terminate the line of the promised Messiah among the Jewish people. He failed, so with the birth of the Messiah at his first coming, he tried again, but without success.

With the ascension of Christ following his resurrection, Satan turned his hostile intentions toward the people of the Messiah. That hostility will reach its peak during the last half of the prophetic week of Daniel, when Satan will be denied continuing access to heaven and will vent his frustration and wrath against God's people on earth. The woman of Revelation 12—a symbol for Israel—will find refuge from his wrath as provided by God, a development that will frustrate the dragon even more. Consequently, he will direct his intensified wrath against "the rest of her [the woman's] seed" who remain in circulation as God's witnesses to the world. These are the 144,000 introduced at 7:1–8.

The next part of the introduction to the bowls brings onto the scene a beast out of the sea (13:1–10) and a beast out of the land (13:11–18)—later identified as Satan's allies and instruments for world domination and persecution of the 144,000 (13:4; 16:13). The beast will ascend to rulership of the world after his death wound heals and will try to obliterate the remaining followers of the Lamb, most notably the rest of the woman's seed.[86] In his cruel treatment of the saints, he will fulfill the wishes of the dragon who energizes him. The false prophet (the beast out of the earth) will be party to this effort to extinguish all living saints as he assists the beast. Through coercion of various kinds he will try to force everyone to receive the mark of the beast. The two villains will not, however, have access to the bulk of Israel, protected in their place of refuge, but they will succeed in martyring the whole number of the 144,000.

The third part of the introduction to the bowls is proleptic. It describes the 144,000 alongside the victorious Lamb on Mount Zion (14:1–5). It anticipates the return of Christ and his residence in

---

[85]See "The Identity of the Woman in 12:1ff."
[86]See "The Beast of 13:1ff." for more details of the beast's identity.

Jerusalem after Armageddon. The resurrected 144,000 martyrs will enjoy ultimate victory over the beast after Christ returns to judge their persecutors and consign them to the lake of fire (19:19-21).

Following the triumphant scene of the 144,000 with the Lamb comes a series of announcements that anticipate the seven bowls (14:6-13), all of which furnish incentives to give God glory by remaining faithful to the Lamb in resisting the beast. The final stage of preparation for the bowls previews the great battle when the Lamb returns to defeat his enemies. A harvest and a vintage foresee the great bloodshed that will result from that battle (14:14-20).

With the background for the bowls in place, John resumes his description of the chronological *events* by encountering the seven angels charged with dispensing the bowls' contents, which are none other than the seven last plagues God will use to complete his anger (15:1). There follow rejoicing in heaven over the last plagues (15:2-4) and heavenly preparations for the plagues (15:5-8). Chapter 16 records the pouring of the seven bowls on the earth. Again, this entails an advance in intensity over the previous series. No longer are the results fractional; these judgments sound the note of finality, and appropriately so. They are God's seven last plagues and will come in rapid sequence at the end of Daniel's seventieth week.

The first six of them include incurable sores on worshipers of the beast, death to *all* sea life, transformation of *all* fresh water into blood, scorching of *all* humanity through the sun's intensity, darkening of the beast's kingdom, and preparation for the doom of earth's kings. The sixth bowl sets the stage for bowl seven by gathering earth's rulers to a spot where they intend to wipe out the remaining saints, but instead experience their own destruction.

In the last part of chapter 16, the seventh angel pours out the contents of his bowl. Then comes a dramatic announcement of the culmination from the heavenly temple, the storm theophany accompanied by the greatest earthquake ever, the division of Jerusalem into three parts, the fall of Gentile cities (especially Babylon), the flight of islands and disappearance of mountains, and a great hailstorm. The last of these provokes the blasphemy of earth's rebels.

Yet these are just peripheral features of the seventh bowl. Its substance is yet to come after a second "bowl" *intercalation*. Before disclosing to John the bowl's contents, one of the angels of the seven last plagues has another lesson in background matters. He must represent to John the separate elements of Babylon, the end-time opponent of God and righteousness, and how they will meet their end. At any given time in history, few would predict the emergence of that city on the Euphrates as an international leader, but prophetic statements of Scripture point to its future rise to power.[87]

The complex of this empire during that final day will include religious and commercial elements as well as the dominating political machine of the beast. Before recounting the end of political Babylon through the seventh of the seven last plagues, the angel traces how the religious and commercial parts of the city and empire will meet their end. Chapter 17 tells about the close relationship between the beast and the false religion fostered by Babylon, and the later breakup of that relationship through which the beast and his allies destroy the harlot, who represents false religion. Chapter 18 reflects God's future dealings with the materialistic side of Babylon. That city, during the last part of the seventieth week, will attain international dominance in commercial affairs, so God's judgment of that side of the world empire's operations will send the rest of the world into a state of shock that will threaten its very existence. This entity will meet its end through burning by direct divine intervention. The anticipated demise of Babylon evokes singing in heaven—four songs because of the city's judgment (19:1–5) and one song looking forward to the marriage of the Lamb (19:6–8). Following these John has a brief dialogue with the angel who has shown him the coming fate of the city.

The end of the Babylonian interlude leads into a disclosure of the *events* of the seventh bowl, the last of the seven last plagues. The bowl's contents consist of eight scenes, each introduced by John's words "and I saw":

1. Second coming of Christ (19:11–16)
2. Summons of the birds to a human feast (19:17–18)
3. Slaughter of Christ's human opponents (19:19–21)
4. Satan's imprisonment (20:1–3)
5. Satan's release and final defeat (20:4–10)
6. Setting of the Great White Throne (20:11)
7. Sentencing to the lake of fire (20:12–15)
8. Sketch of the new Jerusalem (21:1–8).

---

[87]See "The Futurity of Babylon in Revelation 17–18."

The description details events whose fulfillment will come in the sequence of the scenes in the text.[88] Christ will return from heaven, accompanied by the resurrected saints, to meet armies led by the beast and false prophet. Before the battle an angel will summon the birds to "the great supper of God," which results when Christ overwhelms the enemy, casting the beast and false prophet in the lake of fire and killing the rest of earth's rebels.

The remaining enemy, Satan, will enter a one-thousand-year incarceration, during which time Christ will rule with his saints in a kingdom that fulfills Jewish expectations based on Old Testament prophecy. When the thousand years end, God will permit Satan's release from the abyss. By that time offspring of the initial believing population in the kingdom will have multiplied and produced many who chose to remain in their unbelieving state. From these unbelievers Satan will recruit a massive army to march against Jerusalem once again. This time fire from heaven will consume the adversaries. Satan at that point will go to his final place in the lake of fire.

The placement of a "great white throne" with God seated on it comes next (20:11–15), in conjunction with the removal of the old creation. From that throne God judges unbelievers, those whose names are absent from the book of life, and relegates them to the lake of fire.

The final scene of the seventh bowl may not seem to be a judgment at first (21:1–8), because it devotes most attention to the beauty and bliss of the new creation, but its final verse (21:8) pays conspicuous attention to those denied access to it because of their presence in the lake of fire and burning sulfur.

To enhance appreciation for the new creation and to contrast the new Jerusalem with Babylon of the old creation, a third "bowl" *intercalation* pictures one of the last-plague angels leading John on a "tour" of the Jerusalem that is to come (21:9–22:5).[89]

4. Epilogue (22:6–21)

To close the book, John furnishes a testimony of the last-plague angel that in essence announces the end of the prophecy begun at 4:1. He adds his own testimony about further interaction

---

[88]See "The Millennial Kingdom of 20:1–10."
[89]See "The New Creation of 21:1ff."

with that angel, who instructs him not to seal the book's contents because of the imminence of events foretold therein. He follows this with the testimony of Jesus, who emphasizes the importance and finality of the prophecy just given. To this John responds, "Amen, come, Lord Jesus." A benediction closes the book.

CONCLUSION

A literal understanding of Revelation erases any questions about the book's coherence, organization, and logic. Its straightforward message is the book's best defense against the maligning it has received because of an alleged incomprehensibility. Usual hermeneutical principles bring out God's plan for the future and the eternal state. No need arises to add to or subtract from what a literal interpretation yields.

Hermeneutical Summary

A comparison of a dispensational view of Revelation with those of my fellow contributors to this volume reveals striking differences, the most notable being the interpretive principles followed by each interpreter. The main issue is what constitutes a grammatical-historical method of exegesis. The other three writers allow for far more symbolism than does a dispensational view. They justify their nonliteral approaches by appealing to the special genre or character of Revelation as apocalyptic. A dispensational view holds that the book is primarily prophetic rather than apocalyptic[90] and that biblical prophecy deserves literal interpretation, just as do other literary genres of Scripture.[91]

To understand any passage of Scripture in a nonliteral way violates principles of grammatical-historical interpretation unless contextual features signal a need to interpret otherwise. The figurative indicators in Revelation 12:1ff., for example, illustrate how grammatical-historical interpretation provides for figurative language when a writer intended something to be a

---

[90]John uses *prophētēs* or its cognates eighteen times in Revelation's twenty-two chapters: *Prophēteia* occurs seven times (1:3; 11:6; 19:10; 22:7, 10, 18, 19), *prophētis* once (2:20), *[rophēteuō* twice (10:11; 11:3), and *prophētēs* eight times (10:7; 11:10, 18; 16:6; 18:20, 24; 22:6, 9). See Thomas, *Revelation 1–7*, 23–29, for other reasons why prophetic genre is preferable.

[91]Ibid., 29–39.

symbol.[92] If a writer intended his words to be understood non-literally, that is the way to interpret them; if, however, he furnishes no such indication, then he meant them literally.

Another way to portray the nature of literal interpretation is through sample comparisons of it with various nonliteral approaches to parts of Revelation.

Preterism. Earlier in this volume, preterist Gentry interprets a reference to clouds in Revelation 1:7 as a nonpersonal coming of Christ. Christ never returned to earth in A.D. 70 personally, so explaining the fall of Jerusalem as his coming violates the principle of literal interpretation. All contextual indications point to a literal and personal coming of Christ in that verse. Gentry calls this a "judgment-coming" of Christ, but the criteria of Revelation also connect a deliverance of the faithful with that coming. Preterism nowhere explains the promised deliverance from persecution that is associated with the coming, for example, in 3:10–11. Gentry's interpretation of 1:7 simply does not fulfill the criteria of literal interpretation of the text. The fact is, the church did not escape persecution in A.D. 70, but continued to suffer for Christ's sake long after that.

Another hermeneutical shortcoming of preterism relates to the limiting of the promised coming of Christ in 1:7 to Judea. What does a localized judgment hundreds of miles away have to do with the seven churches in Asia? John uses two long chapters in addressing those churches regarding the implications of the coming of Christ for them. For instance, the promise to shield the Philadelphian church from judgment (3:10–11) is meaningless if that judgment occurs far beyond the borders of that city. Besides, 3:10 tells of an hour of testing that will come on the *whole inhabited earth*, not just on Palestine. Literal interpretation does not foist on the text an unnatural meaning as does preterism, but allows the text to speak for itself. To explain the effects of a "cloud coming" to Palestine on these seven distant cities as "severe aftershocks" is a weak effort to veil the hermeneutical flaw of reading into the text an idea that is not there.

Idealism. Idealist Hamstra acknowledges the prophetic style of Revelation, but what does he mean by "prophetic"? How can the symbols be prophetic and yet have "no historic connection with any particular event"; and contrariwise, how can they "find

---

[92]E.g., see above under the heading "Identity of the Woman in 12:1ff."

fulfillment in an historical event or person without exhausting its meaning"? Not only is that combination puzzling, but it also ignores the nature of prophecy. Predictive prophecy in the Bible has fulfillments in history that are specific, as the predictions in Isaiah 53 of the Messiah's sufferings. In fact, credentials of the true prophet of God are the exact fulfillments of his prophecies, according to Jeremiah 28:9: "The prophet who prophesies about peace will be recognized as one truly sent by the LORD only if his prediction comes true" (cf. Deut. 18:22). Prophecies of generalities that are void of meaningful details, that can by glossing over specifics find application to any number of historical instances, hardly merit the name of biblical prophecy. The predictions in Revelation are not about general types of happenings, but about specific events yet to be fulfilled.

Progressive dispensationalism. Progressive dispensationalist Pate with his "eclectic approach" tries to mix "the best" of preterist and idealist hermeneutics with a literal approach. His appraisal of what is "best" in those two systems distorts whatever elements of literalism he retains. He attempts to justify his "already-not yet" hermeneutical key by recourse to Revelation 1:1, 3, 19, but he reads into those verses a meaning borrowed from Oscar Cullman. He connects the "already" aspect with the last days inaugurated by the death and resurrection of Christ. That leads him to have John prophesying about events that lay in the past by the time he wrote Revelation, whether Pate dates the book in the 60s or the 90s (oddly, he seems to prefer both dates).

For example, Pate sees the second seal as predictive of wars occurring between A.D. 41 and 54, dates long before John wrote the book. He also equates the third seal with famines happening in A.D. 42, 45–46, 49, and 51, predating the writing of the book once again. He finds prophetic fulfillments of the fifth seal in conjunction with persecutions in Acts, events dating from before A.D. 35 until approximately A.D. 58. All these "fulfillments" transpired *before* John penned the prophecies.

Does biblical prophecy consist of predicting past events? Of course not. That is not prophetic genre; it is a species of historical narrative, which is not the nature of what the text of Revelation says about itself. Besides partaking of the weakness of idealism—that is, finding repeated "fulfillments" by glossing over details of prophecy—the progressives oppose a fundamental characteristic of prophecy, that of prediction.

Progressive dispensationalists also inherit the weaknesses of preterism by positing a possible early date for the writing of the book and identifying specific fulfillments in connection with the wars leading up to A.D. 70. Those conflicts affected only a small fraction of the world's population, but the seal judgments, for example, will impact the whole world. How could one-quarter of the world's population have perished when the Romans besieged Jerusalem in the first century? The answer is that they could not. The only possible fulfillment of that prophecy lies yet in the future, unless one chooses to ignore the literal meaning of 6:8.

Someone may propose that an interpreter will find whatever he wants to find in Revelation. A reconstructionist—that is, a preterist—will find a way to relegate the book to past fulfillment because of his predisposition that the Christian message will gradually improve society as a whole, a message that is incompatible with Revelation if its fulfillment lies in the future. An amillennialist—that is, an idealist—will find fulfillments throughout the church age because of a preunderstanding that the Millennium is present already. An "already-not yet" inclination will find past, present, and future fulfillments in the book because of its inclination to merge covenantalism—that is, idealism and/or preterism—with dispensationalism.

The grammatical-historical way to approach the book is to put one's predispositions aside and let the facts of history and principles of grammar within the book speak for themselves. Recent hermeneutical trends have pushed aside this time-honored quest for objectivity, but they have done so through allowing intrusions by man-made and man-centered philosophical emphases.[93] Inclusion of human preunderstanding has no place in biblical interpretation. To call a system of hermeneutics that has undergone changes—that is, through an inclusion of preunderstanding—"grammatical-historical" is anachronistic. To do so is to apply an old name to a new system of interpretation and is altogether misleading. A dispensational view of Revelation strives for objectivity by putting aside all preunderstanding and bias, so that the text of the book may speak for itself. That is grammatical-historical interpretation historically construed.

---

[93]Thomas, "Current Hermeneutical Trends," 249–55.

Nearness and Imminence of Christ's Return

Preterism makes much over an alleged time limit placed on the coming of Christ in Revelation and in the Olivet Discourse. Gentry says that "soon" (Rev. 1:1) and "near" (1:3) could not cover nearly two thousand years, but require that the coming take place "in *their* [John's original audience's] lifetime." He cites Matthew 24:34 to parallel Jesus' teaching with Revelation, interpreting "this generation" to refer to the lifetimes of those who heard him speak.

Jesus' own teaching reflects the error of that interpretation, however. Repeatedly, he taught that no person, not even he himself, knew in advance when that coming would happen: "No one knows about that day or hour, not even the angels of heaven, nor the Son . . ." (Matt. 24:36); "Therefore keep watch, because you do not know on what day your Lord will come" (24:42); "The Son of Man will come at an hour when you do not expect him" (24:44); "Therefore keep watch, because you do not know the day or the hour" (25:13); "It is not for you to know the times or dates that the Father has set by his own authority" (Acts 1:7).

The preterist is guilty of the very error against which Jesus warned, namely, that of setting a time frame within which his coming must occur. A preterist might reply, "But Jesus did not forbid specifying a year or a period of years within which he would come; he only spoke of the day and hour." That response resembles the justification for date-setting given by some who have set dates for Christ's return during the closing decades of the twentieth century. The rejoinder to that response is that the day or the hour includes references to the week, month, year, and period of years that include the day and hour. Jesus declared that no one knew (or knows) in advance when he would (or will) return.

Preterism also ignores the context of the Olivet Discourse. Just before Jesus spoke of "this generation" in Matthew 24:34, he had told a Jewish audience, "*You* will not see me until *you* say, 'Blessed is he who comes in the name of the Lord'" (Matt. 23:39, emphasis added). The Jewish nation of that day certainly did not meet that criterion in A.D. 70. They did not at that time say, "Blessed is he who comes in the name of the Lord," so they obviously did not see Jesus at that time. The fulfillment of that prophecy is yet future.

Jesus clearly used the second person plural "you" in Matthew 23:39 to speak of the Jewish nation corporately, without limiting the pronoun to a particular generation of Israelites. That is the sense he gave to the expression "this generation" in 23:36 and to the "you" and "your" in 23:37–38. He did not limit the expressions to his immediate listeners, but used them as representatives of the nation that will in the future meet the criteria described in the series of verses. The setting in which Jesus gave the discourse must determine the interpretation of his words. Only in the future will a generation of Israel say, "Blessed is he who comes in the name of the Lord." That will be the generation that Jesus speaks about in 24:34.

Jesus taught "soonness" without setting a limit on how soon his return would come. He alerted his followers to expect him at any moment, but to remain faithful and stay busy until that coming occurs. He also warned the unfaithful of an impending judgment to fall on them unless they repent. According to a dispensational view, that twofold lesson of comfort and warning in the Olivet Discourse also summarizes the message of Revelation.

CONCLUSION

This volume has come to a conclusion, and the readers will now have to decide for themselves which of the viewpoints presented here best understands Revelation. My suspicion, however, is that each of the approaches represented will have had something important to say to them about the last book of the Bible, and accordingly deserves to be heeded by its audience.

Perhaps the appropriate way, then, to conclude this work is to summarize its contents, and to do so by rehearsing the significance of the beginning of Revelation—1:1, 3. The reader should have gathered that the starting point is the key to understanding the Apocalypse, for all else proceeds from that. How one views these verses and the statements that "these things" (the events of Revelation) must "soon" take place and that the time of their fulfillment is "near" governs one's subsequent approach. Otherwise said, how one begins his or her study of the book of Revelation is how one most likely will end it.

Thus, *preterists* take these opening verses to mean "immediately," so that, on their reading of the book, things did indeed happen quickly, at the fall of Jerusalem in A.D. 70. *Idealists* also take these verses at apparent face value, interpreting the events of the Apocalypse as immediately occurring and continually unfolding in history. *Classical dispensationalists* believe the teaching about a twofold return of Christ accounts for 1:1, 3. Thus the Rapture can occur at any moment (imminency), which will then set in motion the prophecies of the Apocalypse. *Progressive dispensationlists*, while agreeing with the concept of the twofold coming of Christ, still think that the already/not yet principle better grasps the meaning of 1:1, 3—those circumstances predicted began to occur in the first century and will continue throughout history, building to a climax.

Having said that, however, is there no unity in the midst of the above diversity? I believe there is. Perhaps 1:19, which has guided the order of the four presentations, provides us with the key: The same God who intervened mightily in the past through Jesus Christ, is at work in the present on our behalf, and will triumphantly conclude his plan in the future. It is this dynamic that affirms our Christian oneness in the midst of hermeneutical variety.

C. MARVIN PATE

SELECTED BIBLIOGRAPHY

Adams, Jay E. *The Time Is at Hand*. Phillipsburg, N.J.: Presbyterian and Reformed, 1966.

Alford, Henry. *The Greek New Testament*. 4 vols. Chicago: Moody, rep. 1958 [1849-1861].

Allison, Dale C. *The End of the Ages Has Come: An Early Interpretation of the Passion and Resurrection of Jesus*. Philadelphia: Fortress, 1985.

Aune, David E. *Prophecy in Early Christianity and the Ancient Mediterranean World*. Grand Rapids: Eerdmans, 1983.

_____. "The Influence of Roman Imperial Court Ceremonial on the Apocalypse of John." *Papers of the Chicago Society of Biblical Research* 28 (1983): 1–26.

Balyeat, Joseph R. *Babylon, the Great City of Revelation*. Sevierville, Tenn.: Onward, 1991.

Barrett, C. K. *The New Testament Background: Selected Documents*. New York: Harper & Row, 1961.

Beagley, Alan James. *The "Sitz im Leben" of the Apocalypse With Particular Reference to the Role of the Church's Enemies*. New York: Walter de Gruyter, 1987.

Benoit, P., J. T. Milik, and R. DeVaux, eds. *Discoveries in the Judean Desert of Jordan II*. Oxford: Oxford Univ. Press, 1961.

Benware, Paul N. *Understanding End-Times Prophecy: A Comprehensive Approach*. Chicago: Moody, 1995.

Blaising, Craig, and Darrell Bock, eds. *Dispensationalism, Israel, and the Church*. Grand Rapids: Zondervan, 1992.

_____. *Progressive Dispensationalism*. Wheaton, Ill.: Victor, 1993.

Bock, Darrell L. "The Son of David and the Saints' Task: The Hermeneutics of Initial Fulfillment." *BSac* 150 (October-December 1993): 440–47.

_____. "Current Messianic Activity and OT Davidic Promise: Dispensationalism, Hermeneutics, and NT Fulfillment." *TrinJ* 15NS (1994): 55–87.

Boyer, Paul. *When Time Shall Be No More: Prophecy Beliefs in Modern American Culture.* Cambridge, Mass.: Harvard Univ. Press, 1992.

Bruce, F. F. *New Testament History.* Garden City, N.Y.: Anchor, 1969.

Buis, Harry. *The Book of Revelation: A Simplified Commentary.* Philadelphia: Presbyterian and Reformed, 1960.

Calkins, Raymond. *The Social Message of the Book of Revelation.* New York: Woman's Press, 1920.

Carrington, Philip. *The Meaning of Revelation.* London: SPCK, 1931.

Chance, J. Bradley. *Jerusalem, the Temple, and the New Age in Luke-Acts.* Macon, Ga.: Mercer Univ. Press, 1988.

Charles, R. H. *Studies in the Apocalypse.* Edinburgh: T. & T. Clark, 1913.

_____. *A Critical and Exegetical Commentary on the Revelation of St. John.* ICC. 2 vols. Edinburgh: T. & T. Clark, 1920.

Chilton, David. *The Days of Vengeance: An Exposition of the Book of Revelation.* Fort Worth, Tex.: Dominion, 1987.

_____. *The Great Tribulation.* Fort Worth, Tex.: Dominion, 1987.

Compolo, Tony. Interview. *The Door.* Sept./Oct. 1993.

Crutchfield, Larry. *The Origins of Dispensationalism: The Darby Factor.* Lanham, Md.: Univ. Press of America, 1992.

Cullmann, Oscar. *Christ and Time: The Primitive Christian Conception of Time and History.* Trans. Floyd V. Filson. Philadelphia: Westminster, 1950.

DeMar, Gary. *Last Days Madness: Obsession of the Modern Church.* Atlanta: American Vision, 1994.

Dodd, C. H. *The Apostolic Preaching and Its Developments.* New York: Harper, 1944.

Düsterdieck, Friedrich. *Critical and Exegetical Handbook to the Revelation of John.* 6th ed. Trans. Henry Jacobs. Winona Lake, Ind.: Alpha, rep. 1980 [1884].

Farrer, Austin. *A Rebirth of Images: The Making of St. John's Apocalypse.* London: Darce, 1949.

Fee, Gordon D. *1 and 2 Timothy, Titus.* Peabody, Mass.: Hendrickson, 1988.

Fee, Gordon D., and Douglas Stuart. *How to Read the Bible for All Its Worth: A Guide to Understanding the Bible*. 2d ed. Grand Rapids: Zondervan, 1994.

Ferguson, Everett. *Backgrounds of Early Christianity*. Grand Rapids: Eerdmans, 1987.

Fiorenza, Elisabeth Schüssler. "The Quest for the Johannine School: The Apocalypse and the Origin of Both Gospel and Revelation." *NTS* 23 (April 1977): 402–27.

_____. *Revelation: Vision of a Just World*. Proclamation Commentaries. Minneapolis: Fortress, 1991.

Fitzmyer, Joseph A. *The Gospel According to Luke X-XXIV*. AB. New York: Doubleday, 1983.

Ford, J. Massyngberde. *Revelation*. AB. New York: Doubleday, 1975.

Friesen, Steven. "Ephesus: Key to a Vision in Revelation." *BAR* 19:3 (May-June 1993): 25–37.

Gentry, Kenneth L., Jr. *Before Jerusalem Fell: Dating the Book of Revelation*. Tyler, Tex.: Institute for Christian Economics, 1989.

_____. *The Beast of Revelation*. Tyler, Tex.: Institute for Christian Economics, 1989.

_____. *The Charismatic Gift of Prophecy: A Reformed Response to Wayne Grudem*. 2d ed. Memphis, Tenn.: Footstool, 1989.

_____. *He Shall Have Dominion*. 2d ed. Tyler, Tex.: Institute for Christian Economics, 1996.

_____. "Postmillennialism." *Three Views of the Millennium and Beyond*. Ed. Darrell L. Bock. Grand Rapids: Zondervan, forthcoming.

Grenz, Stanley J. *The Millennial Maze: Sorting Out Evangelical Options*. Downers Grove, Ill.: InterVarsity, 1992.

Hailey, Homer. *Revelation, an Introduction and Commentary*. Grand Rapids: Baker, 1970.

Harrington, Wilfrid J. *Understanding the Apocalypse*. Washington, D.C.: Corpus Books, 1969.

Hemer, Colin J. *The Letters to the Seven Churches of Asia in Their Local Setting*. JSNTSS 11. Sheffield: Univ. of Sheffield Press, 1986.

Hendriksen, William. *More Than Conquerors: An Interpretation of the Book of Revelation*. Grand Rapids: Baker, 1944.

_____. *Three Lectures on the Book of Revelation*. Grand Rapids: Zondervan, 1949.

Hillers, D. R. "Revelation 13:18 and a Scroll from Murabba'at." *BASOR* 170 (April 1963): 65.

Holwerda, David E. *Jesus and Israel: One Covenant or Two?* Grand Rapids: Eerdmans, 1995.

Ice, Thomas D., and Kenneth L. Gentry Jr. *The Great Tribulation: Past or Future?* Grand Rapids: Kregel, 1997.

Jeremias, Joachim. *Jerusalem in the Time of Jesus: An Investigation into Economic and Social Conditions During the New Testament Period.* Philadelphia: Fortress, 1969.

Johnson, Alan F. "Revelation." *The Expositor's Bible Commentary.* Ed. Frank E. Gaebelein. Grand Rapids: Zondervan, 1981; 12:399–603.

Knight, George W., III. "The Scriptures Were Written for Our Instruction." *JETS* 39 (March, 1996): 3–14.

Kuyper, Abraham. *The Revelation of St. John.* Grand Rapids: Eerdmans, 1964.

Ladd, George Eldon. *Crucial Questions About the Kingdom of God.* Grand Rapids: Eerdmans, 1954.

_____. *A Commentary on the Revelation of John.* Grand Rapids: Eerdmans, 1972.

_____. *The Presence of the Future.* Grand Rapids: Eerdmans, 1974.

Lindsey, Hal. *The Late Great Planet Earth.* Grand Rapids: Zondervan, 1970.

Marshall, Alfred. *The Interlinear Greek-English New Testament.* 2d ed. Grand Rapids: Zondervan, 1959.

Merriam-Webster's Collegiate Dictionary. 10th ed. Springfield, Mass.: Merriam-Webster, 1993.

Metzger, Bruce M. *A Textual Commentary on the Greek New Testament.* London: United Bible Societies, 1971.

_____. "Revelation, The Book of." *The Oxford Companion to the Bible.* Ed. Bruce M. Metzger and Michael D. Coogan. New York: Oxford Univ. Press, 1993.

Milligan, William. *The Revelation of St. John.* London: MacMillan, 1886.

_____. *Lectures on the Apocalypse.* London: MacMillan, 1892.

_____. *Discussion on the Apocalypse.* London: MacMillan, 1893.

_____. *The Book of Revelation.* New York: A. C. Armstrong, 1903.

Minear, Paul S. *I Saw a New Earth: An Introduction to the Visions of the Apocalypse*. Cleveland: Corpus, 1968.

Moffatt, James. "The Revelation of St. John the Divine." *Expositor's Greek Testament*. Ed. W. Robertson Nicoll. Grand Rapids: Eerdmans, n.d.

Moo, Douglas J. "The Case for the Posttribulation Rapture Position." Pp. 169–211 in *The Rapture: Pre-, Mid-, or Post-Tribulational: Essays by Reiter, Feinberg, Archer, and Moo*. Grand Rapids: Zondervan, 1984.

Moore, A. L. *The Parousia in the New Testament*. NovTSup 13. Leiden: E. J. Brill, 1966.

Morris, Leon. *The Revelation of St. John*. TNTC. Grand Rapids: Eerdmans, 1969.

Mounce, Robert H. *The Book of Revelation*. NICNT. Grand Rapids: Eerdmans, 1977.

Moyise, Steve. *The Old Testament in the Book of Revelation*. JSNTSS 115. Sheffield: Academic Press, 1995.

Mulholland, M. Robert, Jr. *Revelation: Holy Living in an Unholy World*. Grand Rapids: Zondervan, 1990.

Mussies, G. *The Morphology of Koine Greek As Used in the Apocalypse of St. John*. Leiden: E. J. Brill, 1971.

Nichols, Stephen, J. "The Dispensational View of the Davidic Kingdom: A Response to Progressive Dispensationalism." *The Master's Seminary Journal* 7/2 (Fall 1996): 213–39.

NIV Study Bible. Grand Rapids: Zondervan, 1985.

Pate, C. Marvin. *Luke*. Moody Gospel Commentary. Chicago: Moody, 1985.

_____. *The End of the Age Has Come: The Theology of Paul*. Grand Rapids: Zondervan, 1995.

Pate, C. Marvin, and Calvin B. Haines, Jr. *Doomsday Delusions: What's Wrong With Predictions About the End of the World*. Downers Grove, Ill.: InterVarsity, 1995.

Perkins, Pheme. *Reading the New Testament*. New York: Paulist, 1978.

Pieters, Albertus. *Studies on Revelation*. Grand Rapids: Eerdmans, 1950.

Plantinga, Cornelius, Jr. *Not the Way It's Supposed to Be: A Breviary of Sin*. Grand Rapids: Eerdmans, 1995.

Poythress, Vern S. "Genre and Hermeneutics in Rev 20:1–6." *JETS* 36 (1993): 41–54.

_____. *Understanding Dispensationalists.* 2d ed. Phillipsburg, N.J.: Presbyterian and Reformed, 1994.

Provon, Iain. "Foul Spirits, Fornication and Finance: Revelation 18 From an Old Testament Perspective." *JSNT* 64 (December 1966): 81–100.

Ramm, Bernard. *Protestant Biblical Interpretation: A Textbook of Hermeneutics.* 3d rev. ed. Grand Rapids: Baker, 1970.

Ramsey, William. *The Letters to the Seven Churches.* Grand Rapids: Baker, 1963.

Richardson, Peter. *Israel in the Apostolic Church.* SNTSMS. Cambridge: Cambridge Univ. Press, 1969.

Ritmeyer, Leen. "Locating the Original Temple Mount." *BAR* 18:2 (March-April 1992): 24–45.

Robertson, O. Palmer. *The Final Word: A Biblical Response to the Case for Tongues and Prophecy Today.* Edinburgh: Banner of Truth, 1993.

Russell, David S. *The Method and Message of Jewish Apocalyptic 200 B.C.–A.D. 100.* Philadelphia: Westminster, 1964.

Ryrie, Charles C. *Dispensationalism Today.* Chicago: Moody, 1965.

Saucy, Robert L. *The Case for Progressive Dispensationalism: The Interface Between Dispensational and Non-Dispensational Theology.* Grand Rapids: Zondervan, 1993.

Schick, Edwin A. *Revelation: The Last Book of the Bible.* Philadelphia: Fortress, 1977.

Scofield, C. I. *Rightly Dividing the Word of Truth.* New York: Loizeaux Brothers, 1896.

The Scofield Reference Bible. New York: Oxford, 1909.

Smallwood, Mary E. *Documents Illustrating the Principates Gaius Claudius and Nero.* Cambridge: Cambridge Univ. Press, 1967.

Swete, Henry Barclay. *The Apocalypse of St. John.* Grand Rapids: Eerdmans, n.d.

Tacticus. *The Histories.* Trans. Kenneth Wellesley. New York: Penguin, 1986.

Tenney, Merrill C. *Interpreting Revelation.* Grand Rapids: Eerdmans, 1957.

Terry, Milton S. *Biblical Apocalyptics: A Study of the Most Notable Revelations of God and of Christ.* Grand Rapids: Baker, rep. 1988.

_____. *Biblical Hermeneutics: A Treatise on the Interpretation of the Old and New Testaments.* 2d ed. Grand Rapids: Zondervan, 1974.

Thomas, Robert L. *Revelation 1–7: An Exegetical Commentary.* Ed. Kenneth Barker. Chicago: Moody, 1992.

_____. "Theonomy and the Dating of Revelation." *The Master's Seminary Journal* 5/2 (Fall 1994): 190–92.

_____. *Revelation 8–22: An Exegetical Commentary.* Chicago: Moody, 1995.

_____. "A Critique of Progressive Dispensational Hermeneutics." Pp. 414–25 in *When the Trumpet Sounds.* Ed. Thomas Ice and Timothy Demy. Eugene, Ore.: Harvest House, 1995.

_____. "Current Hermeneutical Trends: Toward Explanation or Obfuscation." *JETS* 39 (June 1996): 249–55.

_____. "The 'Comings' of Christ in Revelation 2–3." *The Master's Seminary Journal* 7/2 (Fall 1996): 153–81.

Townsend, Jeffrey L. "The Rapture in Revelation 3:10." In *When the Trumpet Sounds.* Ed. Thomas Ice and Timothy Demy. Eugene, Ore.: Harvest House, 1995.

Turner, David L. "The New Jerusalem in Revelation 21:1–22:5: Consummation of a Biblical Continuum." Pp. 264–92 in *Dispensationalism, Israel and the Church.* Ed. Craig A. Blaising and Darrell L. Bock. Grand Rapids: Zondervan, 1992.

Unjhem, Arne. *Book of Revelation.* Philadelphia: Lutheran Church Press, 1967.

Vanderwaal, Cornelis. *Hal Lindsey and Biblical Prophecy.* St. Catherines, Ont.: Paideia, 1978.

_____. *Search the Scriptures: Hebrews–Revelation.* St. Catherines, Ont.: Paideia, 1979.

Von Mosheim, L. *Historical Commentaries.* Vol. 1. Trans. Robert S. Vidal. New York: Converse, 1854.

Vos, Louis A. *The Synoptic Traditions in the Apocalypse.* Kampen: Kok, 1965.

Walker, Peter W. L. *Jesus and the Holy City: New Testament Perspectives on Jerusalem.* Grand Rapids; Eerdmans, 1996.

Walvoord, John F. *The Millennial Kingdom.* Findlay, Ohio: Dunham, 1963.

_____. *The Revelation of Jesus Christ.* Chicago: Moody, 1966.

Walvoord, John F., and Roy B. Zuck, eds. *Bible Knowledge Commentary: Old Testament.* Wheaton, Ill.: Victor, 1985.

Wilcock, Michael. *The Message of Revelation.* Downers Grove, Ill.: InterVarsity, 1975.

SCRIPTURE INDEX

SUBJECT INDEX